The Colne
by
Boat, Bike & Boot

THE COLNE

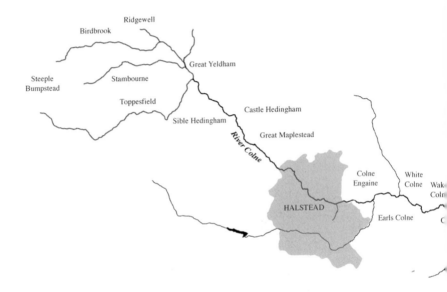

Published by
David Cleveland
2013

Front cover picture: *The author approaching Chappel viaduct.*
Back cover picture: *The author leaving Brightlingsea ferry.*

Cover design by Adam Rickwood

THE COLNE
by
Boat, Bike & Boot

Ken Rickwood

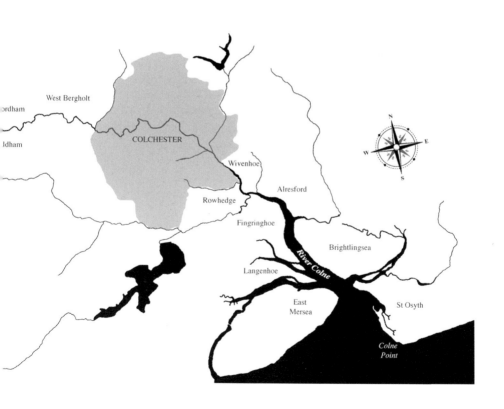

Published by
David Cleveland,
Manningtree, Essex

ISBN 978-0-9558271-6-7

© Ken Rickwood 2013

First published October 2013

British Library Cataloguing-in-Publication Data
A catalogue record for this book is available from
the British Library

Designed by Ken Rickwood
Printed in England by Lavenham Press Ltd

CONTENTS

ACKNOWLEDGEMENTS

This book would not have been possible without the help of many people, past and present. I have consulted many books and those listed in the bibliography have all provided me with useful information, but many more have provided an odd snippet here and there. I am indebted to the many individuals who have helped me and I hope that if I fail to mention a name, where I should, it will be forgiven. I have found that most villages have an enthusiastic local historian, many of whom have helped me a great deal.

I have tried to ascertain the copyright of all the pictures that I have used and included a picture credit list on page 379. Those unattributed are either in my own collection or photographs I have taken during my travels researching this book.

Individuals and organisations whose help I would like to acknowledge are: Adrian Corder-Birch, Brian Alderman and Earls Colne Heritage Museum, Brian Flemming and Colne Engaine History Society, Colchester Local Studies Library, Chris Thompson, Dave Russell, Derek Snowling, Derek Tumber, Derak Smith and Brightlingsea Museum, Essex Record Office, Jenny Kay and Fordham Local History Society, Jim Smith and Halstead & District Local History Society, John Collins and the Nottage Maritime Institute, John Stewart, Margaret Hedges, Patricia Burton-Hopkins, Patrick Denny, Paul Gallifant, Peter Noakes and West Bergholt Local History Group, Phyllis Hendry and St Osyth Museum & Archives, Ros Watling and Rowhedge Heritage Trust, Roy Fulcher, Suffolk Record Office, Tony Millat and Mersea Museum and the University of Essex. Extracts from Ordnance Survey maps are reproduced with the kind permission of Ordnance Survey

I must make special mention of David Cleveland for his constant encouragement. Finally to my wife, Maureen, who has endured many years of my wanderings and endless hours of solitude while I slaved at the computer, then tirelessly read my drafts and contributed many useful suggestions.

INTRODUCTION

This book is about the Essex Colne, a river that has been explored by boat, bike and boot by an Essex man who has spent a lifetime discovering its treasures and secrets. This is not the only river to bear the name Colne. There are river Colnes in Hertfordshire, Lancashire and Yorkshire; and a Coln in Gloucestershire. It is thought that the name is derived from an old Celtic word that simply means 'water'. The antiquity of this name has given the Essex river the unique privilege of having four parishes and a town all named after it: Colne Engaine, Earls Colne, White Colne, Wakes Colne and the ancient town of Colchester.

The Essex Colne is an extraordinarily ordinary river. By international, even national standards it is but a small lowland trickle, yet it is the longest all Essex river, passing through some of the most beautiful scenery in the county and the oldest town in the country. Its catchment area includes the driest place in Britain and the annual rainfall anywhere along its course rarely exceeds that of many places in Palestine. Despite this, the river has had a profound influence on the landscape and the people inhabiting its banks. First settled by Stone Age peoples, it later became home to one of the most powerful pre-Roman tribes in Brittain. Since then, it and its tributaries have powered over forty mills and it has been crossed by bridges built of wood, iron, stone and brick. On its banks ships have been built, coins minted, fabrics fashioned and more besides.

Within its diminutive length of forty-two miles the Colne exhibits the geogrphical characteristics of all rivers. A valley is divided into four sections each with its own particular features, which inevitably blur at the edges. The stages are: the young, the middle-aged, the old and finally the tidal estuary.

The young stage includes all the rivulets that join together to form a recognisable river. Several headwater streams that rise in the chalklands of north-west Essex form the young stage of the Colne. These join together and, below Great Yeldham, the river has acquired the characteristics of middle-age. Here the river has grown to a size where the water and materials carried in it have helped to form the landscape. The river now flows in a recognisable valley and has acquired a floodplain. As the Colne flows through the Hedinghams, Halstead and the Colnes to Fordstreet it is joined by several tributaries that add to its flow; its essential characteristics of a meandering river flowing across a floodplain, bounded by hills, remain the same. Although Essex is generally regarded as a flat county, the Colne has worn away a valley with sides that are far from flat. This fact is best experienced by exploring the valley by bicycle.

Below Fordstreet the river enters its third stage. Here the valley floor widens and the landscape through which the river flows has been formed largely by what has been brought down by the river. By the time the Colne reaches Colchester it enters its fourth and final stage as it becomes tidal and flows into its estuary, passing Rowhedge, Wivenhoe and Brightlingsea to Colne Point where it enters the North Sea.

This book is an exploration of the Colne made by boat, bike and boot, parish by parish, as it meanders its way from salt to source. There is so much of interest along the way that I have been able only to include a small selection of facts and anecdotes, some of which I hope will be of interest to the reader. I have chosen to travel upstream, seeing the landscape and riverside settlements from the river in much the same way as the first adventurers and settlers encountered the valley.

CHAPTER I

St Osyth

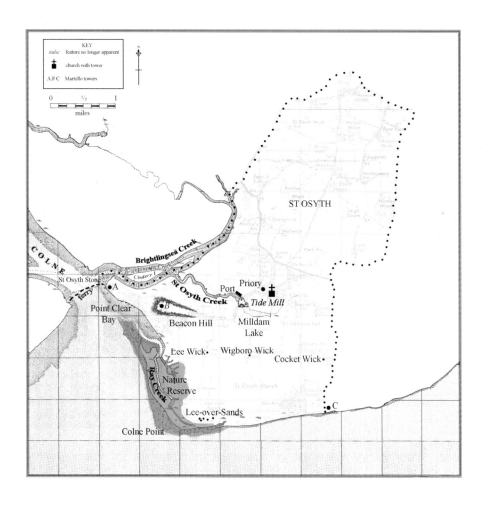

St Osyth

In ancient times St Osyth was known as Cice or Chich; it is thought that this refers to the twisted or crooked creek. It is recorded in Domesday that the manor of Cice had a mill in Saxon times. It is very likely that this was a tide mill. The suffix 'St Osyth' was added much later in recognition of the devout Christian, Osyth, who was beheaded in Cice in 653. The official name is still Cice St Osyth, although the ancient name is never used and the locals call their village 'Toosey'.

The 1848 Whites Directory describes St Osyth as a large, picturesque village with a mill standing on a brook that falls into a navigable creek. The parish is one of the three largest in the county. It extends south to St Osyth Point that juts into the ocean at the mouth of the river Colne near St Osyth Marsh and contains 1,677 souls within its 8,433 acres of land.

Now the winter population is over 4,000 but this increases to over 40,000 during the summer months.

Essex is a watery county. It is almost completely bounded by water with the Thames to the south, the Stour to the north and the Lee to the west. To the east its peninsulas and islands merge into the North Sea giving it the longest coastline of any English county. Between the Tendring peninsular and Mersea Island is the mouth of the longest all Essex river, the Colne.

The Tendring peninsula is the most northerly of the Essex peninsulas and is home to the county's most sandy beaches at Walton-on-the-Naze, Frinton-on-Sea and Clacton-on-Sea. At the peninsula's southernmost extremity the sand has almost run out as it competes with the more familiar Essex coastline of mud and marsh. Here at the mouth of the Colne estuary is where my journey started. I arrived early on a mid-November morning. The sky was grey: the silent, all-enveloping grey that dissolves the sky into the land somewhere indefinable in the distance. As the warmth from an invisible sun lifted this veil of grey towards itself the strange silhouettes of the buildings of Lee-over-Sands were slowly revealed. This attractively named seaside resort, nestling behind Colne Point, was conceived in 1932 when a company started the development of, what was intended to be, a rather up-market holiday resort with its own golf club and airstrip. The grand venture failed and now all that remains are a few ramshackle buildings behind the Colne Point Nature Reserve.

This is all of Lee-over-Sands, ideal for those who like isolation
and easy access to Colne Point Nature Reserve. (2011)

The Essex Wildlife Trust manages the 683 acre (273 ha) area of salt marsh and shingle spit as the Colne Point Nature Reserve. This is the last remaining habitat of shingle and salt marsh that once existed along much of the Tendring coastline. During the late 19th and early 20th centuries seaside holiday developments brought dramatic change to this coast. But there are no caravans here, just a few scars of earlier industrial activity of gravel removal and extraction. This is an ongoing activity along the estuary and as we travel along the river we will see abundant evidence of both working and abandoned sites. Here, in 1910, Samuel West set up a firm to take sand and gravel from the shore. Although this activity was called into question many times by the Parish Council, the work continued until the outbreak of WWII, only to be restarted afterwards. This commercial beach robbing finally ceased in the 1950s leaving an area that is now rich in plants and animals, including many nationally and locally rare species.

I have travelled on many of the sea walls of Essex, sometimes on foot but frequently with my trusty bicycle. Today I had my bike and started what was to be the first of many Colneside journeys with my wheeled friend. I have found that most sea walls are well used near access points and, when there

Loading barges with gravel at Sam West's jetty in Ray Creek at Colne Point. Much of this was transported to Dagenham to be used in the construction of the Ford Motor Company's factory. (1933-6)

4

are not too many people about, are easy to cycle on. Then beyond the point where most visitors retrace their steps, the surface becomes more uneven and the path less well defined: cycling here needs more concentration with less opportunity to look around. There are also long stretches of wall seldom visited by anyone, sometimes overgrown, sometimes so deeply rutted that pushing or carrying my bike is the best option.

While loitering in the Nature Reserve I had noticed that against the flat skyline of the sea wall was the occasional silhouette of a cyclist. I was soon to become one of these.

I left Lee-over-Sands along the sea wall footpath. I have heard tell that when this was being constructed in 1953 signs of an ancient building were discovered. It is thought that this was Roman in origin and may have been a watchtower or navigational aid for vessels sailing up the Colne.

The sea wall is built between the salt marsh of the nature reserve and what was St Osyth Fresh Marsh. For centuries this was grazing land but, following the rebuilding of the sea wall, the area was drained and is now used for arable crops. As I approached the higher land - well not much more than a metre higher - the footpath left the sea wall and headed inland towards Lee

Sam West's long abandoned jetty at the head of Ray Creek, now on the Essex Wildlife Trust's Colne Point Nature Reserve.. (2011)

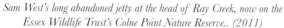

Wick Farm. On this November day I could see from the sea wall that the path, or where the path should have been, was now a very muddy field in which winter wheat was just emerging. I had just read on an information board that the average annual rainfall here is only 19 inches (482 mm) making it the driest place in Britain. The same board informed me that the majority of field boundaries are of prehistoric or Roman origin. I ignored the signpost and diverted around one such boundary. The wide grassy field margin allowed me to keep my feet free from mud, and it also provides habitat for voles and other small mammals feeding the expanding barn owl population.

I was now enjoying the cool autumn sunshine as I made my way to Lee Wick Farm, a fine Georgian building on a long established farm site. I have been told that in this area the name 'Wick' can mean 'sheep pasture' or 'farm'. When I compared old maps with new ones I found that the addition of 'Farm' to several of the 'Wicks' in this area is a very recent development. This leads me to favour the 'farm' meaning. A look at my map showed me that Lee Wick stands five metres above sea level and, on this contour, to the east you will find Wigborough Wick, Cockett Wick and the ancient Jay Wick, now something completely different. It seems our forebears knew where it was sensible to build. This sense appears to be sadly lacking in many of today's developers who happily build behind a sea wall hoping that it will protect their investment. When they are long gone others will wallow in the water that will inevitably one day reclaim this marshland.

From Lee Wick I took the path to Beacon Hill, a spur that extends to the Colne at Point Clear Bay. This promontory is over 10 metres high and overlooks the estuary. Its commanding position has long been used for the defence of the Colne. The present housing development occupies the site of another wick, Blockhouse Wick, a farm that took its name from the blockhouse that once stood on this hill. A blockhouse is a military term for a small, isolated fort in the form of a single building. Henry VIII built many, as part of his defences protecting important maritime approaches. The Colne estuary was defended by one at East Mersea and another here on Beacon Hill. It is thought that this one was a hexagonal timber construction that housed several cannon.

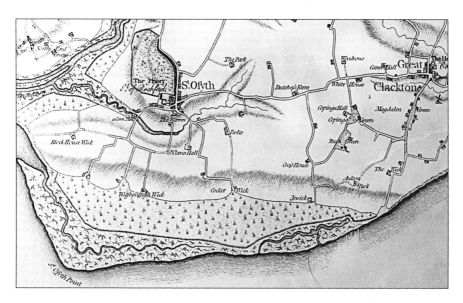

This 1777 map shows the sea wall, fresh water marsh and the wicks, all on the higher ground.

Two hundred years or so later Beacon Hill became the site of a Martello Tower. These forts were built during the early years of the 19th century as defences against a possible attack by Napoleon. A chain of 103 towers was erected to protect England's south and east coasts between Seaford in Sussex to Aldeburgh in Suffolk. Each tower was constructed from about a million bricks with walls about three metres thick and twelve metres high surmounted by a gun platform. The south coast towers were given numbers and those on the east coast had letters. In the parish of St Osyth there were three towers: A, B and C. Tower C still stands but is no longer in St Osyth; it was lost to the neighbouring parish when Clacton Urban District was created in 1937.

Tower B stood on Beacon Hill and stayed in the parish a little longer. When the threat of invasion had passed this tower, along with many more, including the other two in the parish, were taken over by the Preventives, the forerunners of the Coastguards, whose duty it was to try to prevent smuggling.

7

Prior to the demolition of tower B in 1967, to make way for a housing development, it was owned by Frank Hyde. The roof of the tower was festooned with aerials that were part of an early radio telescope. Frank used this in 1959 to make the first amateur observations of the Crab Nebula. His vast experience in pioneering this field of amateur astronomy led him to write his definitive guide *Radio Astronomy for Amateurs*.

Below Beacon Hill, Point Clear is crammed with caravans and an assortment of holiday homes many of which appear to have grown out of beach huts. They are protected from the sea by a concrete sea wall along which I walked to Martello Tower A. This is one of the 47 surviving towers and since 1986 has housed the East Essex Aviation Museum.

By the tower is the *Ferry Boat Inn* that is close to a ramp over the sea wall. This leads to the ferry, which I will come back to later when I continue my exploration of the Colne, but before I do, I will explore the village of St Osyth.

The path from the ferry ramp continues for a short distance along the concrete sea wall past more beach huts which are gradually being expanded into houses. The concrete gives way to grass as the wall follows Brightlingsea Creek past Cindery Island and then along St Osyth Creek to the port. For much of the way this is a wide post-1953 wall but the stretch beyond the caravans and golf course is little used, narrow and overgrown. The surface was muddy and as I did not want to slide off the wall I chose to walk. The path emerges by a small collection of houseboats and on the other bank is the ancient port of St Osyth. Today this is little more than a boatyard at the head of the tidal creek that is now much

Martello Tower A at Point Clear, now the East Essex Aviation Museum. (2011)

more silted-up than in the days of trade. At certain states of the tide, Thames Barges can still reach this port and several take advantage of its sheltered position and traditional boatyard to over-winter. Boats have been built here for centuries but the yard has had a checkered history. It has been opened and closed several times, and it has built various craft including barges and houseboats, folkboats and yachts. After the most recent period of closure it was reopened in 1987 and now specializes in restoration work, for which it has gained a high reputation. A notice board in the yard proudly boasts '*St Osyth, a port since 1215*'.

Sea going vessels were prevented from travelling further up the creek by the milldam. This was built to create a reservoir of seawater to power the tide mill that once stood here. There is a record in Domesday of a mill in Cice (Chich), the former name of St Osyth. This was almost certainly a tide mill. During the Middle Ages there are further references to a tide mill that belonged to the Priory. This was rebuilt in 1732 and worked until 1929. It was unusual in that its two undershot wheels were powered by water flowing from a large man-made milldam lake covering four acres (1.6 ha).

The development of St Osyth beach started in 1927. This view of beach huts overlooking the Colne estuary was taken looking towards Beacon Hill that still has its Martello Tower. (1937)

Point Clear from the air, home to 300 chalets and 1800 caravans. The Colne estuary is at bottom right and many moorings can be seen in Brightlingsea Creek. (2007)

In its later years the mill was not very profitable and when it finally closed its owner, George Summit, tried various schemes to make money. These included using the millpond as a boating lake, opening a café, and when the lake froze over, he tried to charge people to skate on it. He was ahead of his time but failed to make enough money to maintain the mill, which gradually fell into disrepair. Then during WWII it was badly damaged by two mines that exploded in the Creek. After the war the preservation societies were aware of the precarious state of the building but failed to act before the January gale of 1962 when the roof was blown off into the road, shortly to be followed by the demolition of the remains.

As the shadows lengthened towards the end of what had been a glorious November day I walked up Mill Street, passed the Georgian Mill House and several cottages to an unassuming 1960s dwelling that has an interesting history to tell.

St Osyth Mill. The Mill House is on the extreme right and the barge Mayflower is moored in front of what is now the boatyard. (1920s)

The tide mill was demolished in 1962. The Mill House is still there and hulks, some awaiting restoration, replace the working barge. (2012)

THE COLNE

In Elizabethan times St Osyth was an isolated close-knit community where inbreeding and incest were not unknown and anybody unfortunate enough to be slightly different and who fell out of favour was easily vilified. So it was that an unusually tall, stooping woman who had claimed to have cured some villagers' ailments was accused of being a witch. In 1582 Ursula Kemp was held in the village lock-up, then imprisoned in Colchester Castle before being taken to Chelmsford to be tried for witchcraft. On the evidence provided by her base-born eight year old son, and villagers, to whom she was related in one way or another, she was found guilty, executed, and forgotten.

That is until 1921 when some bones were discovered in the garden of a cottage in Mill Street. These were carefully exposed revealing a skeleton with pronounced curvature of the spine. The burial was not in consecrated ground and was orientated in a north-south direction, unlike the normal east-west direction found in churchyards. Also the ankles, wrists and elbows had been fastened down with iron spikes. This was often the practice when burying a witch as it was thought to prevent her spirit rising to haunt or annoy. The owner of the cottage, Mr. Brooker, was far from annoyed at this discovery in his garden and set about cashing-in on his find. He built a wooden frame around the skeleton in the grave and fitted a double trapdoor enclosed in railings. For a number of years he charged visitors a fee to see the skeleton, told them stories and sold postcards as a memento of their visit. It became quite an attraction with charabanc trips run from Clacton and other

The skeleton discovered in Mill Street in 1921, thought to have been that of Ursula Kemp.

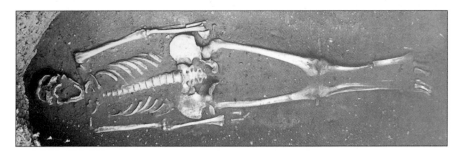

towns in the surrounding area. All this came to a sudden halt in 1933 when Mr. Brooker's cottage burnt to the ground. There were many in the village who were superstitious enough to claim that the end of Mr. Brooker's good fortune was the result of the witch's vengeance. Following this catastrophic event the grave was filled in and once more forgotten.

Then in 1964 prior to a new house being built on the plot, the skeletal remains, along with the iron spikes were removed from St Osyth and taken to the Witches Museum in Cornwall. Here they were exhibited for thirty-three years before being sold to a private collector. More recently a local film maker, John Worland, whilst making a film about the Ursula Kemp story, located the remains and arranged for a forensic examination to be performed. The bones were dated to between 1560 and 1600 so fitting the date of Ursula Kemp. But the evidence from the pelvis and structure of the bones indicated that they were those of a young male of about twenty years. Having been a curiosity and visitor attraction for the best part of the 20th century, the remains of this unknown man were eventually returned to St Osyth and buried in 2011. So ends the remarkable story of Ursula Kemp.

Continuing along Mill Street the road follows the priory wall and then, around a bend, the impressive gatehouse comes into view. This was erected in 1475 and is regarded as the finest medieval gatehouse in the country.

The history of this religious site goes back to the legend of St Osyth. The story of this Saxon Saint has been retold so many times that fact and fiction have become somewhat confused. A brief summary of the story is that Osyth was the daughter of Readwald, the first Christian King of East Anglia. From an early age Osyth was devout and expressed the wish to live the contemplative life but her father's political ambitions involved unifying the Kingdom of the East Angles with the neighbouring Saxons. To this end Osyth was betrothed to Sighere, the Christian King of the East Saxons. During the wedding feast Osyth escaped and took the vow. Sighere was remarkably understanding and respected her piety by giving her land in the northeast of his kingdom at Cice, where she established a nunnery. Some years later the nunnery was sacked by a band of marauding Danes. Osyth refused to give up her faith with the result that her head was struck off. Then, as the story goes, Osyth picked up her head and carried it some way to the nunnery where she knocked on the chapel door before finally collapsing.

Some years later in 1118, an Augustinian Priory was established on the site of the nunnery. The first Prior became Archbishop of Canterbury and eventually the Priory became one of the richest monastic houses in the country. It is thought that St Osyth's remains were moved to the Priory as, at the time of the dissolution in 1539, the inventory included '*the skull of Seynt Osithes closyed in sylver parcel gylte with a crown of sylver gylt to sett upon the sayd skull garnisshyed with counterfett stones.*' Following the dissolution, the Abbey was held by a succession of powerful families until the 1860s when it was sold in 28 lots, mostly to tenant farmers who became the landowners. The Priory buildings became a residence and farm of about 430 acres, much as it is today. This site houses one of the most impressive groups of medieval buildings in Europe. Somewhat controversially, the present owner wishes to further subdivide the Priory lands to develop them for residential purposes.

It is now time to leave the parish of St Osyth and continue my journey along the Colne. To do this I will return to St Osyth Stone to board the ferry to East Mersea.

left: The 13th century seal depicting St Osyth. This was found in the early 19th century near Colchester.

top right: St Osyth Priory Gateway. (1830)

lower right: The Priory was last opened to the public in 1998; the Gateway is undergoing essential maintenance. (2012)

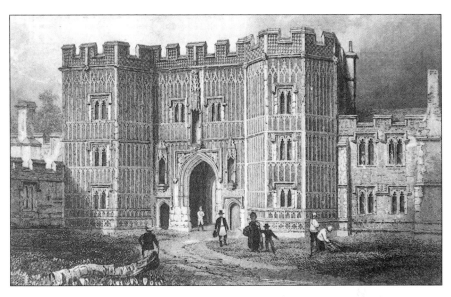

The author at St Osyth Stone, about to board the ferry for East Mersea. (2012)

CHAPTER II

East Mersea

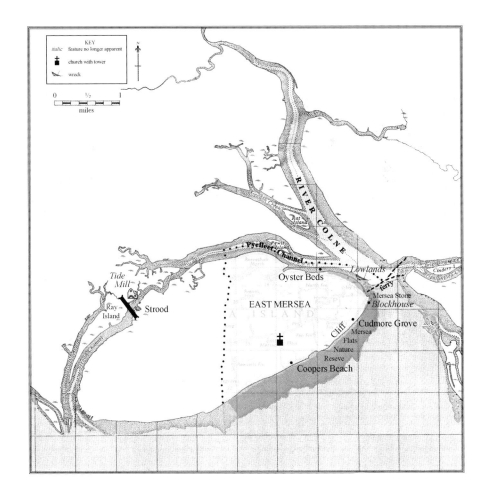

East Mersea

The name Mersea is derived from the Saxon 'Meres-ig' which means 'island in the mere'. In ancient settlement names an 'ig' or 'island' frequently refers to 'dry ground surrounded by marsh' as well as 'island' in the modern sense. In Old English a mere could be anything from a 'pool' to a 'pond' or 'lake'.

In 1848, William White says that the parish of East Mersea occupied 1,820 acres including 500 acres of low marshes and saltings on Pyefleet Creek; there were 331 inhabitants.

By 2011 the population had dropped to 266. This must be somewhat of a record for a parish that is within 50 miles of London.

The ferry crossing from St Osyth takes about 10 minutes. I was accompanied by another cyclist and a young family just going for the ride. As we approached Mersea Stone a small group of people were waiting on the shelving beach to make the return crossing. They joined the young family on the ferry as I left to explore Mersea Island. This is 4½ miles long and 2 miles wide, it gently rises to a height of about 70ft (21m) and is the most easterly inhabited island in the British Isles. The island is divided into two parishes: East and West. The principle settlement is in West Mersea, an ancient fishing community that is now popular with sailors and holidaymakers. Although of a similar acreage, East Mersea is a much smaller and more scattered rural community. It is the East with which I am more concerned as it forms the boundary of the seaward extremity of the Colne estuary. Quite where the estuary ends and the sea begins is debatable. I landed at the eastern extremity of the island at Mersea Stone. Inland from here is definitely the Colne. Seaward is shown on charts and maps as Brightlingsea Reach and I consider this is part of the Colne estuary. This is why I am planning to walk from the Stone along the seaward side of East Mersea, then cross the island to the landward side and return beside the Pyefleet back to the Stone.

Looking across the Colne estuary to Beacon Hill in St Osyth from Mersea Stone. The WWII pillbox in the foreground is the latest defensive structure built on this site to protect this important waterway. (2011)

THE COLNE

Mersea Stone is not any upstanding single stone, or even an outcrop. It is just a collection of small stones - some would say pebbles - that form a stony spit at the end of the island. It has long been of strategic importance for the defence of the Colne. On the orders of Henry VIII a blockhouse was built here to defend the Colne against possible attack by the French or Spanish. This wooden structure was triangular with sides of about 100 yards (90 metres) surrounded by a defensive ditch and would have housed twelve cannon. The fort was neglected or repaired at various times, depending upon the state of readiness the country found necessary. It was used during the civil war when it was held by the Parliamentarians to prevent supply vessels reaching the besieged Royalists in Colchester. All was then quiet until the Napoleonic wars when once again the site was brought into service by the building of a gun battery. Most recently a pillbox was constructed during WWII.

This area no longer serves any defensive role other than that of defending the wildlife habitats of the Estuary. Mersea Stone falls within the East Mersea Flats Nature Reserve which together with Brightlingsea Marsh and Colne Point, form

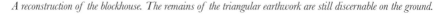

A reconstruction of the blockhouse. The remains of the triangular earthwork are still discernable on the ground.

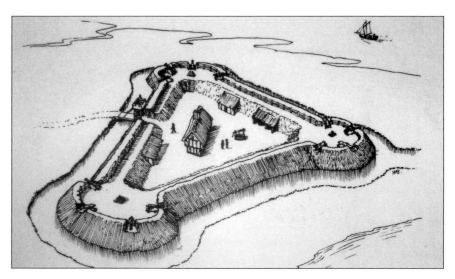

the Colne Estuary National Nature Reserve. The estuary contains a rich variety of habitats of tidal creeks, mudflats, sand and shingle beaches, saltmarsh, sea walls with borrow dykes and grazing marsh.

From Mersea Stone I walked along the path through the marsh to the sea wall, where the way became dry and surfaced, to cope with the ever increasing number of visitors. On the landward side of the sea wall is a water filled dyke. This feature is called a 'borrow dyke' and is common where saltmarsh has been reclaimed from the sea. They are formed when the clay and silt is excavated for the construction of the sea wall.

At the end of the dyke the land rises to form a cliff above which is Cudmore Grove Country Park. Since 1974 this 35 acre (14 ha) site of former arable land has been managed by Essex County Council as a recreation and conservation area. I have been visiting this site since the 1950s when there was a footpath through the cornfields to the beach below a constantly eroding cliff. In that time I have seen the cliff-top recede by at least 100ft (30m) and the cliff edge pillboxes have appeared to move down the beach, as the sea erodes

The three Colne estuary reserves: Mersea Flats, Brightlingsea Marsh and Colne Point.

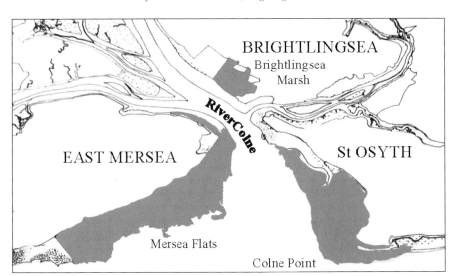

everything else from around them. If you visit this site at low tide you will see rows of stakes stretching out over the mudflats. These were placed there some years ago and were originally interwoven with conifer branches. The idea was that at high tide, sediment in the water would settle and eventually raise the level of mud sufficiently to enable saltmarsh vegetation to stabilise the area. This does not appear to be happening and the cliff continues to erode. I'm sure that the geologists do not mind, as with each cliff fall there is the possibility of further finds of fossilised bones. The soft rocks in the cliff were laid down some two million years ago during the Pleistocene era, these were then overlain with gravels during the Hoxnian interglacial period some 300,000 years ago. Fossilised remains of shark teeth, small mammals, birds and molluscs are not uncommon finds. Identification of these has led scientists to deduce that at the time the climate was more extreme than it is today, with hotter summers and colder winters. Further along the beach is the site where impressive fossil remains of hippopotamus, monkey and elephant have been found. These have been dated to a more recent interglacial period some 100,000 years ago, when the climate here was sub-tropical.

I continued my walk along the beach with the vast expanse of the glistening Mersea mud on my left, but now with the extensive Coopers Beach Caravan Park on my right. Eventually I came to the end of this extensive site with its

East Mersea Flats below Cudmore Grove. The remains of the pillbox on the beach once stood on the clifftop. (2011)

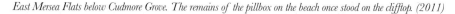

Recent erosion of East Mersea Cliffs. (2011)

seaside facilities of amusements, swimming pool and eating and drinking establishments. I turned inland and followed the track up to East Mersea church.

Parts of the present church of St Edmund date from the 12th century, but it stands on a more ancient site that was originally surrounded by a moat, parts of which can still be seen. This is thought to have been a Viking camp occupying about 5 acres (2ha), dating from the late 9th century. I wonder if it is just coincidence that the later church was dedicated to St Edmund, who was killed by the Vikings because he refused to renounce his Christian beliefs. The story of Edmund is based on considerably more fact than that of St Osyth. The Young Edmund was crowned King of the East Angles on Christmas Day 855 at Bures and reigned for fifteen years before being executed by the Vikings. His followers took his body to Bury, which later became known as Bury St Edmunds. He still has followers today, many of whom think that this particular saint is the rightful patron saint of England, as indeed he was before the Norman Conquest. St Edmund, Patron saint of England and his emblem, the white dragon on a red background, was one of the many obvious signs of Anglo-Saxon England that the conquering Normans tried to remove. Gradually over a period of two hundred years or so the English St Edmund, martyr, was usurped by the far less-deserving St George, a Roman soldier adopted by the Norman Crusaders as the saint who, they claimed, led them to victory.

In more recent times East Mersea church is remembered for its Rector the Reverend Sabine Baring-Gould who was the incumbent here between 1871 and 1881. Baring-Gould was a prolific writer of hymns, his popular titles include *Onward Christian Soldiers* and *Now the Day is Over*. He also penned many novels; one of his early successes was *Mehalah*. This Gothic novel, set in the marshlands of Mersea is said to have its principle characters based on the author's observations of local people.

I left the church by following in the footsteps of Baring-Gould along the path that goes past the Hall, along the most direct route to Mersea Stone. This would have been the first leg of the frequent journeys made by Baring-Gould to London. In the 1870s the most convenient way to make the journey

Crossing the Strood. This Primrose Bus was painted yellow as were all the busses operated by the Mersea, Colchester & District Transport & Bus Co. Ltd., based at the Primrose Garage in West Mersea High Street from 1918 until 1935 when the company was taken over by Eastern National. (c1920s)

from East Mersea was to take the ferry to Brightlingsea to meet the train to Colchester and then on to London. I did not walk directly back to the Stone but turned along Shop Lane and then along the footpath towards Pyefleet. This is the waterway that separates Mersea Island from the Mainland, the channel flows through the wide expanses of forlorn saltmarshes with their low lying islets that are the setting for *Mehalah*.

The channel is crossed by a tidal causeway known as the Strood. At one time it was believed that this was originally a Roman construction. One of the many stories associated with the Strood involves the appearance of a Roman centurion who walks the Strood in certain misty conditions. It is now thought that the Roman access to Mersea was by way of a ford and that a causeway was not required. Over the centuries, following the Roman withdrawal from Britain, rising sea levels made access increasingly more difficult. Archaeologists have now established that the original Strood was a timber causeway built by the Saxons between 648 and 702, possibly for access to an important religious establishment on the island.

As the sea level continued to rise the original crossing was repaired and rebuilt, but the name 'Strood', thought to be derived from the Saxon word 'strod' meaning marshy land, has remained the same.

Early in the 18th century, a long, narrow tidal water reservoir was dug beside the Strood. This was to power the tide mill built in 1734. By 1769 this was described as 'the late Stroud Mill'. This implies that the mill worked for less than 35 years, giving this mill the dubious distinction of having the shortest lifespan of any Essex tide mill.

Just beyond the Strood is Ray Island. Since 1970 this uninhabited marshland island has been owned by the National Trust and managed as a nature reserve. The warden is of the opinion that the evidence of an early building on the island supports the theory that Baring-Gould's *'small farmhouse built of tarred wreckage timber, and roofed with red pantiles'* is based on the folk memory of a real building that stood on the island long before his time. Before I go back to *Mehalah* I need to describe what was before my eyes as I walked along the sea wall beside the Pyefleet.

The oyster beds here have a long history. It is thought that oysters were harvested here before the Romans arrived. There is documentary evidence from 1189, when Richard I granted the fishery to the Borough of Colchester in return for the town sending men to help build Dover Castle. Mersea is regarded as the centre of oyster culture in England and in its heyday in the 1830s there were over 500 smacks and 2,000 men involved in the oyster fishery. Since then the industry has declined and in 1920 the Native Oyster was almost eliminated by disease. After re-stocking, the recovering industry was again in trouble in the 1980s when pollution from the anti-fouling agent TBT drove the oyster almost to extinction. The use of this chemical has now been banned and the oyster fishery is thriving once again. There are now two types of oyster in the waters off Mersea: the Native, with its flat shell that takes five years to grow to maturity and can only be harvested and eaten when there is an 'r' in the month; and the faster growing Rock oyster with its crinkly shell that matures in three years and can be harvested and eaten all year round. The dredged oysters are sorted and the mature oysters are moved to the creek-side to fatten before being collected, then washed and kept in clean flowing water for 48 hours before they are ready for sale.

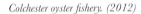

Colchester oyster fishery. (2012)

Since 1540 the oyster season has been opened with the traditional Gin and Gingerbread ceremony led by the Mayor of Colchester. He and other civic dignitaries sail from Brightlingsea to Pyefleet Creek for the first dredge and to declare the oyster fishery open. (c1900)

Since 1964 the lease of the Pyefleet fishery has been held by Colchester Oyster Fishery Ltd. who grow and supply Colchester Native Oysters and Rock Oysters to the public, trade, wholesale markets and many prestigious London hotels.

For a long time I was hesitant about calling the Pyefleet a tributary of the Colne. It could be considered an area of sea as it connects the Colne Estuary with the Blackwater Estuary to make Mersea an island. What persuaded me was the fact that below the ebbing and flowing saltwater is a constant flow of freshwater supplied by the rivulets that drain in through the marshes from the surrounding land. The 19th century bargemen and WWI sailors knew about this. They went to the entrance of the Pyefleet to collect freshwater by using large cast-iron bells that were lowered to the bottom.

I had now reached the point where the Pyefleet ends and I was actually walking along the bank of the Colne. Within a short distance, quite close to the shore, I saw a few metal struts poking out of the water. These are the crumbling remains of *SS Lowlands*, the only wreck in the Colne that is marked on the chart. How the ship became a victim of the notorious Mersea mud is a fascinating story. In fact there have been many stories, some woven into yarns involving gold and silver bullion, told by local boatmen to visitors to add value and excitement to their boat trips. We will never know the whole truth but the bones of the story have been unravelled by local maritime historians. The 260ft (78m) steel steamship *Lowlands* was built in 1888 in West Hartlepool. Her last voyage was to be in March 1916 when she sailed from Hull with a cargo of timber. Two days later she was torpedoed off Margate and left to sink. Luckily her cargo of timber kept her afloat and no lives were lost. She was picked up by a tug and towed into the Thames and beached on Mucking

As the tide ebbs, oyster pits are slowly revealed in the Pyefleet Channel as it wends its way through mudflats and saltmarsh to the Strood. (2011)

The remains of the gantry on SS Lowlands *wrecked here in 1916, a long-time favourite roost for cormorants. (2012)*

Flats with other craft damaged by enemy action. Here *Lowlands* was declared a total loss and her cargo removed. The story then becomes a little vague but sometime later a salvage firm patched her up and proceeded to tow her to the Colne, whether to be broken up or repaired is unclear. All went well as far as Colne Point where, for reasons unknown she was beached. The naval authorities were not happy with her position and ordered her removal. The tow was continued, now under the direction of a Colne River Pilot. It is possible that the vessel's pumps failed, or for some other reason the pilot decided the ship would have to be beached again. Consequently he headed for the Brightlingsea shore but the Harbour Master would not allow this and directed the vessel to East Mersea. Now this is where things began to happen that were to determine her fate for the following ninety-six years and more. At high tide she was towed out of harms way on to the mud close to the shore. Unfortunately as the tide ebbed she slipped into the navigation channel and her temporary patches burst leaving her to be sucked into the

A seaworthy SS Lowlands *in Bristol Docks. (c1900)*

Mersea mud. There followed at least two attempts to raise her and one to blow up the vessel but she was well and truly stuck. Then during **WWII** when all metal was required for munitions a further salvage attempt was made but once again the Mersea mud won. Despite being marked with lights and buoys and everyone using the Colne claiming to know the whereabouts of *Lowlands* there have been several near misses by trading vessels and some reports of glancing blows by river barges.

The sea wall path was soon crossed by the path that would have been Baring-Gould's direct route to the ferry. In those days the long established ferry departed from the hard at the end of this path, that is now just down from the sea wall. The ferry was operated by William and Anne Baker who lived on an old barge moored by the hard. Baring-Gould's frequent visits to London meant that he got to know them well. Anne Baker exhibited many of the colourful characteristics that Baring-Gould used in a character in his novel. Perhaps more significant is that William had a thirteen year old daughter, Mehala. Although by now she was living in Brightlingsea, Baring-Gould would have known her. Her name at least could well have been the inspiration of his fictional heroine.

The ferry continued to operate until the closure of the railway to Brightlingsea. Then after several years without a ferry the service was reopened in 2002. Now in its tenth year of operation the custom built 21ft (6.3m) boat complete with ramp to allow easy access for wheelchairs and cycles is supported by local people and a growing number of holiday-makers. I left Mersea on the ferry, full to capacity, to continue my story in Brightlingsea.

The waiting room and ferry from East Mersea to Brightlingsea operated by Mr. Mole. (c1935)

Today there is no shelter for passengers awaiting the ferry to Brightlingsea. (2012)

CHAPTER III

Brightlingsea

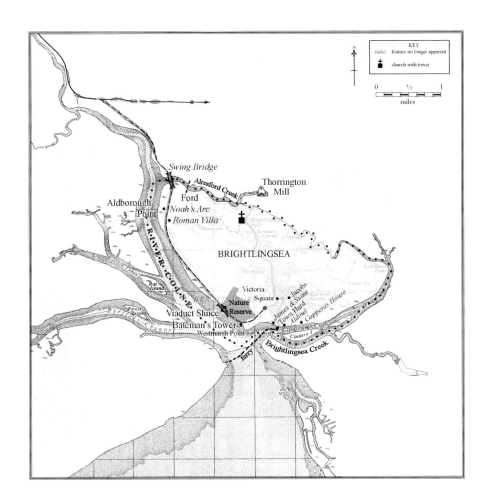

THE COLNE

Brightlingsea

The name is thought to be derived from three Saxon words meaning 'the island belonging to Brychta's or Brightic's people'.

At the time of the Domesday Survey the manor was held by King William and contained one mill.

Brightlingsea has the unique distinction of being the only Cinque Port in Essex. Since 1360 it has been a 'Limb of the Cinque Port Liberty' affiliated to Sandwich.

In 1848 William White described the parish as a considerable fishing village of 2,045 souls and 3,093 acres on the eastern side of the estuary of the river Colne. Extending about 3 miles along the banks of the Colne, it is bounded on the north by Alresford Creek and on the south by Brightlingsea Creek. Being almost surrounded by these creeks, it has been considered an island and, at high tide, can only be reached by the single road from Thorrington. It has long been associated with the oyster and sprat fisheries.

The population in 2011 was 8,076 and the town is largely a dormitory for Colchester.

There are two approaches to Brightlingsea, one by road and one by sea, or, as it is said, "by the front door or the back". I entered by the front door on the ferry from East Mersea.

The port of Brightlingsea has a long history. It is perhaps fortunate that it was never developed into a major sea port. The natural harbour has played an important part in the town's history. Its most recent claims to fame were during the Miners' Strike of 1984 when attempts to import coal were thwarted by picketing miners, and again in 1995 when the export of live animals for slaughter in Europe was stopped by a series of protests by people who thought the practice was cruel and inhumane. The protests resulted in nearly 600 arrests and became known as the battle of Brightlingsea. Today the harbour is mostly given over to leisure craft, although there is a little commercial activity of which some is associated with the offshore wind farm industry. The enormous piles of scrap metal for export, that decorated

Brightlingsea's 'front door'. The Town Hard and distinctive Anchor *building with ferryman, Peter Harry, in the foreground. (2012)*

the quayside for many years, have been replaced by equally sized heaps of woodchip awaiting export to Europe to be burned in power stations. And of course there are the foot-ferry operations to Point Clear, East Mersea and Colchester via Wivenhoe and Rowhedge.

In the days when the ferryman had to row his boat, sometimes in a fast flowing tide, the precise time of arrival was not predictable. This was well known to the railway staff and it was not unknown for the Station Master to hold the train or even the engine driver to pull back into the station if a rowing boat was seen in the mouth of the creek. I will return to the informal nature of the running of this railway later but first I will explore the town.

For many years the almost island of Brightlingsea was a scattered farming community clustered around its eight greens. There was also the natural landing place at the confluence of the Creek with the Colne, this meant that there has always been some fishing and other maritime activity in the parish even before there was a town. This did not develop until the 19th century

By the time that this photograph was taken Mr. Horatio Mole had operated the ferry by oar and sail between Brightlingsea and East Mersea for 52 years. (1933)

when the unprecedented demand for oysters led to the expansion of the industry and the growth of three of the island's greens into the town of Brightlingsea. As the fishery grew so did the demand for vessels and the long-established boat building activity expanded to fulfil this requirement. This meant that later in the century, when the activity of leisure yacht cruising and racing boomed, Brightlingsea had all the boatbuilding skills and associated industries to become one of the prime centres of this industry. At its peak well over a hundred yachts were overwintered in mud berths along the creek. The annual fitting out and crewing of these 100 to 200 ton vessels provided employment for getting on for a thousand Brightlingsea men.

By the 1930s Aldous had become the largest yard on the Essex coast. It extended upcreek from the hard and occupied an area of 15 acres (6ha) with three slipways. During WWII the yard had up to 660 employees and built over 400 craft and repaired or refitted many more. This level of activity was not maintained during the post-war years when the yard built workboats,

The ferry is now run by Brightlingsea Harbour and operates between the town, Point Clear and East Mersea. (2012)

Steam yachts laid up in their winter berths. (1930)

tugs and ferries mainly for Commonwealth countries. Eventually decreasing order books led to the closure of the yard in 1962. The site then became a general industrial estate where, today there are a few companies that supply some of the needs of the leisure boat industry. A small part of the site is used by the Colne Smack Preservation Society that was founded by Jim Lawrence in 1971. The traditional Colne smack was developed over a period of time, so that by about the year 1900 it was regarded as the perfect fast and functional boat that two or three men could handle while sailing and fishing at the same time. At its peak there were over 150 of these craft operating out of Brightlingsea but the introduction of motorised vessels meant that by the 1970s, there was the real possibility that the traditional smack would pass into the history books. The Heritage Dock has helped to ensure that this did not happen by saving at least eighteen of these vessels, and these will be seen sailing on the Colne for many years to come.

The road that leads into this industrial area is Copperas Road, named after an earlier industry that flourished here for over 200 years. On the first edition of the Ordnance Survey map published in 1805 the only feature marked on the creek is the Copperas House.

The story of how this industry arrived in Brightlingsea is interesting. Chemical compounds of various metals with sulphur are collectively known by the ancient name of *vitriols*. They are used in the production of inks and dyes. The methods of making them were known to the Babylonians and they

Enthusiasts working on a traditional Colne smack in the Aldous Heritage Dock. (2012)

were used in Europe by the Greeks and Romans. During the 15th century the production and movement of these substances was restricted by a Papal monopoly. When this was tightened during the following century, Henry VIII, and then Elizabeth I, granted considerable state subsidies to entrepreneurs in an effort to find a local source of these substances, which were essential to the country's important wool industry. The initiative was successful and the copperas industry arrived in Brightlingsea. The earliest written record of this is that of the death of a copperas maker in the town in 1638.

Within the London Clay that is exposed on many of the beaches of Essex can be found stones that are often in the shape of broken twigs. This is because they are in fact just that: pieces of wood which over the course of geological time have become fossilised and pyritised, that is changed into iron pyrites or copperas. These stones were gathered by hand or dredged in large numbers in several coastal districts where the copperas was washed from the clay by the tide. The gathered material was taken to a copperas house where

The Edwardian Anchor *Hotel beyond the hard at high water. (c1910)*

the manufacturing process was carried out. On a large floor copperas stones and pieces of scrap iron were made into piles. These were then moistened with water. After a few hours the action of air and water on the copperas produced green vitriol (ferrous sulphate) and sulphuric acid, which reacted with the scrap iron to produce even more green vitriol. This was drained off into lead tanks where it was heated to produce green vitriol crystals. These crystals, although very impure, were adequate for dyes used in the woollen industry, the tanning process and in the production of inks. From the 17th until the 19th century the copperas industry in southern England prospered, and Brightlingsea was one of the chief places where it was carried out.

At the head of the hard where I had arrived, is the building known as the *Anchor*. The outward appearance has hardly changed since it was built as an hotel in 1903, even though it has now become apartments. This cannot be said of the site to the left of the hard. This is the site of the former James's yard and Stone's yard that became James & Stone Ltd

The Anchor, *the site of an inn since 1805, converted into apartments in 2001. (2012)*

Reg White (1938-2010) memorial. (2012)

1963 Little Americas Cup 1964 Little Americas Cup
1964 Hornet World Champion 1965 Little Americas Cup
1966 Little Americas Cup 1966 Yachtsman of the Year
1968 "B" Class World Champion 1968 Little Americas Cup
1969 Tornado World Champion 1973 Tornado European Champion

1976 Tornado European Champion
1976 Tornado North American Champion
1976 Tornado World Champion
1976 Yachtsman of the Year 1976 M.B.E. New Years Honours
1979 World Tornado Champion 1981 National Champion

Olympic Gold Medallist 1976

in 1942. Together the yards handled 547 vessels during the war years. Many people know of this yard as the home of the Brightlingsea One Design (BOD). This class of clinker built wooden dinghy was designed by Robbie Stone in 1927 and is still regularly raced on the Colne. One of its most famous sailors was the Olympic Gold Medallist and several times World Champion, Reg White. Reg was born in Brightlingsea in 1935, the son of an oyster merchant. He grew up on the foreshore and was interested in boats from an early age. From school, he was taken on as a boatbuilding apprentice at James & Stone's yard. At the same time, he sailed his father's BOD with considerable success. He went on to become involved with the building of catamarans. This led to a partnership which later became the Brightlingsea boat-building company, Sailcraft Limited. The company's boats were developed to new levels when the Tornado was selected for the 1976 Olympics, and at the same time Reg went into training to represent Great Britain. He was rewarded with a gold medal and was made an MBE for his contribution to the sport.

The plaque on the restored Wreck House. (2012)

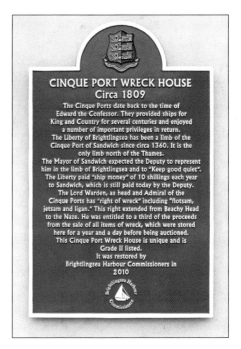

Not far from the Reg White memorial there remains a little bit of old Brightlingsea. Squeezed and belittled by new development is the ancient wreck house. This was where items salvaged from wrecks were stored for a year and a day before being auctioned. Because of the unique status of Brightlingsea as a Cinque Port, a third of all wreck proceeds went to the town. The building was restored by Brightlingsea Harbour Commissioners in 2010.

Brightlingsea Marina on the site of the former James & Stone shipyard. (2012)

The James & Stone yard managed to stay in business until 1989. The site has now been redeveloped as a marina. I had first seen this development several years ago from East Mersea and thought how incongruously its steel piling and out-of-scale buildings sat in the landscape. Sometimes the facilities that new developments provide enhance local communities, so it was with an open mind that I first visited Brightlingsea's new marina. Unfortunately, close inspection confirmed my first impressions of a wholly inappropriate development. The area was cold and impersonal with access to the waterside severely restricted. I left the newest building in the town as quickly as possible for the oldest.

The town's most noteworthy house is known as *Jacob's*. This is not only the town's oldest house but possibly the oldest surviving wooden house in England. Said to have been built in the 13th century it takes its name from the original owner, who was probably the builder of the house. It consisted of one large room open to the roof, the fire being a brazier on the floor, and the smoke escaping through a smoke hole in the roof.

The east and west wings were added soon after, making it into a fine example of a 14th century timber-framed 'H' shaped dwelling. During the 15th century a ceiling of beautifully carved and moulded oak was built into the hall, dividing it into two rooms, one above the other. The decorated brick turret, with its spiral staircase in the corner of the forecourt, was built for the purpose of getting into the room above. The house as seen today from the High Street was in fact the back of the house, which actually faced the sea. The estate extended considerably on either side, and reached down to the waters edge. Over the next 200 years or so the house deteriorated, and eventually was divided into seven 'lets'. The west wing was almost entirely rebuilt, converting it into three cottages. The front of the house now faced the roadway. It was plastered all over and the upper stories, which projected at each end, were underbuilt with brick. A shop was erected between the wings and various other changes and additions were made, rendering the house unrecognisable both inside and out.

Then, by an incredible twist of fate in 1919 the house was accidentally 'discovered' and the uncovering began. The shop was pulled down and most of the inside and outside plastering was removed. In 1932 the Ancient Buildings Trust bought the property and shortly afterwards repairs were started. Under the plaster facings between the beams were the original wattle and daub walls in an excellent state of preservation. It seems incredible that

'Jacob's' *before restoration, with the shop built in 1895.*

'Jacob's' *shortly after restoration. (c1920)*

'Jacob's', *possibly the oldest timber framed house in England. (2012)*

hazel sticks bedded in stiff clay and dry cut grass could have lasted for at least 600 years. Everything has been done to preserve the building as a perfect example of early English architecture and, with the addition of the modern conveniences of a bathroom and electricity, the house can be run efficiently.

From 'Jacob's', I made my way along the High Street to Victoria Square. It is difficult to imagine that before Brightlingsea developed as a town this was Lower Green, one of the eight greens in the parish. The others are Bell Green, East End Green, Church Green, Pigs Cote Green, Gandergoose Green, Street Green and Hurst Green. It is only Hurst Green that today is recognisable as a largely unencroached green. The town of Brightlingsea has a High Street of real shops that cater for all the needs of the local community. This gives it a homely, old fashioned feel. It is the sort of town one expects to find on an island or at the end of the line: Brightlingsea is neither but almost both.

As I continued past the Square I passed the museum and the town's community centre. This is built on the site of the former railway station. The original station was a dismal draughty wooden building that, to no-one's regret, caught fire on New Years Eve 1901. A new station was opened in 1904

The new Brightlingsea station. (1904)

and this served the town until the line was closed in 1964. Then, regrettably, four years later the building was severely damaged by fire and demolished the following year.

Slightly beyond the site of the station is the old embankment. This is now a footpath which makes it possible to walk virtually the whole length of the old railway from here to the site of the former swing bridge at Alresford creek. I pushed my bike up on to the path and could see the embankment stretching out along the bank of the Colne. For the first few hundred yards the path runs more or less beside Promenade Way. This road terminates at Bateman's Tower Café where I had a light lunch before visiting the tower.

John Bateman, or the 'Old Squire' as he became known, was one of Brightlingsea's best loved benefactors. He arrived in Brightlingsea in 1871 at the age of 32 and lived in the Hall until he died in 1910. During this time he contributed much to the town. On the revival of the Cinque Port Liberty, he became Brightlingsea's first Deputy and held the office for nine of the years between 1887 and 1903. He presented the town with the Deputy's badge and chain of office, which is still worn by the Deputy today. To the visitor his most conspicuous legacy is the tower built at Westmarsh Point, at the confluence of Brightlingsea Creek with the Colne. This was built as a grandiose beach hut in 1883 as a folly for his daughter to use while recuperating from consumption. The tower is said to be a fine example of the use of Roman cement and originally it had a conical cap. This was removed during WWII so that the Royal Observer Corps could spot enemy planes approaching from the Continent. In 2005 the Heritage Lottery Fund helped finance the refurbishment of the tower and this included the fitting of a replica of the original roof. The tower is now used by many local sailing organizations to administer races. During race days, the public can visit the tower, whose new roof makes it a popular gallery from which to watch the races.

opposite upper: An early view of Bateman's Tower at the confluence of Brightlingsea Creek and the Colne. (1920s)

opposite lower left: Bateman's Tower had its conical cap removed in 1940 to enable the Royal Observer Corps to spot enemy aircraft during WWII. (1960s)

opposite lower right: Bateman's Tower was refurbished in 2005 when a replica conical cap was added but no attempt was made to correct its 5^0 lean. (2012)

Today the tower's strategic location makes it a useful navigation aid to sailors. It is thought that this position, or somewhere close by, was that of the vanished Henry VIII artillery earthwork and timber blockhouse which, along with those at Point Clear and East Mersea, were built to guard the mouth of the Colne.

I left Bateman's Tower and rejoined the path on the old railway embankment. Over the years I have visited Brightlingsea many times but the last time that I travelled this particular route along the Colne was in 1955. I was then on a slow train easing its way back to Wivenhoe. In those far off days I was one of two schoolboys who had managed to save up enough money to buy a *Weekly Runabout* train ticket for the sum of ten shillings and sixpence (52½p). This entitled the holder to travel on any railway in Essex, and we were determined to do the lot. It was during this week that I made my one and only trip to Brightlingsea by train.

The line has an interesting history. Around the middle of the 19th century there were several proposed schemes to bring a railway to Brightlingsea. The one that came to fruition was that proposed by George Bradley, a Yorkshire based solicitor. It appears that George's hobby was collecting Manorial rights. He was the proud owner of several of these in the counties of Yorkshire, Lincolnshire, Suffolk, Somerset and Hampshire. His first one in Essex was to be the lordship of the manor of Brightlingsea. George Bradley was an ambitious man and often sold on some of his Manorial rights at a considerable profit but his plans for the Brightlingsea venture were for something different. Here he saw a way to get in on the bourgeoning railway boom that was sweeping the country at the time. Accordingly he went about acquiring the land along the bank of the Colne between Brightlingsea and Wivenhoe. Then, in 1861, the Wivenhoe & Brightlingsea Railway Company (W&BRC) was formed. The proposed route was to follow the river. The track would be laid on an embankment that would also protect the low-lying marshland from inundation by the sea. There were those who said that Bradley's real aim was to provide a cheap sea wall to protect his lands, but the real reason was sprats. Such were the catches by the Brightlingsea fishermen that the fish were being spread on the fields for manure, yet there was an insatiable fish market not 60 miles away in London. There was already a railway to Wivenhoe and the only obstacle on

Bradley's proposed route was Alresford Creek. This was to be crossed by an iron viaduct that incorporated a swing bridge to allow the passage of vessels into the Creek. There were two other viaducts on the line, but these were low and of timber construction. All these works were completed within five years and the line opened in 1866.

The railway had a chequered history. There were good years when the sprats came and the oysters flourished, in addition to a growing holiday trade. But the line was to suffer the perils of flooding throughout its lifetime; first in 1874 then every few years until 1903 when half a mile of track was washed away. The repaired and raised railway did not flood again until 1928.

Then there were minor incidents until 1953 when the damage was so devastating that the future of the line was in doubt. However it was rebuilt and reopened after nearly a year to a great fanfare and celebrations at Brightlingsea. During the 1950s passenger numbers remained reasonable

The wooden viaduct, now replaced by a raised sea wall and Viaduct Sluice. (c1955)

and oysters were still being transported to London. Then the severe winter of 1962 all but wiped out the oyster trade and, in common with many branch lines throughout the country, passenger numbers fell. These factors, together with the high operating costs of the swing bridge, led to the closure of the line in 1964 as part of the Beeching cuts.

I cycled along the course of the old railway with the river on my left and Brightlingsea marsh on my right, to my first stop at Viaduct Sluice. There was no trace of a viaduct, or any feature in the landscape to warrant such a structure. However when the railway was built it was considered necessary to build a low wooden structure across the creek that drained the marsh at this point.

The marsh is now the third site of the Colne Estuary Nature Reserve, the others being at Colne Point and East Mersea. Here a major part of the reserve is the 50 ha of grazing marsh that was first reclaimed from the sea in the 16th century.

The path along the sea wall to the end of the nature reserve is well used as part of the circular route around the marsh. Beyond the reserve the surface is considerably more bumpy, but as there was nobody else using it I continued to make slow but steady progress on my bike. Every now and again there are traces of saltmarsh on the riverside of the wall. This natural intertidal zone can act as a very effective soft sea defence, but as the land sinks and the sea level rises the saltmarsh tries to move inland. If it is prevented from doing this by a sea wall then it is gradually washed away. This not only means that important habitat is lost but that the sea defences are exposed to ever increasing erosion from the sea. It has been estimated that if no action is taken, Essex could loose all of its saltmarsh within a few decades. I noticed that the sea wall along this part of the Colne is being strengthened with concrete blocks to protect a few acres of reclaimed arable land. I wonder for how long this short-sighted and expensive policy can continue.

There are the remnants of a small area of saltmarsh at Aldeboro Point. To the landward side of the sea wall is the area known as Noah's Ark. The origin of this intriguing name is, according to Edward Dickin in his *History of Brightlingsea*, named after a sailing collier that was, 'carried over the sea wall by a northwest gale and an exceptionally high tide.' It appears that the vessel could not be economically refloated, so windows and doors were fitted and the hulk became a dwelling. By the time Dickin wrote his book in 1913 the hulk had been replaced by a cottage of the same name. Today there is no dwelling on the site but the converted collier was not the first building to stand in the area, for Noah's Ark is the site of a Roman villa. This would have been a desirable position at the time, affording views up and down the river as well as being virtually opposite the important early Roman settlement at Fingringhoe Wick. The site was discovered during WWI when this area was used as a training area for soldiers before going to Flanders. In the water-filled creeks and grey mud they practiced digging trenches and tunnels. Some of these trenches cut through walls and pavements which, subsequent archaeological investigation revealed, were the remains of a substantial Roman dwelling with tessellated floors and heated by a hypocaust. All traces of the Roman villa have been lost in subsequent quarrying activity but traces of the WWI activities can still be seen in the regular patterns left on the marshland landscape where tunnels and trenches have become creeks.

Towards the mouth of Alresford Creek and the location of the former swing bridge, the footpath veers inland following the sea wall along the Creek. The last 50 yards or so of the old embankment are now so overgrown as to be impassable. I left my bike on the sea wall and wound my way across the marsh to the remaining piers of the bridge. From here I could see across the Creek to two similar piers on the Alresford side. If I had been able to cross I could have continued to follow the bank of the Colne.

The bridge is long gone but I have read of the perilous exploits of the young boys who crossed the Creek by way of the disused structure. I will return to the bridge later when I am in Alresford. Meanwhile I collected my bike and followed the creekside path to the tidal ford. Today it is not the tide that makes this ford impassable, but the deep accumulation of mud on its approaches. It is still a right of way and is crossed every now and again by 4x4 enthusiasts and adventurous walkers who don't mind mud up to their waists. This is the ford that gives Alresford its name, again something that I will come back to in the next chapter. I had no option other than to cycle along the rough and uneven unmade road that leads inland to the working gravel pits near Moverons farm. From here the road is surfaced and joins the main road at All Saints' church.

The regular creek pattern of WWI practice trenches at Aldboro Point. (2012)

This, 'the mariners' church on the hill', has stood here, over a mile from the present town for some seven hundred years. It is thought that in the 14th century Brightlingsea was a village of some 500 people. As was usual in those days, the lord of the manor built a church near his home and no doubt some dwellings clustered round the church. On at least two occasions during the 20th century large pits were discovered in the churchyard. These contained considerable numbers of skulls and bones, apparently all buried at about the same time. A possible explanation is that these were victims of the Black Death of 1349 when about half the population died in a very short space of time. Communal graves were probably the only way of coping with such a disaster. It has been suggested that the remaining population left the plague stricken area and migrated to the waterside. Or it could be that the population remained scattered and did not nucleate again until the Victorian period as suggested earlier.

What is notable about the church is its unique frieze of memorial tiles to Brightlingsea men who have lost their lives at sea from 1872 to the present day. Each of the 212 tablets gives the name, date, and a short account of the disaster. This remarkable collection of memorials was instigated by Arthur Pertwee, who was the vicar from 1872 till 1917: a devoted priest who was very much involved with and loved by the seafaring community in his care. There are many stories concerning this greatly revered priest and his selfless exploits. One of his regular activities was to climb the 127 narrow spiral steps

Part of the unique frieze of 213 memorial tiles to Brightlingsea men who lost their lives at sea. (2012)

to the top of the 94ft (28m) church tower on the stormiest of nights, to swing a hand lantern as a beacon to the ships near enough to see 'the mariners' church on the hill'.

From the church on top of the hill there is a cyclepath beside the busy road that is Brightlingsea's back door. I sped down here to the low-lying marsh that joins Alresford Creek to Flag Creek that flows into Brightlingsea Creek which all goes to make Brightlingsea virtually an island. This is where I strayed into the parish of Thorrington for a few hundred yards before I turned into the entrance to the mill. This is built on Alresford Creek and is where I crossed into my next Colneside parish of Alresford.

The dark flint flushwork of All Saints' church tower is the finest example in Essex. (2012)

The first and last of the tiles that make up the unique frieze of memorial tiles to Brightlingsea men who have lost their lives at sea during the last 140 years. (2012)

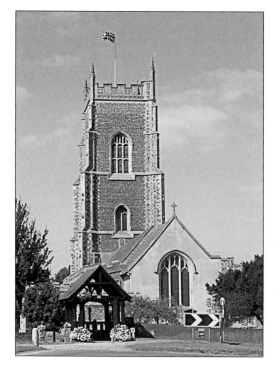

CHAPTER IV

Alresford

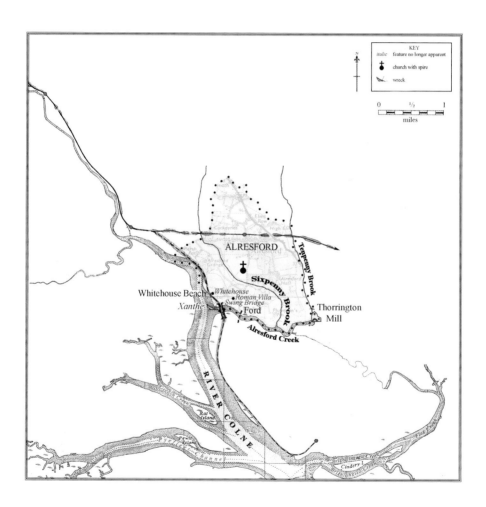

THE COLNE

Alresford

The name could be derived from either a persons name, Aegel's ford; or from the Old English Alor for Alder, the ford by the Alder trees, Alors ford.

In 1848 William White says that the parish has 289 souls and 1,427 acres and describes it as follows, 'this pleasant parish is watered by two rivulets, which fall into a creek of the Colne. The creek is fordable at low water; and from this ford and the alders still growing near it, the parish had its name.'

The population in 2011 was 2,009 and is centered about a mile north of the creek around the railway station.

Thorrington Mill happens to be built on the Thorrington side of Alresford Creek. Former mills could well have been on the Alresford side. This, apart from its inherent interest, justifies its inclusion in this chapter. Above the mill Alresford Creek becomes the attractively named Tenpenny Brook. There has been a mill on this site since Domesday but the present mill dates from 1831. Earlier mills could well have straddled the creek as there is a will from 1558 containing a bequest of a half share in a watermill at Alresford. Other early records show that during the 1820s the mill was equipped to grind Roman cement. This is a type of cement that was widely used before the invention of Portland cement in 1850. It was made by grinding the soft rock called septaria found near Harwich. Thousands of tons of septaria, or cement stone, were dredged off Harwich by fleets of smacks in the 19th century. At its peak the cement industry employed over 500 men and supplied much of the cement used for the stucco so much in fashion during the Regency period.

In 1926 Thorrington Mill ceased operating as a tide mill when the wheel failed. Alresford Creek was navigable to barges for a few more years while the mill was powered by a portable steam engine. (1928)

THE COLNE

The existing mill was built as a corn mill and its three pairs of stones were driven by a 16ft (4.8m) diameter breastshot waterwheel powered by the tide. The twice-daily tide filled the millpond where the water was held until the tide half-ebbed. It then powered the millwheel for the hours until low water. The regular flow of the tide provided a more reliable source of power than that from many streams and rivers or the vagaries of the wind. Harnessing the energy of the tide has always been a fascinating challenge. In these days when the effects of global warming and the consequences of over reliance on fossil fuels are becoming ever more apparent, it is surprising that more effort is not made into developing ways of harnessing the energy available from the regular and predictable rise and fall of the tide. The principle is ancient and there are many tide mills recorded in the Domesday Book. The existing Thorrington Mill was built at the beginning of an age when sea-borne transport was becoming important and it was the growth of this trade that led to the enlargement of many tide mills. It also spawned the development of many ingenious ways of overcoming the limited working hours of these mills; and these hours would get an hour later every day, necessitating some night shifts every other week. As far as is known none of these methods were used at Thorrington. Here the miller had access to a nearby windmill, until it was blown down by a gale in 1869. In some other places systems were developed that could keep the mill wheel turning twenty-four hours a day. Indeed one was in operation in Liverpool from 1796 until 1827, but these systems were abandoned with the arrival of steam-driven auxiliary engines; another technology that was never adopted at Thorrington, although it was powered by a portable steam engine for a few years following the collapse of its breastshot waterwheel.

Following its life as a working mill the building was left to decay until it was bought in 1941 by Tom Glover. He restored the fabric of the building and used it as a seed store before passing it into the hands of Essex County Council in 1974. Under the direction of the County Council's millwright, the mill was sympathetically restored and the millwheel turns once again. For those who are interested in seeing the restored machinery or just enjoy ancient buildings, the mill is open to the public on the last Sunday of each of the summer months.

Thorrington Mill. On the left is Alresford Creek, silted up and overgrown with reeds. The once tidal millpond is now filled by Tenpenny Brook on the right. (2011)

The milldam bridges Tenpenny Brook and leading from it is a footpath that follows the sea wall along the side of Alresford Creek. This was once a well-used tidal channel. I could see no sign of the disused Church Dock that was used by barges for the farm trade. I soon came to Sixpenny Brook, which rises in the neighbouring parish of Elmstead and flows right across the parish. When I crossed above its mouth, now a sluice in the sea wall, it was but a trickle as it flowed into the Creek.

Restored machinery in Thorrington Mill. (2008)

Sixpenny Brook as it trickles into Alresford Creek with All Saints', Brightlingsea, beyond the vanished Church Dock that stood on the other side. (2011)

Beyond Sixpenny Brook the Creek widens and in the distance I could see the masts of the many pleasure craft that are now moored in its sheltered waters. These are managed by the Alresford Creek Boat Owners Association who also keep the Alresford side of the ford fairly clear of mud to facilitate the launching of dinghies.

The ford is an ancient crossing place and could well have been in use since Roman times. It was certainly on the toll road that once ran from Alresford to Brightlingsea, when a man was employed to sweep the ford. Until WWI the ford was one of the six places in the Creek where stackie barges loaded. The Great War brought many changes to the area, one that was favoured by the locals was an engineers training exercise that resulted in a pontoon bridge across the creek. To their dismay this was dismantled at the end of the war. Then WWII brought more changes, this time the frequent use of

Clearing the mud from Alresford ford in 2008.

the ford by the army kept the mud at bay. After the war the occasional use by vehicles kept the ford reasonably clear for a few years. I have been told that it was quite possible to walk the ford until the 1960s. Since then, at times, the accumulation of silt has risen to a depth of 3ft (0.9m) or so, making a crossing hazardous if not impossible. Every now and again crossings are attempted by groups of walkers or owners of specialist vehicles. In 2008 a group of 4x4 owners used a mud-plough to clear the ford from the Brightlingsea side and for a while afterwards the crossing remained passable.

St Peter's Church, Alresford, before the fire in 1971　　*St Peter's after the disastrous fire in October 1971*

The ruins of St Peter's Church. The parish is now served by the new church of St Andrew, built nearer the centre of the village. (2012)

Ford Lane leads up to the village and is well used by people visiting the Creek. The lane passes working quarries, and near here is the site of another Colneside Roman Villa, discovered in 1884. Further along the lane is the ruin of the parish church of St Peter. This was built about 1320 in the early decorated style and it burnt down in 1971.

Back at the ford I was close to the rusting remains of the aerial cableway that was used from 1932 until the late 1960s by the Alresford Sand and Ballast Company to transport material from their quarries to barges moored at the jetty in the creek. The quarries are still being worked but now everything that leaves the site does so by road.

The mouth of Alresford Creek as it enters the Colne is 430ft (129m) wide and for 100 years was crossed by an iron bridge. When the Wivenhoe to Brightlingsea railway was opened in 1866 the local press described the iron viaduct as 'one of the most important structures of its kind in this part of

The aerial cableway in operation, viewed from the jetty.

Barges at the jetty during its working life. A loaded bucket hanging from the aerial cableway is just arriving at the jetty.

the Kingdom'. Because the Creek was navigable the centre section could be swung horizontally through 90 degrees to allow vessels to pass. An official called the Bridge Pilot operated the bridge, which he would open by walking

The remains of the aerial cableway with the working pit beyond. (2011)

The Alresford Sand & Gravel Co. jetty in Alresford Creek. Barges were loaded here from 1932 until the late 1960s. (2011)

The Bridge Pilot posing on the swing bridge at Alresford Creek. (1905)

along the track to the centre pier where he would insert a large T bar. He then rotated this, which through a system of gears would slowly revolve the central spans of the bridge to the open position. This was basic human powered Victorian engineering: one man moving a structure weighing several tons supported on a ball race that contained ball bearings the size of footballs. If the bridge was to remain open for any length of time the Pilot's assistant would row out to rescue the Pilot from his marooned position. If the bridge was open and a train was due the two men would row out to the central pier and the process reversed. The Bridge Pilot would then ride across the bridge in the cab of the train. In fact his duty was to ride across the bridge on every train to enforce the speed limit, initially 10 mph, later reduced to 5 mph. The Pilot's other duties included rowing out to the bridge mechanism to oil the mechanical parts, a job constantly needing to be done due to the corrosive salt spray and high winds. The bridge was demolished three years after the line was closed in 1964 and all that remains today are the concrete piers at each end of the viaduct and the skeleton of the boatshed.

There is still a path that follows the trackbed to the side of the creek where the embankment suddenly stops as it crumbles down to the remaining

One of the last steam trains to cross the swing bridge. (1950s)

A motor barge passes through the open swing bridge, it was opened to allow barges to reach the quarry jetty and Thorrington Mill.

Looking across Alresford Creek, all that remains of the viaduct and swing bridge are the piers on either bank. (2011)

concrete piers. I sat below the Tamarisk trees that have taken over the embankment and looked across the Creek and over the Colne to Fingringhoe. This has long been a favourite place for birdwatchers. In the mud just off here are the rotting remains of the smack *Xanthe*, a fast little vessel built at

Beside the remaining bridge piers is all that remains of the Bridge Pilot's boatshed. (2011)

Looking towards Fingringhoe Wick over Alresford Creek as it joins the Colne. In the foreground are the ribs of the Colne smack Xanthe *poking out of the mud. (2012)*

Rowhedge in the 1890s. When her working life of fishing for winter sprat, or stowboating as it was called, came to an end she was moored here just inside the mouth of the creek. In her dying years she was used as a floating bird hide before gradually falling to pieces forcing the ornithologists back onto the riverbank. Today all was quiet apart from the wind gently rustling the trees above and tumbling wavelets below. This tranquil setting was interrupted now and again by the clatter of the flapping corrugated iron on the rusting boat shed on the creekside. This was built by the Railway Company and was where the boat used by the Bridge Pilot was kept.

From here Brightlingsea is so near yet so far. But this may change if Sustrans can raise the funds. Sustrans is a leading national charity working for a sustainable transport network in the UK. To facilitate more convenient and safer cycling, an expanding network of cycle routes has been developed. Many of these have been made possible by the construction of facilities at particular locations. A local community initiative for a cycle route between Brightlingsea and Wivenhoe included a proposal for a cycle/footbridge across Alresford Creek. This scheme received Sustrans backing and was one of two proposed schemes in Essex on the reserve list for funding from the £50 million grant made to Sustrans in 2007. It is just possible that this proposal will be funded sometime soon.

I continued my journey along the bank of the Colne. The path from here to Wivenhoe is most attractive at all times of the year. First there is the miniature oasis of loveliness known as White House Beach. Here a grassy clearing within a spinney descends to a sandy beach sandwiched between areas of saltmarsh but, for all the beauty of this place, it hides a tragic tale.

In earlier days this lonely spot, just up river from Alresford Creek was overlooked by Copyhold Cottage. This was lived in by a family of fishermen named Welham who worked a smack from the beach where the small shingle spit soon became known as Welham's Hard. Then the railway was built with its track running between the hard and the cottage. The Welhams seemed to have adapted to this inconvenience and the cottage took on the somewhat grander sounding name of the White House. Then a double tragedy struck the family. In 1897 Samuel Welham was lost at sea and a year later the family

The White House. (1880s)

White House Beach with Tink's boat moored on the marsh beyond. (2011)

smack was washed up onto the marsh by an exceptionally high tide. Samuel's sons decided to dig around her so that she would float out on the following tide. This was to compound the family tragedy, as during the digging-out the smack slipped and fell to one side tragically crushing one brother to death.

This aside, numerous folk have had many a happy time here. The proximity of the beach to the railway made this an attractive picnic destination. Never an official stop, the train would halt and whole Victorian families would 'jump for it' to spend a day on the beach. When it came to getting home, a wave to the engine driver was all that was needed to stop the train for day trippers to clamber aboard. For many years members of the Welham family would be willing to boil a kettle for those who wanted tea. It appears that by the turn of the century the Welhams had left the White House which was then used for a few years by groups of visiting artists. By the 1930s the house had gone but remnants of the orchard remained as did the trains' informal stopping. This unofficial process continued way after the W&BRC was taken over by Great Eastern and eventually LNER. It is said that during the summer months of the inter-war period, nearly every train stopped for picnickers and swimmers at White House Beach.

This is still an attractive and popular place, but now most visitors arrive on foot, a few by bike and a few by boat. One man who has taken a liking to the place is Tink. He lives here summer and winter with only his dog for company. When I passed this spot on a cold December day his bike and trailer were on the riverbank. A single plank of driftwood led on to his solitary craft where there was a wisp of smoke wafting skywards from the stovepipe.

The line of the old railway and sea wall hug the riverbank to the end of the spinney. Here the river turns to the west leaving the railway embankment to continue straight across the marsh to Wivenhoe. The footpath follows the sea wall and a little further on I left the parish of Alresford. During my progress along the riverside path I have often looked across the water and glimpsed many structures, from bird hides to gravel workings on the other bank. I will look at these more closely before I take up the story of Wivenhoe. To get to the other side of the river I will take the ferry from Wivenhoe to Fingringhoe, and return to this seawall much later.

Looking towards the Colne along the Alresford parish boundary. (2011)

CHAPTER V

Fingringhoe & Langenhoe

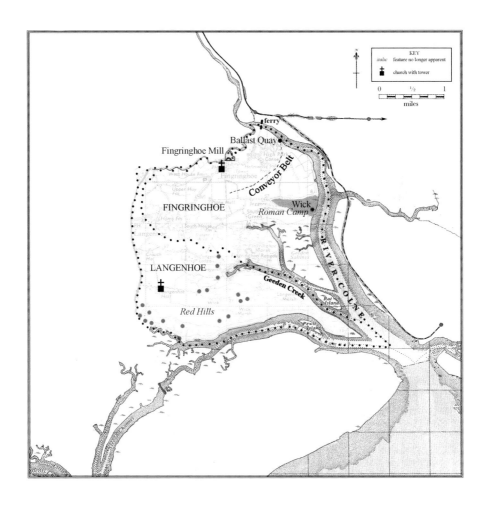

THE COLNE

Fingringhoe & Langenhoe

The name Fingringhoe is Saxon and was first recorded in 975AD. It could mean the hill-spur belonging to the descendants or followers of Fingringas, or a man of similar name, or could be derived from the Old English word for finger, from the finger of land that diverts the Colne eastwards between Roman River and Geedon Creek.

In 1848 William White describes Fingringhoe as 'a pleasant village on the south side of Roman River, and on the west side of the vale of the Colne. It contains 581 souls, and 2,863 acres of land extending more than a mile eastward to the banks of the river Colne, where there is a ferry to Wivenhoe. On the Wick farm, old coins, foundations of buildings, and other ancient relics, have often been found.'

Fingringhoe does not feature in the Domesday survey but Langenhoe is described as having one mill and a salthouse.

The name Langenhoe could be a description derived from the Old English 'lang' meaning long and the 'hoh' meaning hill-spur, the long hill.

William White describes the parish as 'a scattered village on a declivity with 161 inhabitants and about 2,063 acres of land, extending eastward to the river Colne, and including 30 acres of waste, roads, and water.'

The population in 2011 of Fingringhoe was 775, and that of Langenhoe 572.

I arrived in Fingringhoe a little muddy. The ferry was reinstated in 1991 and is operated at weekends by a small group of volunteers. At Wivenhoe the ferry is easily accessed by way of a wooden jetty built out from the quay. On the Fingringhoe side the landing is a simple gravel hard. This has been used for centuries and was rebuilt when the ferry reopened twenty years ago. While the ferryman held the bow against the hard by chugging the outboard against the incoming tide, I made my precarious descent into the several inches of silt that had accumulated on the hard. I was passed my bicycle which I carried up to drier ground. I wiped the worst of the mud from my shoes in the grass and set out to explore Fingringhoe.

In contrast to the bustling waterfront of Wivenhoe there is absolutely nothing at the Fingringhoe riverside, no Ferryboat Inn, no building of any

The Wivenhoe - Fingringhoe ferry arriving at the muddy hard. (2012)

description, just the end of Ferry Road that heads straight across the marsh. As the road begins to rise toward the village there is a footpath which leads to Ballast Quay. This path follows the edge of the marsh a short distance before rising to Ballast Quay Farm. Although now designated as a footpath this has many of the characteristics of an ancient track that once followed the course of the river. I wheeled my bicycle along here until I reached the sewage works where millions of useful bacteria are quietly purifying the water before it is discharged into the river. From here the track becomes a concrete road leading up to the farm.

To the left is Ballast Quay, built in 1708 to supply ballast to sailing ships in the coal and timber trade. It has since been used for many years to load barges conveying gravel from the nearby pits to London. It is now the only commercially operating quay remaining on the Colne. Twenty-five years ago, in 1988 the Colne was one of the busiest waterways in East Anglia.

Overlooking the sewage works and saltmarsh to Wivenhoe from the footpath between Ferry Road and Ballast Quay; all the buildings are on the other side of the river in Wivenhoe. (2012)

Ballast Quay, Fingringhoe, the last working commercial quay on the Colne. (2012)

The ports on the river handled over a thousand ships, mostly from European countries importing a variety of cargos that included timber, coal, soya, wheat, fishmeal, bricks, granite, starch and fertilisers. There were some exports of peas, feed-wheat and barley. Today the only commercial cargo is sand and gravel exported from Ballast Quay to London by J J Prior.

J J Prior have a long association with the area. James John Prior was born in Essex in 1844. At the age of twenty-six he founded his own business which soon expanded to contain several farms, steam vehicles and sailing barges. After WWI the company developed the river transport side of the business and built up a fleet of a dozen or so motor barges that were mainly used for the transport of sand and gravel. In 1934 the founder's grandson, Bert, bought a sand marketing company at Fingringhoe and so began the long and fruitful association of the company with the area. By the 1990s the company was being run by Bert's grandson, Peter, who has since moved the company headquarters to Fingringhoe.

The company currently operates a fleet of five motor barges working in the Colne. Each has a crew of three and between them, they transport 200,000 tons of material to London each year. In Fingringhoe the company now employs 12 men and several sub-contractors from the local area. Gravel

The sailing barge Centaur, *built in 1895, seen here loading sand at Ballast quay Fingringhoe. (1954)*

is extracted from the quarry and transported by a conveyor to Ballast Quay where it is processed ready for shipment to London to be used in building projects, most recently for the 2012 Olympic facility.

For each ton of material sold, the company pays £1.95 to the Government Aggregate Sustainability Fund. This is like the lottery fund in as much that areas

Sand and gravel are excavated using a loading shovel and hydraulic excavator with a bucket that can hold 3.5 tonnes. Here a loading shovel feeds the conveyor belt which carries the material approximately 1 km to the processing plant at Ballast Quay. (2012)

affected by aggregate extraction can bid for money to enhance their local facilities. The *Access Fingringhoe* project has been funded in this way. Within this project pre-extraction archaeological digs have been funded and when workings are finished, habitats for wildlife have been established. Also access and appreciation of the area has been enhanced by the creation of walks and the provision of information boards. The project has involved many local groups and its legacy of improved access to the countryside, increased local biodiversity and improved education will benefit the area for generations to come.

From Ballast Quay Farm I proceeded up the hill to High Park Corner where I turned left into Brook Hall Road. I was now on part of the 'Gravel Pit Trail', a circular walk established as part of the *Access Fingringhoe* project. The road soon ends and a bridleway continues through the former gravel workings. The path descends gently into an area of ponds and cliffs that is being colonised rapidly by wildlife. Mingled with the birdsong is the squeaking and rattling of the conveyor that now transports gravel from a new pit further inland to Ballast Quay. The bridleway continues to Fingringhoe Wick, the site of much earlier gravel workings.

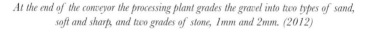

At the end of the conveyor the processing plant grades the gravel into two types of sand, soft and sharp, and two grades of stone, 1mm and 2mm. (2012)

Across the estuary to Alresford and Brightlingsea, from the Fingringhoe bridleway to the Wick. (2012)

The Wick is an interesting site with a long history. Following the retreat of the latest Ice Age glaciers the area of tundra was first colonised by birch, then pine, followed by oak. This primeval woodland was first visited by early man as a hunter. Later, areas of woodland were cleared for farming. Stone Age tools from both of these eras have been found on this site. It is not known if there was a Bronze Age settlement in Fingringhoe, but the presence of suspected red hills and the finding of a socketed axe head from this period suggests that Bronze Age people were living in the area before the Romans arrived.

This is when we know for certain that the Wick area was inhabited. It is believed that this was the site of a small river port; it is known locally as Bacon or Beacon Town. Its function was to serve the legionary fortress and later Roman colony at Camulodunum (Colchester). The remains of a 2 acre (0.8ha) enclosure and several substantial houses, together with numerous finds of coins and military equipment, indicate that this was an early Roman site. Beacon Hard, a 40ft (12m) clay bank embedded with Roman tile and brick, is probably the remains of the landing place where men and materials were transhipped from wind powered vessels used for the sea crossing from the continent, to smaller vessels that could be manoeuvred more easily by oars along the shallow and narrow waters of the Colne.

Following the departure of the Romans it is very likely that the area reverted to woodland and then later, in more settled times, to farmland. The earliest map of Fingringhoe made in 1751 shows Wick farm, and by the turn of the 20th century the farm is described as consisting of a house with farm buildings in 515 acres (206ha) of arable, grassland and saltings, the bulk of which was Geedon Marsh.

During the following years some fields were sold to an adjoining farm and Geedon Marsh was sold to the War Department. In 1921 the remaining 100 acres (40ha) or so were sold to a gravel extraction company. The site was then worked by several companies until it was exhausted in 1959.

Shortly after this, the area was acquired by the Essex Wildlife Trust and has been managed by them ever since. The upheaval produced by excavation and the processing of gravel had created an industrial wasteland which, with judicial management, has been transformed into an area of habitats that include foreshore and freshwater lakes with swathes of gorse, open grassland and wooded thickets between. This reserve has become home to a host of invertebrates, wild flowers, birds and mammals. It is enjoyed by many visitors each year who come to pursue their own interests, or to learn by following the way-marked routes, or attend one of the many specialized events.

The ballast loading jetty at Fingringhoe Wick was converted for use as a hide for watching wading birds. It has not been used since the late 1990s when it became unsafe. (1999)

THE COLNE

The wreck of the sailing barge Fly, *built as a 'stumpie', that is without a topmast, in 1899 and used for the transport of sand and ballast until she was beached in 1936 at Fingringhoe. (1999)*

In the visitor centre I took a well earned rest with a welcome cup of coffee, while looking out over Geedon Marsh. There are always binoculars and frequently telescopes that visitors can use to observe the wildlife. At high tide it is possible to distinguish Rat Island, this lies between the Colne, North Geedon and South Geedon creeks. It is now a nature reserve but in former times Black-headed gull eggs were collected by the bucket load. These were regarded as a delicacy, rather like quails eggs, and were sold to prestigious hotels and restaurants in London and elsewhere. Not all of the eggs were collected by professionals as John Hedges recalls in his book of memories, *The Wanderer.* In this, he describes a childhood adventure involving bicycles, an inflatable rubber boat and thousands of gulls screeching above, as eggs floated from their nests, and two boys had to be rescued by a passing yacht, all due to an unusually high tide.

Beyond Geedon Creek is Langenhoe Marsh which extends to the Pyefleet Channel. Most of this, along with the rest of the marshland visible from the Reserve observation room is owned by the Ministry of Defence, who use it as a training area with live firing. If you approach the Geedon creeks by water you are informed by notices on two bright yellow buoys that this is a restricted access area and that if the red flags are flying you could be surprised by loud bangs. This occurs with such frequency that the gulls now totally ignore the acoustic intrusion into the hushed silence of the marsh.

Langenhoe Marsh is a finger of watery land that extends down to the Colne which, for half-a-mile or so, forms the parish boundary. It is hard to imagine that this deserted and desolate place was once the site of one of our earliest industries. For many years the origin of the Red Hills on the Essex marshes was a mystery. The original height of these hills is difficult to estimate because of their location. Some have been partially or completely eroded by the sea or submerged in accumulations of mud, and where the sea has retreated the material forming the hills has invariably been carted away by farmers as a suitable substance to lighten their heavy inland soils. Hills have been found with estimated diameters from less than 20 metres up to over a 100 metres. The hills were first systematically investigated towards the end of the 19th century and then over the following half century the story of their origin slowly emerged. It is now thought that for a period extending for over a thousand years starting from sometime around 100 BC, the estuaries and marshes of Essex were the centre of a thriving salt industry. Over three hundred sites have been identified, with seventeen of these in Langenhoe.

It is thought that during high tide, seawater was trapped in clay pans cut into the saltings where it was left to partially evaporate in the sun. The resulting brine was transferred into crude clay pots where it was heated over open fires. When evaporation was complete, the pots were broken open and the salt removed. On the sites where this happened the remnants of coarse pottery vessels, ash and scorched clay gradually accumulated and grew into the Red Hills.

Today there is no industry in Langenhoe, in fact there is not much to Langenhoe at all. Most of the habitation is now in the north of the parish where it is indistinguishable from its neighbour, Abberton. On the main road from Colchester to Mersea the names of the two parishes appear on the same village sign. The parish boundary follows the middle of this road which means that those travelling towards Colchester pass through Abberton but those going to Mersea are passing through Langenhoe. Yet this quiet, nondescript parish did enjoy a short-lived period of fame when pictures of its church appeared in the national papers. This was in 1884 when Langenhoe was at the epicentre of the strongest earthquake to strike mainland Britain. Measuring 5.1 on the Richter scale, well over 1,000 buildings were damaged. These included twenty churches and the one to sustain the most dramatic damage was at Langenhoe. A report at the time stated: *'The Reverend Parkinson was sitting in the rectory when the earthquake struck. He felt "a violent shock." The whole house shook for a few seconds shattering the chimneys, cracking ceilings and collapsing part of the roof. On emerging from the rectory, the Reverend beheld the sad sight of the church. "It*

The earthquake damage to Langenhoe Church, part of the tower collapsed through the roof of the nave. One of the parishioners is shown with his tricycle. (1884)

The interior of Langenhoe Church shortly after the earthquake struck at 9.20am on 22 April 1884.

seemed utterly ruined" he later said, "some tons of the stone battlements of the tower had been dislodged. These had fallen with great force upon the nave, which was almost entirely destroyed." The interior suffered further still. "Roof timbers and masonry had smashed the pews and pulpit. The altar was buried under debris and the choir gallery had been ripped from its wall foundations.'"

For a while Langenhoe was known as the 'Earthquake Church'. The damage was so severe that the whole building was demolished and rebuilt using much of the old stone and original material. The 15th century windows and doorways were reused and the 500-year-old doors were rehung, as was the bell. All this was accomplished in two years and the new church was re-opened in 1886.

The rebuilt Langenhoe Church. (c1900)

Its troubles were far from over as it later acquired the reputation as one of the most haunted places in England. This was as a result of a number of disturbing happenings experienced by the Reverend Ernest Merryweather, Rector there for twenty years. Many of these could be attributed to a combination of a poor quality rebuild and the interpretation by the Rector of 'things that go bump in the night'. Never the less the last service was held in 1959 and the church was closed. The reason given at the time was that the building was too dangerous. This prompted a BBC ghost hunting team to spend the night there in 1961 with the result that absolutely nothing happened. Meanwhile the authorities decided that funds were not available for the necessary repairs to the dangerous building so plans for demolition were put in place. This was carried out in 1962, a mere 76 years after being rebuilt. The parish was united with Abberton, but the Parish Council still maintains the graveyard.

From the Wick I made my way back to Fingringhoe village centre. Here we have all the elements of the quintessential English village: church, pub,

Langenhoe graveyard has no visible remains of the church amongst its few scattered gravestones. (2012)

green and pond. It is no wonder that the centre of this village is classified as a conservation area.

Few churches can boast the combination of setting and architectural features present in St Andrew's Fingringhoe. Pevsner described it as 'visually quite exceptionally exceptional' and Scarfe in his guide to Essex as 'irresistibly beautiful.' The building is mainly 15th century brick and stone with a tall, attractive west tower of knapped flint and stone.

Close by the church is the pub, the *Whalebone*. This has been in existence since at least 1735. It was refurbished in the early 19th century and has undergone several 20th century alterations. It has been suggested that despite the presence of a whale jawbone on the premises at various times during its life the name could have been derived from the Saxon word 'valbon' meaning welcome.

Between the pub and the church are two more features of the village centre that are worthy of note. First the oak tree that has such a setting and girth that it is certain to have been the subject of stories and legends for a very long time. The village story is that the tree is supposed to have grown from an

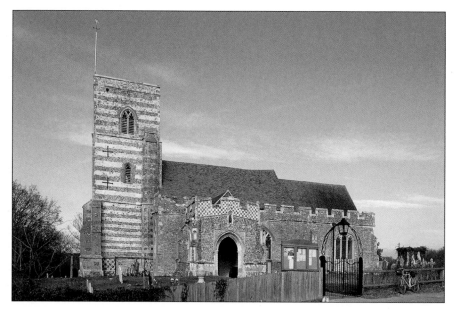

The 'irresistibly beautiful' St Andrew's, Fingringhoe. (2012)

acorn placed in the mouth of a pirate who had been hanged in the village. It is thought that this may be based on a folk myth dating back to the time of the Danish invaders of the dark ages. The present tree is of unknown age but probably dates back to around 1500.

Beside the oak is the village pond, this was once of great importance, not only to Fingringhoe but also to several neighbouring villages. The spring that feeds this pond was the source of the most highly regarded water in the area. For those further afield who could not collect their own water, it was delivered by pony and trap at a cost of a halfpenny (¼p) a bucket. Then in the 1970s health inspectors deemed the water not fit to drink and the spring head now carries a warning sign. I am not sure if there is a real health risk or if this is more to provide a defence in the case of possible litigation.

Before I leave the village centre I will mention the story of one of its former inhabitants, Connie Kent. One of the village buildings that has

The Whalebone *now with a pub sign and a clear view of the church. (2012)*

The Whalebone *with the church behind the tree and smoke from the cottage chimney. (c1900)*

now been demolished is Church Cottage, this appears on the extreme right of the early 20th century picture of the village. This was once the home of Connie Kent. By the time that this former actress, whose stage name was Vera Verchayle, moved to the village she had developed somewhat reclusive habits. She was often seen about the village with her stooping gait and ear trumpet but rarely communicating with anyone. When she had not been seen for some time it was assumed that she had gone away. By 1949 the ravages of animals, children and others had made the apparently abandoned Church Cottage so neglected that it was considered dangerous and required demolition.

When the police searched the building prior to demolition, in an upstairs room of the cluttered, mouse and rat infested dwelling they found what looked like the remains of clothing. Upon closer inspection this contained traces of hair and a skeleton. It was assumed that these were the remains of Connie Kent who had last been seen in the village a full ten years previously in 1939. The story jogged a few people's memories and it transpired that before Connie took to the thespian life she was a local woman, born in the village in 1871.

The discovery of the skeleton generated quite a lot of press interest and inevitable speculation. I have read many of these reports; some proclaim suicide, others murder, all more newsworthy than natural causes. The articles that appeared in the local paper, the *Essex County Standard,* not only report the facts but ridicule the London journalists with their fervent imaginations. Never the less there are some mysteries surrounding the case. It seems unlikely, but not impossible, that a body could remain in a house for ten years before being discovered, despite being searched on at least two occasions. Of more concern is that the forensic examination of the skeleton did not positively conclude that the remains were those of Connie Kent. One wonders if the Essex Police were reluctant to accept the Scotland Yard findings because this would have changed one solved case into two unsolved cases. We will never know the truth of the mystery of Church Cottage. Cuttings from the local press make interesting reading and are included here for you to draw your own conclusions.

Fri 25 March 1949

Connie Kent Case Nears End
Police say 'We rule out Murder'

But unanswered questions remain

County Pathologist Dr. F. E. Camps was working yesterday to establish finally whether Connie Kent died a lonely natural death in her tiny Fingringhoe cottage or whether she was murdered.

But, from all evidence so far gathered, the Police do not believe there is any question of foul play and they expect Dr. Camps' report to reveal that the only mystery surrounding the death of this cultured village recluse is: how could her death, within a stone's throw of the local inn and the village school, have remained unnoticed for 10 years?

Villagers had passed the cottage scores of times without suspecting, until on Tuesday they saw police officers searching the cottage to discover what they are convinced is the skeleton remains of the "missing" woman, ex-actress Ada Constance Kent, who in 1939 vanished from village life.

After that the cottage was searched three times in three years, first by Mrs. Mary Maskell, now dead, one of Connie Kent's few friends, then by Mr. Bernard Constable, the Village policeman at that time, and finally by, P. C. Harrington. That was seven years ago.

Although there have been many wild rumours and murder theories have been advanced in the National Press the police have no reason to suspect foul play. At an early stage in the inquiries, Supt. Totterdell told the "Essex County Standard," "it may be that she collapsed and died a natural death, but of course we cannot rule out the possibility of foul play." But on Wednesday evening the Chief Constable of Essex (Capt. F. R. J. Peel) dispelled all doubts by authorising the following statement, "The police are not working on the lines of suspected murder."

In the meantime Dr. F. E. Camps is preparing a report which will be presented to the Deputy Coroner for North-East Essex (Mr. F. E. M. Puxon) at an inquest which will be held in a few days time. Dr. Camps took away from the cottage some hairs found adhering to the skull and some more hair found on a hair brush belonging to Miss Kent as an aid to identity.

Since so much publicity was thrown on Church Cottage and Miss Kent, many telephone calls and letters have been received at Colchester Police Station from all parts of the country from people claiming to have known Miss Kent. Hundreds of letters found in the cottage have yet to be examined.

This is how the tumbledown cottage, half as high as the shrubs which had overgrown it, looked when police first entered to search for clues about the disappearance of its occupier, whose full name was Ada Constance Kent.

For 10 years the interior had remained just as she had left it. The bed was still made up and books and ornaments still adorned the sideboard and cupboard.

Her supper tray was on the oak dining table. A toast rack was stained with rust, and all that rats and mice had left of the toast were crumbs.

Police Took Photographs

There was a book of Shakespeare's plays lying near a little paraffin lamp. Her slippers were inside the fender. Part of the roof had come through on to the furniture and the police took away letters, papers and photographs, some of which show Miss Kent in theatrical dress. Outside the cottage stands a wall built by Miss Kent herself with concrete and old tins.

Rumour had it on Monday that the police would drain the pond, but although reporters, photographers and would-be sightseers hung about all day there was no police activity in that direction.

Supt. Totterdell, who is chief of the Essex C.I.D., paid a brief visit to the cottage and then went away to check up on her acquaintances who, it was thought, might be able to help them in their inquiries.

A Major Kent has been spoken of in the village. He is believed to be her only relative and he was last heard of in Surrey a few years ago. On Wednesday a police officer left Colchester for Somerset House to endeavour to trace him. It is believed that he has been on the stage during recent years. The police have been hampered in their inquiries by the fact that Connie Kent was, somewhat of a recluse. "She did not mix with us" said a neighbour.

Two schoolboys on Tuesday volunteered the information that they had been in the cottage about 12 months ago and had seen the skeleton.

Just Faded Away

The intriguing part of this 10-year old story is that until the other day when P. C. Webb discovered that children had broken into the house no one had worried about Connie Kent .

Long ago the Lexden and Winstree Rural Disrtrict Council, who had condemned the cottage, wiped off rate arrears because they could not trace her. A police chief said, "at the time she vanished no doubt inquiries were instituted and we may have been satisfied at the time. Unfortunately during the war many of our records went to the salvage drive."

Mr. Alfred Hasler, licensee of the nearby Whalebone Inn, said that Miss Kent used to buy cigarettes at his house. She was well educated and had travelled a lot in her early days.

Mrs. Wade, the 74 year-old occupant of a neatly-thatched cottage next door, said that Miss Kent never said much about herself. "She just passed the time of day when I saw her in the garden. But she did mention on one occasion that she had a relative abroad."

Police inquiries extended to Wivenhoe where she used to rent a house on the Quay before coming to Fingringhoe in 1932 and she was a familiar figure there on the quayside.

She has a deposit account of £50 in the Co-operative Savings Bank. That has never been touched and interest has accumulated.

"She Was Good-Looking"

Mrs. A. W. Cranfield, of Rowhedge, an acquaintance, said the cottage was previously occupied by Miss Kent's grandmother and mother before she went to reside there. ''She was: a cultured woman and very good-looking like her mother," said Mrs. Cranfield.

In her early days Miss Kent was on the stage and it was round about 1932 that she went to reside at Church Cottage after her stage career had ended.

She is said to have been born at Ferry Hill, Fingringhoe. A visiting card found by the police revealed that her stage name was Vera Verchayle and in the cottage are photographs of her in theatrical dress.

Mr. Robert Clench, a special constable in 1939, said that Miss Kent had told him that she was one of the original suffragettes who chained themselves to the railings outside the Houses of Parliament. " The last time I saw her," he added, "was when she handed in a faulty gas-mask. After that she disappeared."

The Legal Aspect

In February 1925, Miss Kent's cottage was inspected by the Lexden and Winstree Council and found to be in the occupation of a Mr. Bertie Evans. The address of the owner was then understood to be Anthony Cottage, Church Street, Coggeshall.

In July, 1925, the Council made a closing order of the property, which was served on the firm of local solicitors acting for the owner. The tenant Evans was given the tenancy of a Council house at Fingringhoe early in 1927.

In February, 1928, the Council Surveyor received a letter from Miss Kent, who then lived at Vine Cottage. Quayside, Wivenhoe, asking for particulars of the repairs necessary to make the Fingringhoe cottage habitable as she wanted to live there. " I wish to live in the house myself," she wrote. "to enable me to spend a peaceful and happy old age." Later the same month the Council Surveyor and Medical Officer of Health met Miss Kent at the cottage and spoke to her regarding the property.

In December, 1929, it was discovered that Miss Kent had herself taken possession of the cottage, and she was informed that the occupation was illegal. The Council did not take any action, however.

From 1929 the story jumps to 1947, when Fingringhoe Parish Council recommended that the cottage should be demolished as it was an eyesore to the village, and in August the Lexden and Winstree Council again considered the condition of the property and posted a notice on the front door of their intention to consider demolition. The solicitors who had acted for Miss Kent were also informed, but a letter from them said that they had last acted for her in 1925 and did not know her present address.

October, 1947, was the last occasion on which the Council considered the matter. It was then decided that in the absence of the owner the matter should be deferred.

The police deny stories that a missing poison bottle was found near Miss Kent's remains, or that there is any question of missing jewellery from the cottage.

Analysis

The mystery of Connie Kent is a mystery no longer - though the strange affair, which will long be remembered and spoken of in Fingringhoe, retains certain true elements of mystery, as well a number of false ones.

Chief true puzzle is:-

How did two people search the house without discovering the body? It is assumed that they must have looked in, and seeing nothing out of order downstairs have left satisfied.

Other supposedly mysterious elements have been nothing more nor less the work of Fleet Street journalists who have this week taken possession of the Whalebone Inn.

One reporter "discovered" a bottle marked Poison and developed a suicide theory on this. Existence of such a bottle is denied by the police.

Another headlined the conclusion that Miss Kent had been murdered - but the theory was entirely his own.

Best effort of all, however, was that of the evening paper which came out with the announcement "Pond Dragged"!

Footnote

The Whalebone has returned to its normal tranquillity. Mr. Alfred Hasler, the landlord, is left with some empty barrels and bottles, a new view on the veracity of London newspapers - and a request to secure the tenancy of Miss Kent's condemned cottage. It came from a Southend pensioner, aged 75!

Notes

(printed elsewhere in the same edition)

Mysteries – False and Real

So Fingringhoe is not after all likely to become another Polstead, nor the lovely village pond with its famous oak to take a place beside the Red Barn in the murkier annals of the Eastern Counties.

What started as one mystery ends as another, after a week during which the village has hardly known itself for journalists and photographers, police cars and idle gapers; a week that will not soon be forgotten.

What happened to Ada Kent has soon been revealed. In fact there is no evidence so far that anything unnatural whatever happened to her though at least one of the Fleet Street newshounds has felt it necessary to justify his expense sheet by making up a murder story, without waiting for the findings of the pathologist and coroner, who are likely to reach a much less lurid conclusion.

What is extraordinary, and does justify curiosity and speculation, is that an old lady can die in a cottage right in the middle of a village, with the Eastern National bus stopping outside the front window and the schoolchildren playing at the back, and lie there for just 10 days short of 10 years without anybody even having the curiosity to look in and reveal her.

Could it happen anywhere but in an Eastern Counties village? I doubt it.

It could not have happened there but for an extraordinary combination of circumstances. This old lady lived alone. She was without relatives to visit her. Tradesmen were not regular callers. She mixed little with neighbours. The rural council had lost interest in the house after condemning it. At least one search seems to have been perfunctory. Another which actually discovered her a year ago went unreported. These points, maybe, are all examples of a crude and primitive side of village life.

Yet even so it remains a phenomenon that this cottage could go unmolested for so long. Having myself lived for nearly 10 years within a quarter of a mile of it, and passed it twice daily all that time, without even hearing so much as the name of its former occupant mentioned, my professional chagrin at my defective news sensibility is qualified by personal pleasure that a community can not only behave so honestly, but can so scrupulously mind its own business. No wonder the Cockney reporters were bewildered!

****

Fri 29 April 1949

Police Still Think Skeleton is Connie Kent

The riddle of the Fingringhoe skeleton has deepened according to a report published during the week which declared that the remains found in the tumble-down cottage at Whalebone Corner are not those of Miss Connie Ada Kent.

According to the report Scotland Yard Forensic Laboratory officials say that the skeleton does not correspond with Miss Kent's height and other known measurements.

But Essex Police say they have no knowledge of any such report, and they still expect that the skeleton will be declared to be that of Miss Kent.

"We are unable to deny or confirm it," said a Police chief, "As far as we are concerned we have received no report from Scotland Yard, and we are still awaiting scientific and medical reports, which are not yet complete. Until then the inquest cannot be held and it will be for a jury to say whether the remains are those of Connie Kent or not."

At Scotland Yard a reporter was told. "This is entirely a matter for the Essex police. We can neither confirm nor deny the report."

May Be Double Mystery

When five weeks ago after a search of Church Cottage, Dr. F. E. Camps, the Essex County pathologist, took away a number of bones it was thought that the 10-year-old mystery of the disappearance of Connie Kent, the ex-actress, had been solved and that death was due to natural causes. But should the report be confirmed, the Whalebone Corner mystery will, far from being solved, prove to be doubled in complexity. The police will be faced with two distinct problems:

Whose is the unknown skeleton in the cottage, and how did some person unknown come to be dead there? And what has happened to Connie Kent?

How Long Has It Been There?

In probing the first problem it would be necessary to decide how long the unknown skeleton has lain in the cottage.

This would present in a new light stories that the cottage had been searched since Miss Kent's disappearance without discovering her body. So long as the skeleton was accepted as hers, it had to be assumed that it had been overlooked in the course of these searches, strange as this seemed in so small a house. The new report suggests the explanation that some other person may have died in the empty house after the search for Connie Kent had ended.

During the early years of the war schoolchildren playing near the cottage complained of an offensive smell, and the headmistress reported the matter to Lexden and Winstree R.D.C., who made a search, without, however, discovering a cause. In the village it is thought that this might date the time of death, though again it is mysterious, that nothing was found in the search.

Jury Will Decide

The second problem may never be solved since the intensive inquiries of recent months have drawn blank, suggesting that nothing was heard of the missing woman since her disappearance in 1939.

But despite all conjecture and the report the police believe that they have sufficient evidence for any jury to be satisfied that the skeleton found under a heap of debris in the cottage is that of Connie Kent.

****

Just beyond the site of Connie's cottage and the Church, a lane leads down to the mill. Since the former mill buildings were converted into residences in 1996, the lane has acquired a gate and speed bumps but Mill Lane is still a public right of way. I descended slowly on my bicycle past the Mill House. This recently restored 17th century building was the home of the mill owner or manager until the closure of the mill. I continued to freewheel to the site of the mill.

The earliest record of a mill on this site dates from 1531 when it was described as 'the newly built mill by Richard Whiter and Robert Cooper'. It is likely that the section of building that straddles the river incorporated timbers from this mill when it was completely rebuilt in 1750. By 1848 a

After WWII there was regular barge traffic up the narrow Roman River to Fingringhoe Mill. This slowly dwindled until 1975 when the last working barge visited the mill. (1955)

Fingringhoe tide mill before the steam mill was added in 1893. (c1890)

The 16th century tide mill, the 19th century steam mill and the first of the 20th century silos, all standing beyond the full millpond. (1939)

The working mill complex, no longer powered by the tide and with an additional silo. (1953)

The large millpool filled with mud within 15 years of the gates being left open permanently in the 1950s. The mill ceased working in 1993 and is now in residential use. (2012)

granary had been added and, in 1893, a coal powered steam roller mill was built alongside the tide mill. This was later converted to oil in 1933 and then to electricity in 1938. The mill was still deriving some of its power from the tide until the early 1940s when the wheels finally stopped turning. The mill prospered longer than most by adopting the speciality of producing cooked flaked maize. This kept the mill working until 1993 when, after over 450 years, all milling finally ceased and the mill was closed. Fortunately before the buildings fell into a state beyond repair they were given listed status and in 1996 work started on converting them to residential use.

The mill sits on Roman River and this forms the northern boundary of the parish of Fingringhoe. As I passed by the restored mill and across the bridge I entered East Donyland, my next parish.

Fingringhoe Mill and Church from Roman River. (2012)

CHAPTER VI

East Donyland & Rowhedge

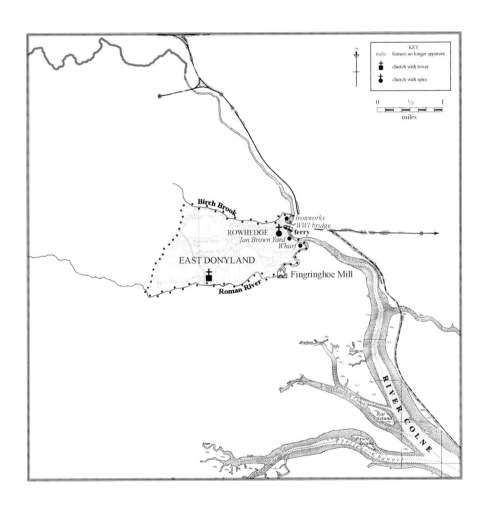

THE COLNE

East Donyland & Rowhedge

It is thought that the name Donyland is derived from Dunna's or Dunning's land. In the late 10th century it was divided into two. The area of West Donyland became part of Colchester, it includes what is now known as Berechurch. East Donyland was centred around the Saxon church of St Lawrence. It is recorded as a small manor in Domesday and by the 14th century was described as one of the smallest and poorest parishes in Lexden Hundred.

By this time the village of Rowhedge was developing in the east of the parish on the banks of the Colne. First recorded in 1346, it is thought that the name is derived from rough hedge. This could have described an early, hedged enclosure. The village grew as the port developed and by the 16th century had become the main centre of population in the parish.

In 1848 White describes the parish of 1,400 acres and 793 inhabitants as a fishing village on the west bank of the Colne.

Today the roughly rectangular parish of East Donyland is bounded by the Colne on the east, Roman River on the south, and Birch Brook on much of the north. A rapidly growing population is filling the redevelopment on the former riverside industrial sites. The recorded population in 2011 was 1,930.

I arrived in the parish of East Donyland by crossing the Roman River at Fingringhoe Mill. In an area so closely associated with the Romans it is tempting to assume that the river is named after them, but this is not the case. It is named after a local family, the Romaynes who were land owners; a John Romayne is recorded in Colchester Court Rolls of 1377. Also it is by no means certain that Fingringhoe Mill has always been so called. In some early East Donyland documents there are references to a mill. This could have been the Fingringhoe Mill that sits astride the parish boundary on Roman River or, alternatively, some or all of these references may refer to other long vanished mill sites along the parish boundary which, for much of its length, is coincident with either Roman River or Birch Brook.

From the mill I took the delightful footpath through woods and over marshes along the bank of the tidal Roman River to its confluence with the Colne. This walk is now named after John Brunning, an enthusiastic local walker and active member of the 'Friends of the Roman River Valley', who was tragically killed in a car accident in 1990. His walk ends at Colneside at the site of the former Colchester Dock Transit Company's wharfs and

Rowhedge Wharf, site of the Colchester Dock Transit Company, now awaiting residential development. (2012)

warehouses. This is now an enormous concrete slab on which there are a few piles of crushed concrete, all that remains of the earlier buildings. This riverside site is awaiting approval for an extensive residential development. I continued along the riverside footpath which is delineated by a white-line close to the edge of the quay. I was now back on the bank of the Colne and was soon at the small inlet accommodating a few moorings by the site of the former Ian Brown Yard. Before I go into the fascinating history of shipbuilding at Rowhedge, I will take a little diversion inland.

From here the old concrete access road, now barred and somewhat overgrown with brambles, bypasses the village and leads up to the Colchester Road. At its end the access road is crossed by a path that leads to the site of the East Donyland medieval church of St Lawrence. The path has all the signs of being an ancient trackway along which many of the former inhabitants of the village would have trudged up to their place of worship.

The medieval church of St Lawrence comprised a small nave and chancel with a small bellcote. It was demolished c1840. From a painting 1816.

In 1838 a new church was built in a more suitable location for the expanding riverside settlement at Rowhedge. The new church was an octagonal construction based on the design of the chapter house of York Minster. It was later described as the 'ugliest parish church in England', and more tactfully by Pevsner as 'quite remarkably original'. At this time the village consisted of a single street parallel to the riverbank and the entire parish had a working population of 202, of which over half were described as dredgermen or fishermen.

From the old churchyard I made my way back to the Colne upon which the riverside community depended. The wharf dates back to the 16th century when it is recorded that seagoing ships unable to reach Colchester Hythe unloaded there. This continued to happen until the 20th century when, in 1984, only 500 of the 2,500 vessels using the port of Colchester actually reached the Hythe. The remaining 2,000 used the quays at Rowhedge or Wivenhoe.

The site of the medieval church, now only St Lawrence's churchyard and East Donyland burial ground. (2012)

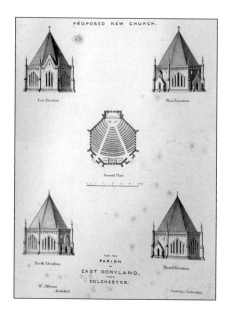

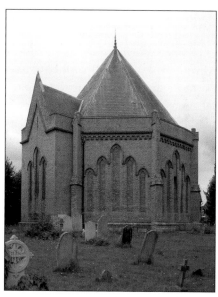

The architect's plans for the proposed new church.   *The 1838 octagonal church of St Lawrence. (2012)*

From late Victorian times until WWII Rowhedge benefited from the yachting boom. As at Brightlingsea, many of these craft were over wintered on the waterfront and provided employment for local mariners. One of the many yachts captained by Rowhedge men was the prestigious Royal Yacht Britannia, owned and raced by Edward, Prince of Wales later King Edward VII and then by George V.

The riverside has been the site of shipbuilding since the 18th century when about five ships a year were being built. These included some as large as the 350 ton vessel built for the East India trade, but the routine work of most of the yards at Rowhedge was building Colne smacks. These powerfully rigged vessels were used for oyster dredging.

The larger smacks that worked far into the North Sea were known as 'skillingers' for their work dredging off Terschelling, a sandbank over 100 miles northeast of Orford Ness. These once common vessels formed

Since 2003 the restored Pioneer CK18 *has been sailing the waters of the Colne and further afield. (2005)*

the largest dredging fleet around the shores of Britain and their work was described as the hardest and cruellest trade that Essex men ever worked.

Of all these deep sea smacks ever built the only one still afloat is the *Pioneer*. She was built by Thomas Harris in 1864 at Rowhedge and worked out of Brightlingsea dredging deep sea oysters. In 1889 she was lengthened by Aldous of Brightlingsea when a wet well was fitted. This is part of the ship that has holes in its planking so that seawater can enter, this enables the catch to be kept alive until the vessel is back in port, making it possible to work further away.

The *Pioneer* stopped working in 1939 when she was converted into a houseboat and moored at East Mersea. Before the end of the war she had broken her mooring and sunk. She remained in the Mersea mud until 1998 when a group of enthusiasts decided to dig out the decaying hulk and restore her to her former glory. Restoration was completed by 2003 and she is now, what is thought to be the last remaining example of a UK sailing fishing vessel with a wet well. The restored *Pioneer CK18* now has a professional crew of three and takes groups of up to twelve, sailing from Brightlingsea for day sails on the Colne and for longer trips in the North Sea.

A quick word about the CK18 displayed on the vessel. All fishing boats must display a number and the identifying letters of their registration port. This is often the first and last letter of the port. Close by we have Harwich, HH, and Maldon, MN, and then between them are the ports along Colchester Creek, CK.

Boatbuilding at Rowhedge was not confined to wooden vessels. By the early years of the 20th century Rowhedge Ironworks was running the upper yard and then during WWII took over the lower yard. Despite their name, they continued to build wooden vessels but their speciality was steel ships. Vessels built for the Navy included habour launches, minesweepers and small tankers. The yard's more specialised projects included steam driven oyster dredgers, paddle steamers and oil tankers. All this activity made the village a very noisy place. What with all the banging and clattering of the shearing and punching machines, together with the eight or more gangs of riveters working for twelve hours a day, Rowhedge was far from being the sleepy riverside village that some people may imagine.

The Pyefleet *steam paddlewheel oyster dredger, built for Colchester Corporation at the Rowhedge Ironworks in 1929. This replaced an almost identical vessel of the same name built at Forrestt's yard, Wivenhoe in 1895.*

The Jackson Pasha, *built in 1932 for the Sudan Government for use on the Nile. She was completely dismantled before being crated up and shipped out. This was the first ever Diesel powered stern wheeler.*

The 200ft (60m) Mahtab-Javed *completed in 1963, the last tanker to be built at Rowhedge.*

The launching of a refurbished Watson Class Lifeboat in 1968.

In 1964 all this noise ceased with the closure of the Rowhedge Ironworks. But some traditional wooden boat building continued at the Lower yard which was taken over by Ian Brown. The mainstay of this firm's work was the maintenance of the RNLI wooden lifeboats. Sadly the long tradition of boatbuilding on the riverside at Rowhedge came to an end with the closure of this yard in 1988 when it was sold to developers. The bourgeoning housing boom had arrived in Rowhedge and continues to this day.

Another activity which has shaped the waterfront of the village is mineral extraction. In 1932 the Rowhedge Sand and Gravel Company began extraction in the parish. The materials were transported by barge to London and elsewhere. In 1946 the company was taken over by F. A. Hunnable and Sons of Braintree who reduced the production of ballast but increased the output of concrete blocks. In the early 1960s a quay 100m. long was built, which was later extended to 150m. This quay with its associated warehouses were taken over by the Colchester Dock Transit Co. in 1972. During the following twenty years or so the port flourished dealing with the ships that were too large to proceed up to the Hythe. In 1988 the port was bought by

Associated British Ports Holdings PLC, who further increased the length of the quays and area of the warehouses. This was to be the final expansion before the port closed in 2001. The buildings became derelict and were demolished in 2012. There are now plans for a residential development on the site.

Rowhedge High Street runs parallel to the Colne and is never far from it. Many of its buildings bear names from the past and there are a few that still function as they always have. One such is the *Albion*. A fine pub still serving traditional ales, close by is a small area of waterfront known as Pearson's Quay. This is named after the owners of the house opposite and was laid out as a small riverside park in 1976 with seats and commemorative sundial. I arrived here at lunchtime in the sunshine and, with the tide lapping at the quayside, I could not pass by the empty seat, so I unpacked my sandwiches, poured a cup of coffee from my flask and placed it on the seat beside me. While admiring an impeccably maintained smack moored to the quay and halfway through my first sandwich, I was approached by the local cat. He nuzzled his cheeks against my legs and as he turned his head to look up at me as if asking to jump into my lap, the curl at the end of his long sinuous tail did a little swish. To the surprise of us both it caught my coffee cup which flew from the edge of the seat. He went. I poured another cup of coffee and turned my attention to the sundial.

The waterfront was laid out as a small park in 1976 and two years later the equatorial sundial was unveiled by Reg White. (2013)

Sundials come in all shapes and sizes and have evolved into quite sophisticated timepieces. Early sundials did not divide the day into equal hours. In fact the Saxons did not have hours at all. They divided their day into eight divisions called tides. The names of some of these tides are still used to describe parts of the day, for example, morningtide and eventide have become morning and evening. All this changed with the arrival of the Normans in 1066 who brought with them the twelve hour system, but it was not until the Renaissance that the art of dialling became established as an important mathematical subject. This enabled sundial makers to adjust the shape and position of the arm, or gnomon as they call it, so that the position of its shadow would read local solar time accurately throughout the year. For the next 400 years or so sundials and clocks were used side by side. When the sun shone, the mechanical clocks were set to local solar time.

The difference of around twenty minutes in solar time between the east and west of the country was of little consequence until the coming of the railways when it was noticed that the outward journey from London to

Rowhedge sundial plaque showing the 'Equation of Time'. During February, up to 15 minutes need to be added to and in October, subtracted from, dial time to obtain an accurate GMT reading. (2013)

Bristol was always shorter than the return journey. Also astronomers had realised that the elliptical path of the earth's orbit around the sun and the angle of our planet's axis of rotation relative to the plane of its orbit mean that, not only do the hours of daylight vary throughout the year, but also it is not always exactly 24 hours between successive noons. All this led to the introduction in 1880 of Greenwich Mean Time, GMT. This is based on solar time at Greenwich adjusted to make the length of every day exactly 24 hours. If you want to set your watch by the sundial then you must take into account the difference between solar time and GMT. This varies with the time of year and is given by the equation of time, helpfully provided on the plaque below the Rowhedge dial. And, if your visit is during the summer, do not forget to rotate the dial so that the pointer at its base is set to British Summer Time, BST, to compensate for the hour's shift between BST and GMT. By now you will have probably realised that clock time is entirely artificial, designed for human convenience and somewhat removed from the reality of the movement of the celestial bodies.

From my seat in the sun I could see the other riverside pub, the *Anchor* with its patrons spilling out on to its quayside tables. Beside this ancient drinking house is the village hard from which, for many years, plied the ferry to Wivenhoe.

A crossing place between Rowhedge and Wivenhoe has existed for centuries. Although there are few early records it is known that by 1718 there was a ferry and a ford. Increased dredging and the replacement of horse transport by motor vehicles in the early 20th century led to reduced use of the ford. By this time the ferry was being run by the Ironworks for their employees, many of whom travelled daily from over the river. Following the closure of the company the ferry was run privately until 1968. Then there was no ferry until 1992 when a group of enthusiasts from both sides of the river began operating a summer weekend service.

Until its resurrection, the ferry ran straight across the river from the ferry hard to Wivenhoe marsh. It was on this marsh that, during the early years of the 20th century, there appeared a huge corrugated shed, and nobody seemed to know its purpose. I will elucidate on this mystery when I get to Wivenhoe.

Rowhedge Ferry Hard with the flat-bottomed ferry boat about to be polled across. (c1910)

Rowhedge Hard with the ferry boat passing on its way to Wivenhoe. (2012)

Before that, I will mention another large structure that was, for a short while, present in both parishes.

One spring morning in 1914 engineers from Colchester garrison arrived in the village with wagons carrying huge bulks of timber and a steam driven piling machine that was to shatter the peace of the village for days to come. At the time it was thought an invasion of the north Essex coast was a possibility. In such an event the rapid deployment of men and armaments from Colchester to the Tendring peninsular would be required. Part of this contingency plan was the building of a bridge across the Colne at Rowhedge. A description of the building of the bridge is recalled by Lesley Southgate in *Rowhedge Recollections*;

"All day long the clanging, hissing and thumping of the pile-drivers were heard all over the village as the foot-square piles were driven deep into the river bed. Pontoons were wallowing all over the water as the "land-sailors" attempted to get the timbers into position. With other children I had much entertainment watching men being inadvertently tipped into the muddy waters. A gap of about thirty-five feet was left open between the two parts of the bridge to allow for the passage of water traffic. On each side of this gap derricks of wood about twenty feet high were built: these allowed for the easy moving into position of the central spans when the bridge was closed. By the sides of the bridge on either side of the gap a quadrant of piles was driven into the mud as a protection against any wayward and erring river traffic attempting to negotiate the manoeuvre through the narrow water-way. As the piling was completed the building of the roadway was begun. The thick planks were neatly assembled and fastened.

High siderails were attached, a guard rail about six inches high and two feet from the edge was positioned which ensured that pedestrians did not get in the way of vehicular traffic. The central spans, when not in use, were stacked on the sides on either side of the bridge. At last the structure was complete.

Of course it was guarded night and day! To house the soldiers on this duty a hut was erected on the Rowhedge side; near this hut stood a huge cauldron which seemed to always be on the boil and sending out appetising smells of Irish Stew. I remember on one occasion seeing the cook take up a stick coated in river mud and giving the delicacy a good stir! The men looked well on it!"

Fortunately the bridge was never required for its intended purpose but it did have its moment of glory when it was formerly opened by King George V in April 1916, on his return from a troop inspection at Clacton. Having walked across the bridge the King decided that he would see for himself the village where the captain and crew of his racing yacht came from.

At the end of WWI it was hoped that the bridge would be kept, perhaps modified to a swing bridge operated by steam power but this was not to happen. The powers that be, considered that such a structure would be a hindrance to maritime traffic, so the bridge was taken down.

The bridge over the River Colne at Rowhedge built by the Royal Engineers in 1914 and officially opened by King George V in 1916.

Today the crossing can only be made by ferry. This now runs from the Rowhedge River Landing Pontoon which opened in April 2006. This greatly extends the time of access to and from the river. It is situated just upriver from the *Anchor* where there is another quayside green upon which is the Rowhedge History Hut. Here the visitor can have a cup of tea and peruse a wealth of local information. From the green there is a public footpath that follows the west bank of the river all the way to Colchester. I chose not to follow this path but left on the ferry to continue my story in Wivenhoe.

The Rowhedge Bridge in the open position ready for the sailing barge to pass through. (1914-19)

The author with his bicycle waiting to board the ferry to Wivenhoe. (2012)

CHAPTER VII

Wivenhoe

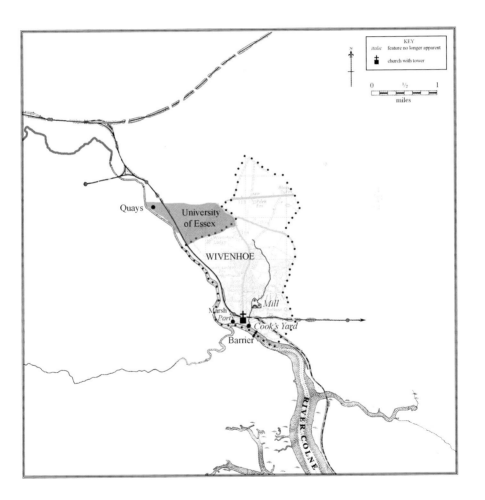

THE COLNE

Wivenhoe

It is thought that the name Wivenhoe is derived from Wifa's hoh, Wifa being a person's name and 'hoh' meaning hill-spur or long hill. It has been variously called Wyneho, Wyfenho and Wyvenho.

The Domesday survey records one mill in the manor.

In 1848 William White described Wivenhoe as 'a large respectable village seated on a picturesque acclivity on the northeast side of the Colne at a point where that navigable river begins to expand into a broad estuary. There is a good quay and it may be called the shipping port of Colchester as many colliers and other large vessels here receive and discharge their cargoes by means of lighters. A constant and extensive fishing trade is carried out here especially in oysters and soles. Great numbers of dredging boats employed in the oyster trade are built here. The parish contains 1,599 inhabitants and about 1,500 acres of land.'

The village has grown from this small riverside industrial village into a town of more than 7,000 people. It has lost most of its industry and many of its shops, but gained an art community and a university. The recorded population in 2011 was 7,637.

The ferry arrived, I unloaded my cycle, and then from the ferry terminus I made my way along the quay and through the redeveloped Cook's shipyard back to the parish boundary, which I had left at the end of Chapter 4.

Between the parishes of Alresford and Wivenhoe there is a narrow finger of land that belongs to Elmstead. When I reached the Wivenhoe boundary I paused, turned and continued my exploration of the north bank of the Colne. Looking upstream from here, there is a nice view of the village, captured in a somewhat romanticised manner by W Bartlett in 1832. Across the river a barge was being loaded at Ballast Quay in Fingringhoe. On my side of the river, directly opposite this quay is what was once a green lane that leads inland. Today there is no evidence of a crossing place here, but where two roads meet on opposite banks of the river it is difficult not to believe that at one time this was the site of a ferry or tidal ford.

Next I came to the redeveloped downriver part of the village. Central to this development is the Colne barrier. Following the closure of Cook's shipyard in 1987, all interested parties came together, and a development plan was drafted. This included a residential area, improved public access to

Approaching Wivenhoe on the ferry from Rowhedge. (2012)

Looking upstream towards Wivenhoe as depicted by W Bartlett in 1832.

the waterfront, a flood barrier and new premises for the sailing club. All this was to be carried out in such a manner as to enhance the existing character of the village and the adjacent conservation area within the Colne Valley as a whole. Negotiations to achieve these bold aims were long and protracted but resulted in a compromise, where all parties achieved something of what they wanted. There is still some local resentment to the barrier. It is seen as a blot on the landscape, built to protect floodplain development in Colchester while the older properties in the village still flood as they always have done. But the sailing club managed to negotiate new premises and the shipyard that had remained derelict for nearly twenty years has been transformed.

The barrier was completed in 1993. It closes an average 40 times a year and it is claimed protects over 2,000 properties from tidal flooding. It is currently undergoing maintenance which includes the refurbishment of the thirteen small radial gates and the large mitre gates across the main channel.

The residential development is ongoing. This is causing some local resentment. Not so much to do with the development itself, but all the to-ing

Approaching the Colne Barrier. Built in 1993 it protects low-lying areas of Colchester, Rowhedge and Wivenhoe from flooding. On average it closes 40 times a year. (2012)

and fro-ing of the construction vehicles through an established and, what was once, a quiet residential area of the village. Ironically, the developers planned to bring the construction materials to the site by way of the river and had already provisionally secured the use of a barge. Then they were prevented from using the river for commercial purposes by the legislation that was used to close the Port of Colchester. Despite the efforts of many people, no way around this ridiculous state of affairs could be found.

I cycled along the mud-strewn road past the growing development into the completed former shipyard area. Compared to the Brightlingsea shipyard development of a similar site, Wivenhoe is a wonderfully pleasant place to be. The whole of the waterside is accessible, there is a new fish dock and information boards with displays which tell visitors about the heritage of the site. All this is set in a varied development with accommodation to suit a variety of tastes.

The area has a long industrial heritage. In the days of sail it was where ballast was loaded into colliers for their return trip to Newcastle after delivering coal to Colchester. It later became the site of the gasworks that opened in 1861. This was on the landward side of the boat building business opened in 1840 by James Husk and run by his family for a hundred years.

This yard built high quality fishing smacks, yachts and other vessels, nearly always of wood. The site and adjoining ship building activities were taken over by Vosper & Co Ltd in 1940 to build motor torpedo boats for the Royal Navy, and high speed air sea rescue launches for the Royal Air Force. In 1947 James W Cook & Co Ltd acquired the shipyards. They developed their barge and lighter activities to become the coaster and motor barge building specialists in the area. The yard prospered for a time but eventually closed in 1986.

Before leaving this site I would like to mention its connection with what was probably the earliest industry to be practised in the village, for it was here that the village brook ran into the Colne. In earlier times the brook was the ancient parish boundary and provided a vital part of the village water supply. It is clearly shown on the early edition Ordnance Survey maps, but is now virtually buried under residential developments. It is still possible to

James Cook's Yard. The gasometers are behind Husk's shipyard, the larger sheds were erected during WWII by Vosper & Co Ltd. (1951)

trace the course of the brook, by following the contours and culverts, as it twists its way up towards the Alresford Road, until it eventually emerges way upstream. On the way it passes Bobbitts Way, named after the former nearby Bobbitts Hole that was located at what is now 36-38 Valley Road. This was, until the 1960s a favourite place for local children to play and families to picnic. The children playing in the brook or looking up the hill toward what is now Dene Park, would have seen no sign of the former importance of this site. It was here, on the brook that stood Wivenhoe Mill. First recorded in 1086 in the Domesday Survey, the watermills on this site ground the flour for the local community until well into the 17th century. Nothing is known for certain about the mill building itself but it was probably typical of the numerous mills situated on the tributaries of the Colne. These early mills were usually single story buildings with an external waterwheel that drove one or two pairs of stones. All the local corn growers in the area would arrive

*Wivenhoe fish dock on the site of
the former Cook's shipyard. (2012)*

The fish dock is surrounded by a mixture of commercial and residential development. (2012)

with their small sacks of corn, and a short time later take away their flour in the same sacks. The miller would, of course keep some for his trouble. These early mills suffered from the same risks as later mills and often had relatively short lives due to fires or the continual shaking from the machinery. Never the less, mills were usually rebuilt on the same site for hundreds of years, as was the one in Wivenhoe. As the population grew, the demand for flour increased and many millers acquired windmills. These were often located on high ground near the site of the watermill and the two mills were operated by the same miller. On many of the sites where the watermill was driven by a small stream, the windmill eventually took over and the original watermill disappeared. This happened at Wivenhoe and by the 18th century the mill was described as a large post mill and was located some 200 yards (180m) up the hill from Bobbitts Hole. Mills are often named after the miller but Bobbitt was never a miller here. Long after the mill had disappeared the area was owned by William Barlett, and it is said that one young member of this family had difficulty in pronouncing the name of his brother Robert, and so Bobbitt lives on.

Milk churns being unloaded for the ferry across to Wivenhoe. (c1914)

Back to the former shipyard, where I continued along the riverside and soon arrived at Ferry House. In what is now a garden there once stood the ferry shelter where passengers waited for the ferry to Fingringhoe. This is where Bethany Street disappears into the Colne. For many years there was a concrete path that led down to the low water mark making it easy for people to use the ferry at any state of the tide. There are still people who remember milk being delivered to the village from a farmer in Fingringhoe. Usually the churns would be unloaded from a cart on the Fingringhoe side to be transported across by ferry. If the cart happened to arrive at a low water neap tide, then the cart could be driven through the river and up into the village. The ferry last left from here in 1952. When arrangements were being made to reinstate the ferry in 1991, the owner of Ferry House supported the use of the old hard but some other nearby residents objected to the proposal because they did not want unsightly queues near their properties! The unsightly queues now mingle with all the other unsightly people outside the *Rose & Crown* where a new jetty was built on the quay.

The ferry shelter. (c1920)

*Ferry House looking straight across to
Fingringhoe Hard. (2012)*

From Fingringhoe looking across to Wivenhoe. The ferryman is Charlie Sainty. (1935)

A view from St Mary's church tower looking across the Colne to the meandering Roman River and Fingringhoe Mill. (1920)

A view from St Mary's church tower looking downriver. The steam yacht moorings have been replaced by the Barrier and the sailing club. (c1912)

I was now on the quay and well into the oldest part of the village. A village that was described in 1997 as 'attractive and interesting without being contrived, not too villagy, not too quaint, but very picturesque'. As I wandered around the jumble of narrow streets behind the waterfront I thought that this description still applies today. The skyline of Wivenhoe is characterized by its 15th century church tower surmounted by its distinctive wooden cupola. It is thought that there has been a church on this site since Saxon times and the views from the tower show what a strategic site this would have been.

I returned to the waterfront and the jetty that has been the ferry terminus for both the Fingringhoe and Rowhedge crossing since the service was reinstated in 1992. Close by is a building known locally as the Nottage. This institute was established in Wivenhoe in 1896 as a result of a bequest by Captain Charles Nottage. Charles was born in 1852 and developed an interest in nautical activities at an early age, before becoming a great traveller. By his late teens he was cruising regularly on a variety of yachts, some of which were crewed by Colnesiders. When he purchased his own yacht in 1885, it was Colnesiders that he chose for his crew. Although a captain, this was a rank related to a commission he held in the Army, but he did have a Board of Trade Certificate empowering him to navigate his own vessel. His yachts, crewed by Colnesiders, were very successful on the racing scene, and no doubt would have continued to be so if ill health had not forced Charles to abandon the sport at the early age of 38. In an effort to find a climate more suitable for his condition he set out on a cruise during which he visited Madeira, Egypt, Australia and the South Sea islands. Eventually, having failed to find relief for his respiratory problems, he returned to England where he died in 1894, aged 42 years. His will contained a variety of bequests including £3,000 to be used

A popular view of Wivenhoe with its attractive array of buildings along the waterfront below a distinctive tower of St Mary's Church. (2012)

to establish a 'Nautical Academy of Colneside' in Wivenhoe. This was to be called 'The Nottage Institute' and to be used for the purpose of 'instructing yachtsmen and other sailors in the science of navigation'. The trustees were given the 'widest discretion' in the establishment and running of the institute, with the provisos that 'no clergyman of any denomination shall be eligible to serve on the management committee' and 'that the institution shall be strictly secular and that no books or periodicals of a religious character are to be placed in any library of the institution'. These provisos arose as a result of the views formed by Charles Nottage during his travels, particularly in the South Seas, concerning the activities of missionaries and religious organisations.

For the first 50 years of its life 'the Nottage' was housed in premises next to the *Black Buoy*. Classes started in 1897 with a fee of 6d (2½p) per week for tuition in navigation. During the ensuing years the classes were extended to include first aid, internal combustion engines, electricity, signaling and technical drawing. Then in 1947 the institute moved to its present location on the quay. Here, in the more spacious premises it was able to add practical classes in traditional boatbuilding to its already impressive list of activities. Today 'the Nottage' provides classes for many Royal Yacht Association (RHA) courses and several general and maritime courses. It is also the guardian of

Captain Charles Nottage,
1852-1894

Since 1947 The Nottage Maritime Institute has been located in a former sailmaker's premises on the quay. (2012)

The traditional boatbuilding area of 'the Nottage'. (2012)

the maritime traditions of the Colne which are accessible through its museum and library. During the summer months the institute is open to the public on Sunday afternoons.

Upstream from the quay is a residential development located in the former port area. Here, some of the earlier buildings have been retained and converted for modern use, so retaining something of the character of this maritime industrial site.

The origin of the upriver shipyard is lost in the mists of time, but what is known for certain is that, during the 18th century, Wivenhoe developed as a port and the upriver shipyard was building smacks, lighters and cargo vessels. Navigation upriver from Wivenhoe has always been difficult and as vessels, such as sailing colliers, became larger, this made it the natural place for them to unload some of their cargo, or lighten their load into lighters, before proceeding to the Hythe in Colchester. The prosperity of the shipyard went up and down as it passed through the hands of several owners. By the time it was being run by Forrestts, who took over in 1888, there were a number of slipways and the only dry dock between Lowestoft and London. This, with its railway sidings leading to the quay, all made for a prosperous time. By now the yard was building both wooden and steel ships for a multitude of customers and purposes. These included lifeboats, tugs, yachts, paddle steamers and many specialised craft.

One of the most unusual was the *Volta*, launched in 1905. This was a submersible built for the British Submarine Company. Because of its small size, a mere 34ft (10.2m) long and 6ft 9in (2m) in diameter, it was called 'the pocket submarine'. Powered by two electric motors, it had a range of 40 miles and was designed to take a three man crew: commander, driver and torpedo-man. Not surprisingly, the British government took a close interest in this vessel and tried to prevent its export. Despite this, or perhaps because of this, the vessel mysteriously disappeared. It has been observed by some that the mini-submarines used by the Imperial Japanese Navy in the early years of WWII bore more than a passing resemblance to the *Volta*.

The launch of the Volta, the only submarine to be built on the Colne. (1905)

Description of the Volta as it appeared in the Engineering Gazette of 10 November 1913.

THE POCKET SUBMARINE

The motive power was electrical, consisting of two series-wound motors of 20 HP., connected in tandem, and so arranged upon the series parallel system as to give a large range of speed. Current was supplied from an 80 volt battery specially constructed to the shape of the boat and fitted in teak cases.

A special feature was made of the starting and controlling resistances, which were wound in watertight tubes, and water-cooled by being fixed in special cavities outside the shell of the boat.

Submergence was effected by a motor pump, by means of which a tank could be rapidly filled or emptied. There was also fitted a small auxiliary motor pump with automatic control, which maintained the boat at any predetermined depth by pumping small quantities of water in or out of the tank as required. The control of this pump was worked by solenoid switches actuated by a pressure gauge of delicate construction, which made or broke the platinum contacts with a rise or fall of six inches of water pressure. The contact dial of this gauge was adjustable so that the instrument could be set to maintain any desired depth.

In order to maintain the boat in a horizontal position when submerged, a travelling weight was provided, which moved on runners the entire length of the boat. As this tramway was situated immediately over the keel it gave rise to a number of problems, as everything else which it became necessary to seat in the bottom of the boat had to be especially shaped to avoid it.

The travelling weight, like the pumps, was actuated by motor power controlled by solenoid switches: these in turn operated in response to the movements of a pendulum. This piece of apparatus was constructed so as to make platinum contact and set the electric current working to move the weight at the least unasked for inclination of the vessel.

The base of the pendulum carrying the platinum contacts was adjustable, so that by moving this base either to left or right, for which purpose a substantial handle was provided, the boat could be made to dive either upwards or downwards at any angle desired.

Another auxiliary machine was designed to continually purify the air absorbing the carbonic oxide gas and replacing it with fresh oxygen. This apparatus was tested by a nine hours sojourn at the bottom of a dock, during which time the crew of three on board played cards, smoked, and by means of a telephone to the bank, ordered drinks, which, needless to say, did not arrive. At the end of the test, the occupants declared they found the atmosphere better than at the commencement, but when the hatch was opened up the first man who entered nearly collapsed, and said other things of the mixed gases which escaped. However, the apparatus undoubtedly worked very well for ordinary periods.

I spoke of the telephone to the surface. This was an ingenious contrivance, fixed outside the boat, and so devised that by turning a handle inside, it became detached, and in case the boat was submerged, would float away to the top of the water with a length of watertight flexible cable connecting it to the boat. In case of serious accident this would not only indicate the spot where the vessel lay, but would also enable the crew to phone their last wishes to the rescuing party.

Another safety device consisted of a heavy weight attached to the bottom of the boat below the keel. The turn of a lever inside the boat would release this, and bring the boat to the top, even when she had made a good deal of water.

The last difficulty to be overcome was that presented by the compass. The submarine, as you will gather by his time was electrical inside and outside. Within a very confined space it contained no less than nine motors, two at least of them being of substantial dimensions. No sort of shielding seemed to efficiently protect the compass. It was even tried outside the boat, the reading being taken by reflection through a window, but all to no purpose. This problem was finally solved by the use of the gyrostat.

The wheel, which was free to move in every direction, was made of forged Delta metal and the rim weighed nine pounds. It was set in motion, at 7000 rpm by a friction drive from an electric motor. Having once been correctly set this gyrostatic compass would point accurately for some twenty minutes, which was considered long enough for practical purposes.

The interior space was extremely cramped but for all that, there was room for each member of the crew to do all that he had to do. Owing to the necessity of keeping the main motors low down in the hull, the main shaft had to be geared to the propeller shaft situated on the axis line. Double helical gear was used, and although every precaution was taken, the noise set up in the confined space made communication by speech impossible, except with the aid of tubes which were installed between the three positions.

In the centre of the boat was a small conning tower. Here the captain stood, upon a platform over the main tank. When running on the surface he could see in every direction through small portholes provided. When submerged, he could make out his course by means of the periscope, or if too low down for this, as when passing beneath a vessel, he would have to calculate his directions. The captain operated the steering wheel and gave directions to the driver or the torpedo man by means of the tubes.

The driver sat in the fore part of the boat, the main controls standing between his knees. Facing him stood the main switchboard. This was fitted with miniature edgewise instruments, and in its construction every possible means was taken to economise on space. To the left of the driver was fixed the automatic and hand tank control gear, and to his right the automatic and hand pendulum apparatus.

The men employed during the trials at sea volunteered for the work, which was unquestionably dangerous. Fortunately no hitch occurred.

During the inter-war years the yard was occupied by a further two companies. During WWII many vessels were built for the Admiralty. There were also some more submarines, but these had no crew and could not be submerged. They were over 100ft (30m) long, made of wood and only existed above the waterline. These dummy vessels were towed to Harwich and located in places so as to confuse and mislead the enemy.

After the war the yard struggled on, before closing in 1961. A few years later the site was acquired by the timber importing firm, J. Gliksten & Son Ltd. The dry dock was filled in, the associated gantry demolished and the quay extended. Timber imports continued to arrive at the wharf until 1992 when it finally closed.

The minesweeper Carhampton *in Wivenhoe dry dock. This was built in 1889 and extended in 1904 to become the largest such facility on the East Coast. (c1947)*

Residential development around the former dry dock site of the upriver shipyard. (2012)

The site has now been developed for residential use, but its heritage has not been forgotten. During the past two hundred years many types of vessel have been constructed here, and this is commemorated on the plaque by the excavated dry dock that now forms a feature in the development.

Beyond the residential development the riverside path continues on to the marsh. This is now a Site of Special Scientific Interest (SSSI) and is home to an abundance of wildlife, including the protected water vole. It has not always been such a haven for wildlife. This former grazing marsh has been used for several purposes. Perhaps one of the most interesting was carried out in a large shed that was erected in 1908 when Jack Humphrys arrived in Wivenhoe.

Jack was born in Hong Kong in 1875, educated in England and became a dentist practicing in London. Then he inherited a small fortune from his grandmother. This enabled him to pursue his hobby of aeronautics. He studied bird flight and experimented with non-powered flight by jumping off cliffs in Cornwall. By 1908 several people had demonstrated the possibility of powered flight and this is when Jack moved his centre of operations to

Wivenhoe. There was considerable secrecy between the early pioneers of aviation and not many people were privy to what went on in Jack's new workshop built on the marsh. He had patented his own airscrew design, control system and flying boat hull. From the local shipyards he was able to recruit craftsmen with the necessary skills to put his ideas into practice. Then on 3rd April 1909 the *Wivenhoe Flier*, known locally as the 'Wiv'ner Airyplane' was ready to launch. From contemporary accounts it is not clear what went wrong, but the result was that Jack suffered the ignominy of having to swim to the bank as the machine sank. The *Flier* was recovered and, following some modifications, several further attempts were made to get the machine airborne but, by 14th May, Jack abandoned his hopes of being the first to achieve a waterborne take-off and landing.

His new ambition was to secure the £1,000 prize for the first British pilot to fly a British aeroplane on a circular flight of one mile. Activity

Jack Humphrys in the pilot seat of the Wivenhoe Flier, *known locally as the 'Wiv'ner Airyplane' ready for take off on the river Colne. (1909)*

in the Wivenhoe workshop was now directed to the construction of a monoplane. This first appeared for trials in a field overlooking Alresford Creek in October. Unfortunately the undercarriage hit a drainage ditch before take-off. Jack was so confident in his machine that he transported it to the first British aviation meeting held in Blackpool. Here bad weather prevented a demonstration of its flying ability. Back in Wivenhoe the machine underwent several modifications but never left the ground. Meanwhile the £1,000 prize had been claimed by Moore-Brabazon flying a machine built by Messrs Short Brothers. Undeterred, Jack went on to build another monoplane to a different design. This had a very large wing area and soon acquired the nickname of *'The Elephant'*. This was to be the last aeroplane to be built at Wivenhoe. In April 1910 Jack left Wivenhoe to join a group of pre-WWI aviators at Brooklands. Here, he and his machine did eventually leave the ground.

The Elephant *in the Wivenhoe shed. Note the remains of the* Wivenhoe Flyer *in the background. (1910)*

Another facility that brought activity to the marsh was the ferry. This operated straight across the river at Rowhedge on to Wivenhoe marsh which was crossed by a toll road to the railway station that bore the name Wivenhoe and Rowhedge. During the thriving days of the Rowhedge Ironworks, many of its workers arrived and departed from the station and rushed across the marsh to and from the ferry

The story of how the railway came to Wivenhoe is interesting and has more than a little to do with the Colne. Colchester has always been an important town and, before the coming of the railway in 1843, the Hythe had been vital to the town's economy. Earlier in the century there had been regular sailings of both goods and passengers to London, Hull and Ostend. All this was threatened by the planned railway that was to connect London

The ferry shelter on the Wivenhoe side of the Rowhedge Ferry.
This group of cyclists are using the ferry on a Sunday in 1959.

Until the demise of the regular ferry service the railway served both communities and the station carried both names. (1952)

not only to Colchester but also to Ipswich, a town with which there had been long standing rivalry. It was also realised that this rival had a deepwater port for which the Hythe was no match. If a deepwater port could be created at the Hythe then this would not only ensure the future of the existing services but also facilitate the transport of goods between ships and London by rail. And so it was that a proposal to build a ship canal between Wivenhoe and the Hythe was prepared by engineer and entrepreneur, Peter Bruff. This is a name that we will come across several times as we proceed along the river. He was involved with so many civil engineering projects in the area that he has been described as the 'Brunel of the Eastern Counties'. Not only was he an extremely competent engineer and passionate about the advantages that civil engineering projects could bring to communities, but he had the ability to persuade local dignitaries and businessmen to back his schemes.

Bruff's scheme was to build a dam at Rowhedge to turn the river up to and beyond the Hythe into a deepwater basin. Access to which was to be via a ship canal, 16ft (4.8m) deep and a mile long built to the north of the existing channel. Despite strong support from the town, the Admiralty turned down the scheme on the grounds that it would be cheaper and more effective to remove an existing lock to improve natural scouring, and to dredge and straighten the existing channel. These improvements were duly carried out but large vessels still had to lighten at Wivenhoe. Several years elapsed, by which time Peter Bruff had developed interests in Walton-on-the-Naze and was promoting the Tendring Hundred Railway. His proposal was now to construct a railway from Colchester to Walton, via Wivenhoe. This was greeted with great enthusiasm by those Colchester interests who had previously been behind the ship canal. The railway reached Wivenhoe in 1863, a full twenty years after arriving in Colchester. Now Wivenhoe became the deepwater port for Colchester with access to the rail network.

At one time or another there has been a railway along most of the length of the river Colne but today it is only the couple of miles or so from Wivenhoe to the Hythe that survives. This stretch of the river is unique in that it has, not only the railway, but a footpath along both banks and a cyclepath.

The Wivenhoe Society Colneside tidy. (2011)

I have been along the cyclepath on numerous occasions, sometimes to reach Wivenhoe and many times to go further afield. The path is part of the Sustrans long distance cycle network, originally *Route 1* from Harwich to Hull, it has since been re-designated as *Route 51*. These routes use a combination of quiet roads and cyclepaths to cover the whole of the UK. It is estimated that the 13,000 miles of this National Cycle Network is used by over a million people every day. The route along the Colne is well used by long distance cyclists, commuters and by families enjoying a sunny summer excursion. For regular users there is always something to see with the varying states of the tide and weather. As I was making this journey one spring morning I was surprised to see many people of all ages wandering about on the marsh. Upon enquiry I discovered that they were taking part in the litter collection day, an annual event organised by the Wivenhoe Society.

Some way along the cyclepath there is a path that crosses the railway by a level crossing. This leads into Wivenhoe Park, now the University of Essex. For many years Wivenhoe parish boundary followed the brook that ran through the park, but now it follows Boundary Road, effectively moving the whole of Wivenhoe Park into Colchester. Never the less, for the sake of its name and long association with the village, I will include it in this chapter.

The park was the home of the Rebow family from 1734 till 1902. The Rebows were an old Colchester family descended from Huguenot refugees, first recorded in the town in the early 17th century. In 1733 Isaac Lemyng Rebow acquired an area of land that was to become Wivenhoe Park. At the time it was known as Bacon's Green and included a 'small country residence' with a deer park. The present house was built around 1760, by the London architect Thomas Reynolds, and the grounds were landscaped with lakes and carriageways by Richard Woods. During the mid 19th century extensive alterations were made to the house. These were carried out under the direction of Thomas Hopper, Surveyor to the County of Essex and a much sought after architect who received royal patronage from the Prince Regent. Originally he proposed pulling down the old George III house and building an entirely new one, but Gurdon Rebow would not allow this. The result was the neo-Tudor mansion that we see today. In 1848 the park was described by White as 'extensive, richly clothed with wood, and embellished with a fine sheet of water, and a stock of deer'.

The visit of Prince Albert to Wivenhoe Park. (1856)

The Rebow's long association with the park ended in 1902 when it was sold to Charles Edmund Gooch. The Park remained in the Gooch family throughout the two World Wars. During WWI the park was festooned with avenues of white tents for troops with all the military paraphernalia associated with horse transport. Occupation of the park during WWII was even more intrusive with camouflaged Nissen huts and concrete tank standings for two Tank Regiments. At the end of the war the park was ploughed and cropped for several years before being laid back to grass.

As part of the expansion of the university sector in the early 1960s it was decided that one of the new 'plate glass universities' should be in Essex. The short list of possible sites included Hylands Park in Chelmsford and Wivenhoe Park in Colchester. To the great delight of Colcestrians, their rivals in the County town lost out when, in 1962, Wivenhoe Park was chosen. Sixty years after his father had bought the estate, Charles Gooch, the younger, sold it to the new University of Essex.

The University campus was designed by architect, Kenneth Capon, who worked in close collaboration with the newly appointed Vice Chancellor, Dr Albert Sloman. The plan was to create a campus to house 20,000 students in a compact area set within the 204 acres of parkland. This bold plan involved the transformation of the small valley below the lake into a multilevel street composed of five quadrangles. Around each of these would be the academic departments, shops, bars and restaurants. The close proximity of all the faculties and facilities was supposed to encourage interdisciplinary activities, a pioneering principle set out by Dr Sloman in the Reith lectures in 1963. The brief given to the architect also included the requirement that 'no student was to have more than a few minutes walk from any one point on the campus to any other'. In order to achieve this it was planned to build twenty-nine high-rise towers close by. In the event only six of these were built. At the time these fourteen storey blocks were the tallest all-brick towers in Europe. This was before the social impact and problems of high-rise accommodation were appreciated. The towers could be seen from Colchester and surrounding villagers, and soon became the symbol of all that went wrong with the University during the turbulent times of the 1960s. Many local people became disillusioned with 'their' university and it took a long time for this, now highly successful institution, to be integrated into the local scene. Over the years the campus has expanded, but not to its original plan. The newer facilities and student accommodation are all low level, exhibiting a variety of modern styles and are distributed throughout the park. Car parks and student accommodation now stretch down onto the floodplain that once separated the campus from the town. This brings me to the University Quays where the riverside cyclepath enters the urban conurbation of Colchester.

The University of Essex with four of its towers built in 1963. More distant in the upper centre of the picture is the student accommodation block, the University Quays, *built in 2000 on the banks of the Colne . (2005)*

The Quays, *student accommodation for the University of Essex built on the banks of the Colne. (2012)*

CHAPTER VIII

Colchester

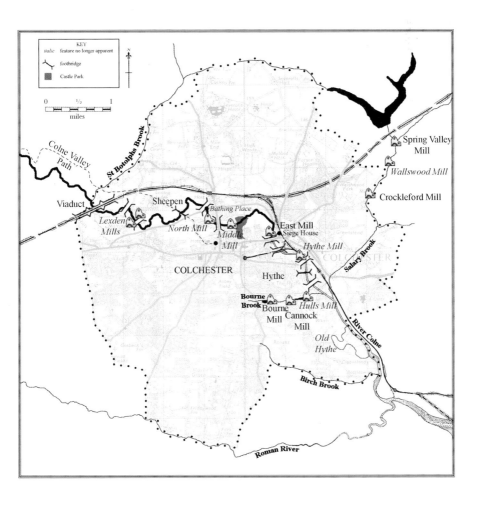

KEY

italic feature no longer apparent

footbridge

Castle Park

0   ½   1
miles

Colne Valley Path

St Botolphs Brook

Spring Valley Mill

Wallswood Mill

Crockleford Mill

Viaduct

Sheepen

Bathing Place

Lexden Mills

North Mill

Middle Mill

East Mill
Siege House

Hythe Mill

Salary Brook

COLCHESTER

Hythe

Bourne Brook

Bourne Mill

Hulls Mill

Cannock Mill

River Colne

Old Hythe

Birch Brook

Roman River

THE COLNE

Colchester

Colchester is on the site of the pre-Roman settlement of Camulodunum; Celtic for 'the fort of Camulos', the war god of the Celts. The Romans built the first British colonia here, Colonia Victrix. The modern name could be derived from a shortened form of Colonia with the addition of 'chester', derived from the Old English 'ceaster' which means a Roman fort. But it is now generally accepted that the first element of the name is derived from the name of the river. Hence, Colchester: the Roman fort on the river Colne.

There were seven mills in Colchester at the time of the Domesday survey: three in the town, two in Lexden, one at Greenstead and one associated with the castle.

William White devotes sixty-four pages to Colchester in his 1848 Gazetteer and Directory of Essex. He describes the town as the largest, though not the 'county', town. Situated on the navigable river Colne, within ten miles of the sea, it has a great corn market, two silk mills and the finest oyster fishery in the world. It is divided into sixteen parishes embracing more than 18,000 inhabitants and an area of 11,770 acres.

The population of Colchester in 2001 was 104,390 since when it has risen to 173,100 by 2011 making it one of Britain's fastest growing towns.

To arrive in Colchester, 'Britain's Oldest Recorded Town', by the Colne is not the most attractive approach. Today it is in the throws of regeneration with much of the detritus of former activities still lingering by the waterside. The residential developments that have been completed usher in a completely new era for the town's former port and industrial area.

This area of Colchester is called the Hythe, formerly New Hythe to distinguish it from Old Hythe, now known as Old Heath. This older hythe, a word derived from the Saxon 'hetha' meaning harbour or landing place, was downstream somewhere between New Hythe and Rowhedge. It was the Anglo-Saxon port for the town. In those days the river followed a tortuous path through the marshes which would have made it difficult for larger vessels to proceed further upstream. Until the 20th century, the course of the Anglo-Saxon river was preserved in the parish boundary which meandered through the marshes. The river was straightened and dredged by the Normans so

Sailing barges at Colchester's Hythe Quay, with some of its numerous warehouses and the gasworks in the background. (c1910)

The Colne Dredger was in constant use keeping the channel clear up to the Hythe. (1985)

Until the 1950s, this chain bucket unloader was used to pump dredged mud from barges into a sludge lagoon. (c1899)

The Colne as it approaches the Hythe. On the left is the former wooden wharf where the silt from the dredger was pumped over the river wall into settling lagoons. This area is now called Hythe Lagoons and is managed as a local nature reserve by Colchester Borough Council. Beyond here are the derelict warehouses on King Edward Quay. (2012)

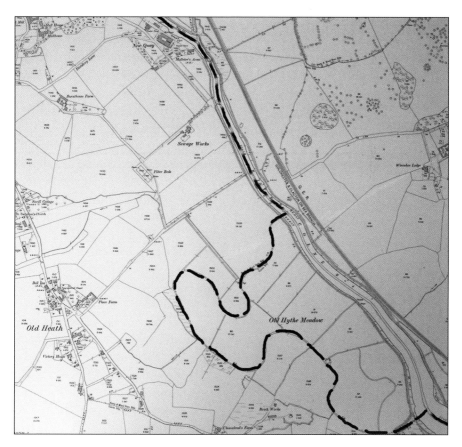

The 1897 OS map shows the old parish boundary between Wivenhoe and Old Heath that followed the tortuous path of the Saxon Colne as it meandered up to Colchester. The course of the river was straightened by the Normans to make it easier for vessels to reach New Hythe.

that by the 12th century the main port could be moved to New Hythe. It is thought that the Old Hythe remained as a landing place for several hundred years. Its last remnants may have been cleared away along with other hazards to navigation that seem to have bedevilled the Colne for centuries. There were constant complaints and disputes concerning the obstruction of the channel with 'weirs, mills, staves and palings'. Over time navigation to the

New Hythe was gradually improved so that by the 19th century the Hythe was vitally important to the town's economy. Its wharfs were extended enabling business and industry to prosper. There were over two-dozen coal merchants, a score of granaries, warehouses and timber-yards along with maltings, limekilns, shipyards and gasworks. All this, with the constant arrival and departure of around 3,000 seamen a year, contributed greatly to the prosperity of the town.

Despite the fact that the town embraced the new industries evolving at the beginning of the 20th century, the Hythe as a port had seen its heyday. Its fortunes waxed and waned until the 1980s when the increased use of rail and road transport and the changing nature of sea-going vessels all contributed to the gradual decline of the port. This along with the constant dredging required to keep the channel free from tidal silt resulted in the port becoming a financial liability to the Council. By the 1990s the port was costing the town hundreds of thousands of pounds a year and an application was made to Parliament to close the historic port. A bill was given Royal assent and in 2001 Colchester lost its status as a port bringing to an end 2,000 years of history.

Coasters at the busy Hythe. (1973)

The most striking vessel at the Hythe today is the former light vessel, now used as a training ship and headquarters of the Colchester Sea Cadet Corps as *TS Colne Light*. This ship was built at Dartmouth in 1954 and served as lightship *LV16* until she was decommissioned in 1988.

Before I proceed further along the Colne I will mention two tributaries that flow into the river along the stretch known as the Hythe. From the north Salary Brook joins by way of a sluice and, not far away, Bourne Brook flows in from the south.

Now there is no commercial activity at the Hythe. The residential moorings and light vessel LV16 *on the left are joined to the residential development on the right by the 1996 Haven Bridge. (2012)*

The headquarters of the Colchester Sea Cadet Corps as TS Colne Light *formerly light vessel* LV16. *(2004)*

First I will explore Bourne Brook. At low tide, beneath King Edward Quay, the tumbling waters of Bourne Brook meet the Colne. It is difficult to believe that this small stream once powered three overshot watermills within its short length of just over a mile. This is a testament to the dam building skills of the medieval engineers who coaxed so much power out of a brook that fell only 100ft (30m) from source to sea level. These mill builders realised that the most efficient method of extracting the energy from a stream with a low flow, but with a good fall, was to use an overshot wheel. This is the situation with many of the mills on the tributaries to the Colne, whereas the Colne itself has much less of a fall but a considerably greater flow, making the use of an undershot wheel more appropriate.

It is difficult to follow the course of the brook up from the Hythe, as it now flows through a culvert and does not emerge until it reaches Distillery Pond. This is the first of the former millponds on Bourne Brook and is formed by an ancient dam. It was near here that the 12th century mill stood, referred to in 1542 as 'Hullmyll'. At various times this had been a corn mill and an oil mill; this leads Benham to speculate that the 17th century watermill built on the dam by John Rootsey was to develop his oil milling activities. The Hull Mills stayed in the family for several generations, until the entire estate was sold in 1801.

Oil milling is an ancient trade. Oil was used by clothiers for treating wool prior to spinning. It was also used in the production of soap, paint and varnish. To produce oil, seeds, usually rape or flax seeds (linseed), were crushed between rollers. The crushed seeds were then cooked to soften them before being put into 9lb (4kg) cloth bags which were placed in a strong wooden trough. The mill lifted stampers which fell under their own weight at about fifteen times a minute until the oil had been squeezed out leaving the 'cake' in the bag.

The estate bought by Richard Carrington in 1801 consisted of 'the Hull Mill and watermill, oil mill and mill house together with millstones, wheels, spindles, cogs, going gears, axle trees and implements.' A few years later the watermill and oil mill were demolished to be replaced by a new water corn mill and a malt distillery. For a few short years the distillery, claimed to be the largest in the country, was producing 40,000 gallons of gin per year. All this came to an end in 1841 when the business was dissolved, its only enduring legacy being the name of the millpond. The corn mill continued to be worked by various millers until it was dismantled in 1896. The mill site entered its final industrial phase from 1900 as a Laundry. The mill buildings were severely damaged by a bomb during WWII and were replaced by a utilitarian brick structure that did nothing to enhance the view across the millpond. The last operators of the laundry were Albany Cleaners who closed in the last years of the 20th century. The deserted site remained derelict for a few years before it was redeveloped as a residential area, part of the Hythe regeneration scheme. Now only the names of the roads hint at the former activities on the site.

The unmade road that gives access to the mill site runs across the dam and then continues beside Distillery Pond and Bourne Brook to Old Heath Road. Here stands the next mill on this diminutive brook, Cannock Mill. We are fortunate that this attractive building has survived in Colchester's expanding suburbs. This is due to the whim of one man. In 1959 Mr. Walter Lock moved into the Victorian Cannock Mill House. For several years, when he rose in the morning he looked out of his window and saw the mill and all was right with the world. Then in 1968 all that changed. He had heard that the owners of the mill, Cramphorns, had plans to demolish the dilapidating mill. Walter thought that the building was too nice to lose so he decided to buy it. At the time he had no commercial plans for the building and when asked why he had bought the crumbling building replied, 'I just think that it looks nice and I want to keep it that way.' The mill site was originally occupied by an abbey mill and during its life was used as both a corn mill and fulling mill. The present building dates from 1848 when it was rebuilt with an overshot wheel by the Pulford family who worked it until 1945. From here on the mill went into its inevitable decline. Bought by Cramphorns it was converted to electricity and worked until 1951. It then became a feedstore and the machinery was removed in 1961, then the wheelhouse collapsed in a thunderstorm and its remains were pulled down. Within a few years the whole building was under threat, only to be saved by Mr. Lock. Walter set about restoring the mill, a project that was to occupy him for over two years. With the help of groups of volunteers, he labouriously

Walter Lock with his newly acquired dilapidated Cannock Mill. (1969)

replaced slates and secured or replaced planks until the job was done. According to his daughter, Carol, he frequently stood and just looked out of the window at what was now his mill, just because he liked it. For the past twenty-five years Carol and her husband, Jack have run their tropical fish business, Dolphin Aquatics, from the mill and have maintained the white weatherboard building to a standard that they are sure Wally would have approved of.

Beside the mill is a narrow path that passes the mill and follows the banks of the brook through what is now called Bourne Valley, a small 25 acre (10 ha) nature reserve owned and maintained by Colchester Borough Council. Much of the walk is boarded through the sometimes boggy valley up to the third, last, and most ancient mill site on the Bourne.

Bourne Mill is probably the mill that was granted to St John's abbey upon its foundation in 1096. The mill takes its name from the bourne or brook on which it stands. Like so many ancient words for watercourses the word 'bourne', originally used to describe a small river, has become the name of many small rivers. In the Colne valley alone there are two Bourne Brooks.

The restored Cannock Mill. (2012)

The Colchester Bourne Brook drains the Abbey fields and, from an early date, was dammed to make a millpond and fishpond. This provided flour and fish for the abbey until the Dissolution. By 1590 the abbey was in the hands of the Lucas family who set about demolishing the buildings and using the stone elsewhere. Sir Thomas Lucas used some in 1591 to construct the exotic fishing lodge and working mill much as we see today. The ornate 'Dutch gables' were there to impress the local gentry who he entertained at banquets held in the lodge. Thomas' son, Charles, took up the Royalist cause during the Civil War and led the assault on East Mills which we will come to later. Soon after the Civil War, Bourne Mill was occupied by Dutch refugees who added clothmaking activities to the site.

Colchester had long been associated with the cloth industry. There are records of cloth being made in Colchester from shortly after the Norman Conquest and the industry soon became established as a major activity in the town. The factors that made Colchester such an important cloth town are largely to do with the Colne. From as early as 1346 Colchester cloth was being exported from the town's port to France. Also, by this time, there were at least eight mills in the town, some of which were involved in the industry. Then, with the arrival of the Dutch refugees and the introduction of Bay and Say making, the industry expanded even more. The quality of these new draperies was such that Colchester cloth appealed to markets all over Europe.

The ornate Bourne Mill built in 1591 by Sir Thomas Lucas as a fishing lodge and working mill. When it ceased working in 1935 it was given to the National Trust. (2012)

Colchester Bay was a light woollen fabric that soon became the favoured material for many items of clothing including shirts and petticoats. It was soon referred to as 'bays', this evolved into 'baize'. Colchester Say was much thicker and was used for Monks habits and the coarse shirts and aprons worn by Quakers.

Colchester cloth maintained its enviable reputation until well into the 18th century. But other regions of the country were competing with newer fabrics and techniques which led to the gradual decline of clothmaking in the town. The last clothmaking mill was Bourne Mill, and this ceased to be involved in the industry in 1840.

We are fortunate to have the recollections of one of the last Colchester men to be employed in clothmaking at the mill. In 1900, Charles Baker, at the age of 76 recalled:

In the year 1826, when I was nine years old, I went to work at Bourne Pond Mill, then held by Peter Devall, Master Bay Maker. I helped sometimes with the spinning, sometimes with the fulling.

The raw wool came to the mill sometimes in the fleece, sometimes from the stapler, but from wherever it came, it was passed first of all through the 'hackler' after which it was oiled. The oiling was done by sprinkling large quantities of linseed oil over it. Next it was threshed with flails and then it was passed through another engine which made it up into "locks" or "slivers". These were, as near as I can recollect, about a yard long and about as large as your finger. It then went into the gin to be spun into yarn. It was never washed until the bay was woven.

The spinning was done by a man who walked backwards, drawing with him a frame which moved on wheels, running on rails. On it were a number of wheels and spindles. The man, as he moved, turned a handle which drove all the spindles on the machine (either 32 or 46 in number, I am not sure which), by means of cat gut strings and also moved the whole apparatus backwards as the threads were drawn out. The wool was pieced on by boys as the threads were spun. After about five yards had been drawn out (or perhaps less, I am not certain as to the length) the machine was pushed up again, the spun threads being wound onto the spindles by the operation. When the spindles were full the yarn was slipped off them and the operation was begun over again.

The spun yarn was sent from the Bourne Pond Mill to the warehouse in Priory Street where the weaver took it in hand. After the wool was woven into bay, it came back to the mill to undergo various finishing processes. Each "piece" of bay was two yards wide and fifty yards long.

The first of the finishing processes was fulling which was carried on thus. We folded a 'piece' of bay on the floor, so that it made a pile about a yard square; and as we did so, we sprinkled it with chamber lye. We then took other 'pieces' and served them in the same way, piling them up as high as we could reach, sprinkling them all the time with the chamber lye. We used to go round to the workhouses and other places to collect chamber lye for which we paid a half-penny a pail.

By the following morning the pile of bays had heated. We then took them and put them, two or three 'pieces' at a time, under the fulling stocks - large wooden beams worked by the waterwheel of the mill - which rubbed them in a certain way, thus 'fulling' or 'thicking' them. The rubbing process continued about half-an-hour when a good stream of water was turned onto the bays to wash them. We used to make the water very foul in fulling. I have seen the Distillery Pond quite white after we had done. Mr. Devall occupied also Lexden Mill, then a fulling mill. There were fulling stocks at Cannock Mill also, but this was partly a flour mill, the two uses to which it was put not interfering with one another.

After fulling the bays were dried on the tenters which were erected at the head of the pond. The lower moveable rail of the tenter could be secured at any desired distance below the fixed other rail, so that the bay could be stretched latitudinally to a certain extent whilst drying. The operation of drying, like that of fulling, was nasty wet work, as it was necessary to carry about the wet pieces of bay.

When the pieces of bay were quite dry they were taken to the bleach house, where they were hung on rails and exposed all night to the fumes of burning sulphur, which made them quite white by the morning.

Next a 'nap' was raised on the surface of the bay by teasing it with the heads of teazles. These came from the Hundreds of Essex, where they were grown. The frame on which the teazle heads were fastened was (as far as I can describe it) a kind of wheel on which the teazle heads were tied between iron rods. The wheel was revolved while the surface of the bay was in contact with the teazles.

Following the closure of the fulling mill the building was disused for a number years. Then the mill was converted for flour milling, a new top floor was added together with a lucam and dormer windows. By 1860 it was operating as a corn mill, which by 1894 was partly steam driven. The millstones continued to turn until 1935 when the building was given to the National Trust and converted into a house.

During the early years of the trust's ownership the three pairs of stones and some of the machinery was removed. The property has not

An engraving of fulling stocks powered by a waterwheel.

Bourne Mill, the lucam was added in the 1800s when the mill was converted into a flour mill. (2012)

Bourne Mill pitwheel is made in two halves; it is 10ft (3m) in diameter and carries 150 teeth. The wallower, attached to the vertical main shaft has 50 teeth and is also made in two halves. (2012)

been used for residential purposes since the 1980s. Since then substantial renovations have been made and a permanent, evolving exhibition about the mill's history has been created. This is now the only overshot mill in the Colne Valley open to the public. The 22ft (6.6m) diameter, 5ft (1.5m) wide overshot wheel can be viewed through a glass panel in the floor where its 64 buckets can be seen being driven round by the millstream. The waterwheel is connected to an iron pit wheel that transmits power to the upright, octagonal main shaft via the wallower; these can be viewed from the lower floor.

Back on the Colne and on the other riverbank is the sluice that lets in the water from Salary Brook. This is longer than Bourne Brook but it has only ever had three mills and only two of them remain, both now private residences. They were at Crockleford, Wallswood and Spring Valley and all three were fulling during the years of the flourishing Colchester cloth trade.

First is the charmingly named Crockleford Mill. This mill was first recorded in 1588 and is believed to have been built by William Beriff, a Colchester clothmaker. It was still working as a fulling mill in 1777, but within twenty years had been converted into a flour mill and then, in 1823, it underwent yet another change when it became an oil mill. It was subsequently used as a chemical works for a few years before spending the last hundred years or so of its working life grinding corn. This it did until 1955 when its overshot wheel finally ceased to turn with the retirement of the mill's last miller, W W Payne. The building is now a private residence.

Not much is known about the next mill on this diminutive brook. Variously known as Wallswood Mill or Middle Mill it is recorded on OS maps until 1921, since when all trace of its existence has gone. Today the location of this mill can be identified as the site of the intersection of four footpaths at the footbridge in the steep-sided valley between Crockleford Mill and Spring Valley Mill.

The third mill on the brook, now just below the Ardleigh reservoir, is Spring Valley Mill. This fulling mill later became a corn mill and had an auxiliary steam plant added to assist the overshot wheel to drive the three pairs of stones that continued to turn until the 1930s. This is an unusual mill in that much of its machinery remains as it was left by its last miller, Tom Glover. During the 1950s the building was used as a studio by the artist Harry Pettit, who lived in the adjacent mill house. During the 1960s the new owner, Gordon Young, made noble efforts to maintain the building but the increased volume of heavy traffic rumbling along the narrow lane was damaging its brickwork

Spring Valley Mill when it was being used as an artist's studio. (1952)

and, despite being a Grade II listed building, a gradual decline set in. Today the mill is in a sorry state, its waterwheel has been damaged by a falling tree and the embanked millpond has been destroyed by the reuse of neighbouring land. The present owner, Ron Vosper has owned the building since 1977. He has tried to maintain this unique, virtually intact three-stone country mill but with little help from local authorities or the national organisations that are supposed to protect our heritage. There is little time left to save this gem from a past era from falling victim to its own slow deterioration.

Spring Valley Mill with slipped tiles, loose boards and scaffolding to support the lucam. (2012)

Now back to the Colne and the Hythe and the journey upstream beyond the Hythe, but first the bridges. Today the first bridge across the river is Haven Bridge. This was built in 1996 to take a new road through the Hythe redevelopment. Its modern single span of concrete deck supported on massive steel beams contrasts with earlier bridges across the Hythe.

The first bridge to be built across the Hythe was at the request of the local residents. In 1407 the Corporation allowed the construction of a footbridge, provided that it was not wide enough for carts and would not interfere with navigation to East Bridge. It took over sixty years of conflict with the town authorities to obtain permission to replace this with a cart bridge. Eventually the responsibility for maintaining the bridge was taken over by the Borough. Very few early bridges had long lives and the Hythe Bridge was no exception. The wooden bridge was repaired or replaced several times before a three arch brick structure was built in 1737. This lasted for a hundred years before being replaced by another timber bridge which itself was soon replaced by an iron bridge in 1878. For many years this was the first bridge across the Colne, but the increasing amount and weight of traffic using it necessitated the building of a new bridge in 1968. This concrete and steel structure now sits adjacent to the earlier bridge which takes pedestrians and cyclists over the river to continue their Colneside journey into the town.

Looking down stream from the parapet of this bridge can be seen the newest bridge across the Colne. This footbridge, the first to be built across the Hythe for over 600 years, was opened to pedestrians and cyclists in 2010. It is designed to provide a link between the housing development on the east bank with the facilities on the west.

Upstream from the bridge the wharfs of the Hythe give way to reed beds. Today there is no trace of the earlier activity that took place here. This overgrown wilderness is the site of the most seaward mill on the Colne.

The three-arch Hythe Bridge existed from 1737 to 1837, depicted here in the print published by Swinburne & Walter. (1825)

In 1878 the first iron Hythe Bridge was opened. (1946)

This is an ancient mill site whose origins are lost in the mists of time, but it was certainly in existence by 1385 when it is recorded as being rebuilt by the Borough. At various periods during its life it was both a corn mill and fulling mill. Town records indicate that it was rebuilt several times and that, by the 17th century, it must have been quite a large mill as it comprised two corn mills and one fulling stock. It is not known if this was a tide mill, using the channel up to East Mill as a pound, or if it was a river mill. In either case there must have been a lock or gate to bypass it because it is known that the river was navigable up to East Bridge. Millers have always wanted to exercise their rights to use the water in the river to power their mills to their maximum advantage. This often led to disputes between mill owners situated close to one another, or with those using the river for navigation. There are records showing that both situations arose with the operators of Hythe Mill who were frequently in conflict with their neighbours at East Mill or those using the river for navigation. Eventually in 1736 the mill was

The Hythe footbridge was assembled on site and then swung into position in 2010. This bowstring truss bridge links the residential developments on Gas Quay to the left with Hawkins Wharf to the right. (2012)

demolished because it obstructed navigation, but this was not the end of industrial activity on the site.

Boat building at the Hythe has always been a minor activity compared with that carried on further downstream. However, a yard operated, somewhat sporadically, on the site of the later Hawkins timber yard, and there was some boat building even further upstream. The work was of an intermittent nature due to the frequent silting of the channel. The following report seems to relate to a field on or near the site of the former mill. 'In 1859 the sailing barge, *Exact* was built on beer barrels in a field above Hythe Bridge. During construction it was found that she was too wide so the boatbuilder took down one side and moved it in, leaving the vessel a little lop-sided. Even then she was too wide to go under the Hythe Bridge which at the time was supported on wooden piles. So she was returned to her berth and that night, builder and owner went to the bridge and trimmed the piles with adzes, rubbing mud

Half the frames of the 102ft (30.6m) cutter Margaret *are in place with the keel and sternpost extending almost to the right of the picture. The vessel would have been launched broadside into the Colne. This Hythe shipbuilding site later became Hawkins timber yard and wharf. (1852)*

into the cut surfaces. At the next tide the barge went under and the owner remarked with satisfaction 'Exact' and so she was thus named.' It would appear that the mutilation of the bridge did not have serious consequences as it survived intact for another eighteen years before being washed away in a flood. It was replaced by the iron bridge that still stands today.

Beyond the former mill site are the remains of the bridge that took the branch line to the quays on the town side of the river. Until a few years ago this bridge was virtually complete but now only the abutments remain. The bridge was built by the Tendring Hundred Railway Company in 1886 and this connection between the rail network and quays on the Hythe was vital in keeping the area functioning as a thriving industrial area well into the 20th century. Further upstream the character of the tidal river changes yet again. The channel passes through wide margins of reed beds and several small streams punctuate its banks. The floodplain on the cycle/footpath side is known as the Moors; it is an informal nature reserve criss-crossed with paths and the remains of earlier watercourses. The course of the river through here was straightened in 1865, a few years before the railway arrived, to allow Thames barges to reach East Mills more easily. The area was once owned by James Paxman, founder of Davey Paxman & Co which was, for more than 100 years, Colchester's largest employer. James was born on Hythe Hill in 1832 and founded his firm in 1865. It pioneered major innovations in steam engines and early electricity generators before becoming a world leader in the design and manufacture of diesel engines. In James' day cattle grazed the Moors and the path, with a picket gate at each end, meandered through small plantations of cricket bat willow and orchards of fruit trees. The cattle have long gone but the trees remain now poking their heads above the undergrowth and still fruiting in this oasis of wilderness in the midst of Colchester's former industrial heartland.

The end of the Moors is marked by another railway bridge across the Colne. Unlike the iron girder bridge that led to the Hythe quays, this one leading to Colchester Town station is still here and still carrying trains. The cyclepath through the Moors joins the riverbank as it passes beneath this bridge to arrive in the area of well-tendered allotments. I have used this path on countless occasions and have always seen at least one of the plot holders working their patch.

Allotments as we know them came into being at the end of the 18th century when a combination of circumstances including rapid population growth, decline of rural industries and enclosure were causing severe hardship and starvation among the rural poor. The enclosure of the countryside removed food production from the many and placed it in the hands of a few wealthy landowners. Not only did the poor lose their land but also their common grazing and foraging rights. It was only when the wealthy realised that they would have to pay increased tax to support the increasing number of hungry, downtrodden and disaffected poor that they began to support schemes to enable the poor to help themselves. One of these was the provision of small plots of land on which they could grow food. These small plots were enclosed in a group and became known as allotments. The idea got off to a slow start but by the end of the 19th century there were nearly a quarter of a million sites. Since then the movement has had a bit of a seesaw existence, tending to become more popular during periods of economic hardship. Now most, but not all, sites are owned by local authorities and are in high demand once again.

Beyond the Colchester Borough Council allotments is East Bay, here there are several buildings of interest and one of Colchester's most historic bridges. Approaching from the allotments you could be forgiven for not noticing a tumbledown wreck of a building between the path and the river. This is the remains of Doe's Mill, an 18th century granary that was later used as a mill for animal feed. By way of complete contrast, on the other side of the path is the excellently maintained East Bay House. This redbrick Georgian house dates from the late 18th century. For nearly fifty years following WWII it was the Colchester Youth Hostel. Before it closed in 1995 it was used by thousands of hostellers either travelling through the eastern counties or visiting the historic town.

The Youth Hostel Association (YHA) opened its first hostels in 1931. A few years later, in 1936, a hostel was opened in Colchester at Middle Mill House. The objective of the organization was 'To help all, especially young people of limited means to a greater knowledge, love and care of the countryside, particularly by providing hostels or other simple accommodation for them in their travels, and thus to promote their health, rest and education.' Accommodation was provided in single sex dormitories and all people staying at a hostel were required to assist in its running by undertaking what were known as 'duties'. These included tasks such as washing up and various cleaning or maintenance jobs. These were allocated by the warden who was in charge of the organisation and management of the hostel. By the outbreak of WWII there were 297 hostels, a third of these were to close during hostilities. Colchester's first hostel managed to survive the war but closed in 1945. During the post-war years there was a resurgence of hostels and hostellers. By 1950 there were over 300 hostels including a new one in Colchester that was opened in 1948 in East Bay House. From the 1970s the YHA has undergone significant modernisation to cope with the changing needs of travellers. Most now offer smaller rooms in place of dormitories and guests are no longer required to perform duties or to arrive under their own steam. In the early days hostellers were expected to arrive on foot or by cycle or canoe. East Bay House is on the banks of the Colne so it is not surprising that some arrived by boat. One such arrival was the warden of the Maldon Youth Hostel who, in May 1949, sailed his dinghy down the Blackwater and up the Colne, completing the thirty-mile journey in eight hours, including lunch ashore at Mersea. East Bay continued to welcome hostellers until 1995 when it was closed, as it was claimed to be too expensive to install the facilities expected by modern hostellers.

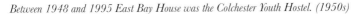

Between 1948 and 1995 East Bay House was the Colchester Youth Hostel. (1950s)

East Bay House, a large late Georgian redbrick house built c1780
behind the WWII crenellated concrete wall. (2012)

In front of East Bay House is one of the most substantial walls in Colchester. This concrete embattled wall, once disguised behind wooden palings was built in 1941 as part of the town defences in case of an enemy invasion. Members of the Home Guard would have been stationed behind this structure to trigger the explosives installed under the bridge and to fire on the enemy as they tried to cross the Colne.

East Bridge is the oldest surviving bridge across the Colne in Colchester. It is believed to stand on the site of a Roman bridge or tidal ford. A bridge on this site has been maintained by the borough since medieval times and was last rebuilt in 1802. This bridge of five brick arches with stone pilasters and an iron balustrade was financed by a turnpike in Lexden Street. The elegance of the elliptical arches with projecting keystones has been somewhat overshadowed by the functional concrete widening which took place in 1927.

Fortunately the iron balustrade and half standard lamps were reused so maintaining the appearance of the bridge from the roadway. Unfortunately, since the beginning of this century, the lamps no longer adorn the bridge due to the mindless behaviour of vandals, who repeatedly demonstrated their strength by toppling them into the river below. These are now just one more hazard for people using the river. When barges were poled up to the mill they had to arrive at the bridge when the tide was high enough for them to float, but not so high that they could not get under. There were several times when they only just made it as evidenced by long and deep scratches on the walls of the central arch. On those occasions the bargemen would need to duck down or lie on the deck, they would then see the inconspicuous plaque high under the arch commemorating the bricklayers, E&R Ewstace, who built this fine structure.

The plaque high under the central arch of East Bridge can only be seen from the river. 2006

When I last rowed under the bridge a few years ago, the tide was high enough for me to rest a while by tying up to the mill wharf. This was built when East Mill was owned by the Marriages, to enable sailing barges to deliver grain and collect flour from their mill. It was constructed at the same time as the river was straightened and improved between the Hythe and the mill in the 1860s. Before this there was no wharf at the mill and early pictures of the site show a gently shelving riverbank. This is an ancient mill site, thought to be one of the three mills recorded in Colchester in the Domesday Survey. Before the Norman invasion it was part of the estate of the richest Saxon lady in the town, Leofleda, but it was first recorded as East Mill in 1331 when it was in the possession of St Botolph's priory. For most of its life it has worked as a corn mill, with occasional periods of fulling. Although this has always been an important mill site, it did not grow into the largest and most long lived in the town until it was acquired by the Marriage

*The five elegant elliptical arches of the 1802 East Bridge
before it was widened and its hump removed. (1927)*

family in 1839. A year later Edward Marriage, the ninth of thirteen children of a Chelmsford miller, moved into the mill house with his wife Lucy. At this time the mill was a white weatherboarded building housing six pairs of stones driven by two waterwheels. Within a couple of years Edward had added an auxiliary steam engine and introduced a flour dressing machine that enabled him to win a diploma at the Great Exhibition of 1851. Shortly after this a plan was conceived to improve access to the mill by building a wharf and straightening the course of the river down to the Hythe. Within a few years these extensive works were completed and the first sailing barge reached the mill in 1865. This method of transporting grain to, and flour from, the mill was to ensure the mill's prosperity up to the end of WWII, by which time other means of transport had become more important. During the Victorian era the mill kept up with the ever-increasing demand, first by rebuilding and

East Bridge was flattened and widened by 7ft 6in (2.25m) at a cost of £11,000 in 1927. It looks much the same today as it did in this 1946 photograph.

enlarging the existing building and then later adding another mill to house a roller mill. By now all trace of the white weatherboard had gone and the site housed a mass of sturdy industrial buildings. During the ensuing years the contribution of waterpower gradually decreased until the early 1930s when the mill was remodelled and the waterwheels removed. By now the East Mills site had become known as Marriages Mills. It became part of the Rank Hovis MacDougall (RHM) conglomerate in 1961 and then as part of this organisation's rationalisation was closed in 1976.

The complex of Victorian industrial buildings, still with the diminutive Mill House that Edward Marriage moved into all those years ago remained empty for several years. There followed various proposals for the reuse of the buildings, eventually the one that succeeded was for a hotel complex. This opened in 1980 but was comparatively short lived and closed in 2001.

The weatherboarded East Mill and the five-arch humped
East Bridge with ford alongside. (1858)

Since then the building has been converted into flats and the site extensively redeveloped for residential accommodation.

At the entrance to the mill site is the historic half-timbered Siege House. This 15th century building was extensively restored by Marriages in 1905 just after they had added it to the East Mills complex. When the external plaster was stripped, the exposed timbers were seen to contain many Royalist bullet holes dating from the Siege of Colchester in 1648. The mill and other buildings in the area were occupied by Parliamentary forces who came under attack when the Royalists attempted a foray out of the town. They were beaten back and after an eleven-week siege the 5,000 Royalists occupying the town surrendered.

Throughout most of its life the river flowed through East Mill then, in 1968, the watercourse under the mill was filled and a new automatic sluice built just upstream to control the river level. Above this, a new water abstraction point was constructed to take water to the Ardleigh reservoir

The weatherboarded building has been replaced by a brick structure and a steam powered roller mill has been installed. A wharf has been built along the river frontage. (1883)

that was completed a few years later. The weir now provides an abrupt end of the tidal saltwater Colne and an impenetrable barrier to migrating eels.

The eel was once common around Britain, being present in most rivers and streams accessible from the sea. This is no longer the case and there is considerable concern about the rapidly declining eel stocks. Eels are migratory and they spend their adult lives in freshwater, returning to the sea to spawn. The theory is that they cross the Atlantic Ocean to the Sargasso Sea, southwest of Bermuda, where they spawn and the larvae are carried by the Gulf Stream back to European shores. Eels in Europe have declined drastically since the 1970s; it is thought that one of the causes is barriers to freshwater migration. This is certainly so in the Colne where, until a few years ago, miriads of tiny eels could be seen floundering in the water below the weir.

For us, unlike the eels, there is a choice of how to proceed further up the Colne. A short distance from the weir it is quite easy to slide a canoe or other

This photograph of the Siege House was taken shortly after it was restored, and the Royalist bullet holes were first marked out in red. It looks much the same today. (1906)

The East Mills site has been completely transformed since 1840 when Edward and Lucy Marriage moved into the diminutive Mill House at the centre of this picture. The weatherboarded mill has been replaced by Victorian brick, the Siege House has been restored and more recently additional residential dwellings have been built on the site. (2012)

East Mill weir, the tidal limit of the Colne, where the freshwater tumbles into salt. (2006)

small portable craft into the river and paddle up to Middle Mill. There is also a riverside cycle/footpath that I frequently use. One of my most memorable journeys along here was made in May 2012.

After two years of exceptionally low rainfall, Essex, along with many other parts of England, was declared a drought area. Then in early May two inches (50mm) of rain fell in two days. The ground was so dry and hard that most of this ran off the fields on to the roads causing many local floods. A day or two later all this water had found its way into the rivers, which suddenly became very swollen. In several places above Colchester the Colne burst its banks and those in the town were just about holding out. I went along to see if the riverside path was still passable. I joined the shared-use path at East Mill where the water was roaring over the weir into the saltwater below. The river above the weir is embanked to keep the water out of the former riverbed. For many years this area was damp and overgrown with willow. Now it is home to riverside dwellings whose front doors are well below the normal river level and considerably below the top of the river embankment. I did not see any anxious residents looking out of their windows, but then they were probably busy moving their belongings upstairs. On this occasion they were lucky. The careful control of the water levels by the authorities just managed to prevent the overtopping of the riverbank.

The raised riverside path through the Lower Castle Park. The town wall is on the left and Middle Mill on the extreme right. (1890s)

As the Castle Park is approached, the area between the embankment and the river widens and includes a riverside lake and an area of recreational grassland. All of this was flooded making the path impassable. I diverted to higher ground before rejoining the river at the lower entrance to Castle Park. For many years cyclists were banned from the park which forced them to detour over the nondescript pre-stressed concrete bridge to the Sports Centre, around the cricket ground and then back to the river at Middle Mill. In 2012, after a long campaign by local cycling groups, the riverside path through the park was designated a shared path. I proceeded along here with the river creeping over its banks on my right and a very soggy Lower Castle Park on my left.

This award-winning park provides a unique historical and recreational facility for the people of Colchester. It has evolved over a very long time. When the Romans established their town on the high ground overlooking the Colne Valley, its most impressive building was

The bridge in Castle Park leading to the Cricket Pavilion depicted in an
Edwardian Postcard as the Constable Bridge. *c1912*

the temple dedicated to their emperor Claudius. This later became
the site of the Norman castle that dominated the area for several
hundred years before being used as a prison and then becoming
ruinous. When, in 1718, Charles Gray built his handsome Georgian
house, Hollytrees, with a new garden in the English Landscape Style,
the castle ruins were part of his estate. During the Victorian era the
land that slopes down to the river was landscaped and opened as a
park in 1892. Then in the 1920s, with a gift from Lord Cowdray, the
Hollytrees estate, including the house and castle, were purchased for
the people of Colchester. Since then the award-winning park has
been a valuable asset to the town. As well as its splendid gardens that
can be enjoyed at any time, the park is the venue for a host of events
that include civic ceremonies, military parades, summer concerts,
festivals and firework displays.

WWII tank traps by Middle Mill pond in Lower Castle Park. (2012)

A tranquil view of the millpond at Middle Mill. The picture shows three Corporation dustcarts; these tumbrels were in use up to the mid 1930s. The four-wheeled cart on the left is thought to belong to the Co-operative Society. (1927)

Around the bend in the river is the rather austere concrete bridge that leads to the cricket pavilion. The first bridge to be built on this site was in the early 20th century when the cricket ground was added to the park. The original wooden structure was often depicted on Edwardian postcards as the 'Constable Bridge' because its design was copied from the bridge at Flatford that features in Constables paintings. When it was time to replace the Flatford Bridge a new bridge of similar design was erected. I think that it is a pity that a similar thing did not happen in Colchester, as the flat, concrete replacement does nothing at all to enhance what could be a beautiful river scene.

A little further on, the river widens as it approaches Middle Mill, and the riverside path passes a few large concrete blocks. These WWII tank traps were to be used to hinder the progress of any enemy vehicles that attempted to use the ancient ford to cross the river at this point.

The ford has been used for centuries and is shown clearly on early OS maps. The route of the ford is well defined but what are not shown are the deep holes in the millpond. There has been a mill associated with this site since Saxon times. Consequently the water cascading over the sluice, or flowing from the waterwheel, has had centuries to scour out a millpond. As the water leaves the turbulence of the millpond much of the scoured material settles to the bottom to create a gravel bank and so create a natural fording place. A ford below a millpond is a picturesque but perilous place and the scene of many an accident for the unwary. As far as the picturesque goes, Middle Mill and its millpond feature prominently in the foreground of Turner's painting of Colchester Castle, and the scene has been the subject of numerous photographs. The perils of the pond have caused many an accident, perhaps the most tragic being the drowning of 21 year-old Joshua Dunt in 1887.

Joshua had recently completed an engineering apprenticeship and, while waiting for a vacancy, was doing odd jobs for a local carrier. On the fateful day, when returning from a delivery, he decided to water his horse by entering the river at the ford. He then made the unwise decision to turn around; his horse lost it's footing and was soon floundering in deep water dragging the

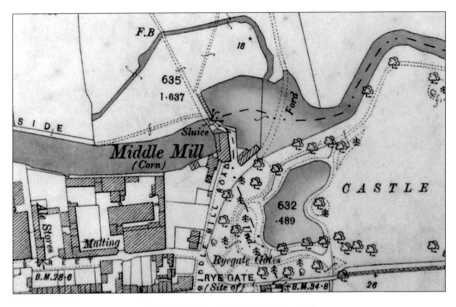

*The 1897 OS map showing Middle Mill
with adjacent mill house and the ford across the millpond,
Castle Park with boating lake and Rye Gate.*

cart and Joshua behind him. Joshua, who could not swim, shouted for help. The miller, Ezekial Chopping, and his workers rushed to the scene with a rope and lifebuoy, but by the time that Ezekial's son, William, had swam out to the struggling Joshua, both he and the cart had completely disappeared below the surface. It was over half an hour before his body entangled with the reins but still clasping the whip was recovered.

Now we come to Middle Mill itself. This is built on an ancient site and for many years was associated with the castle and sometimes was referred to as King's Mill. For most of its long life it was a corn mill but there have been times when it was a fulling mill and sometimes both. In the 15th century it was described as a double corn and fulling mill, but by the 19th century it was a corn mill and in the hands of the Chopping family. The millstones kept grinding and demand was such that by 1886 an auxiliary steam engine had

This view of Middle Mill, taken from across the millpond, shows the watermill with the chimney of the auxiliary steam plant behind. The taller, more distant chimney is that of the silk mill. Although built on the banks of the river it was only ever powered by steam. (c1900)

been installed. The mill worked until 1933 when Richard Chopping sold the mill as a going concern to Marriage's who stripped out the machinery and transferred its trade to East Mills. A year later the empty building was acquired by Colchester Borough Council who used it for storage. Unfortunately they allowed the fabric of the building to decay until they could claim that its upkeep would be impractical, which led to its demolition in the 1950s. This neglect is described by Benham as an outstanding example of 'vandalistic myopia by a local authority'.

The site was tidied up when the mill weir was restored in 2000 but I think that the Council could do more to make amends for their earlier neglect. Historically, the owners of mills have utillised their sites to maximum advantage and used their source of free energy for whatever was the most profitable. Today, we live in a world of ever-increasing energy prices;

this, together with advances in technology, has made small-scale lowland hydroelectric schemes financially viable. Many people who have stopped by Middle Mill must have wondered why we do not make use of all the energy going to waste as the water cascades over the weir. I was pleased to see, on a recent visit to Guildford, that on the site of the Town Mill, on the river Wey, a modern generator has been installed. Since 2006 this has contributed over a quarter of a million units per year to the town's power requirements. Closer to home a high efficiency turbine has been installed at Flatford Mill on the river Stour. This is expected to contribute significantly to the energy requirements of this extensive National Trust Site. The Colne is a relatively small lowland river, but it does convey over twenty billion litres of water through Colchester every year, and none of its energy is captured. Even though this may only yield a relatively small amount of energy, every little helps and the town would not only benefit from the energy but also be seen to be making an effort to reduce its carbon footprint.

The Castle Park entrance known as Rye Gate was built in 1892, near the site of the medieval gate. (2012)

Close by Middle Mill is the site of one of the original Roman gates in the town wall. During medieval times this became Rye, or River, Gate and was taken down in 1659. The present Victorian Rye Gate was built near the site of the medieval gate and was presented to the town when the park opened in 1892.

I left Middle Mill along the riverside path on the town side of the river. The new housing development being built at the beginning of this path is considerably more attractive than the following office blocks and multi-storey car park that overshadow the river. But then, this has never been a particularly picturesque stretch of the river. During the Victorian era the site was occupied by a steam powered, brick built silk mill and was later occupied by the brewers Green King who used it as a malting ale and porter store. This area probably saw its first industrial activity during the Roman period. Recent excavations on a nearby site have revealed evidence that this section of the river could well have been used as a Roman landing place. It is very likely that all the stone and other building materials needed to build the town were unloaded here. Then, later, all those goods that were transhipped at Fingringhoe would probably

Middle Mill House that was the town's Youth Hostel between 1936 and 1945.

have arrived here, as this is the nearest place that the river gets to the Roman town on the hill. The site could well have been used throughout the Roman period and possibly until changes and silting of the river forced river craft to unload much further downstream at Old Heath.

Beyond the office blocks there are residential apartment blocks that overlook North Bridge and the oldest surviving riverside cottages in the area. It has long been thought that there was a Roman bridge near the site of the present bridge. If the Roman bridge was in line with the Roman North Gate it would have been slightly downstream of the modern bridge. Some evidence to support this idea was discovered in the 1950s when workmen digging a hole for the fuel tank for a garage discovered a row of oak piles aligned across

The new cast iron North Bridge shortly after it was erected in 1843. The cottage nearest the bridge, with the jettied upper storey, was demolished when the bridge was widened in 1903.

the mud of the ancient riverbed. Unfortunately the archaeologists were not informed, in case the work was held up, but this story supports the generally held belief that there has been a bridge hereabouts since Roman times.

North Bridge has belonged to the town since medieval times. First recorded in 1189, it has been repaired and replaced several times in its long history. In 1696 it was repaired using stone from the partially demolished castle; less than a hundred years later it had been replaced by a three-arch brick bridge. The existing iron bridge was built in 1843 to cope with the increased traffic between the town and the newly built North Station. All the ironwork for this graceful bridge was cast in Colchester at the foundry in Abbeygate Street run by Richard Coleman. In 1903 the bridge was widened for the town's new tramway. Since

The elegant North Bridge with the adjacent cottage before the flood defence wall was built. (2001)

An anxious resident watches as the river level rises. These cottages have stood here for centuries and in earlier times their residents survived the occasional flood. Now they are protected by a wall built in 2003. There is a little irony in that, the more building there is on floodplains, the higher the water level rises in the river and this actually increases the risk of flooding to all low lying areas. (2012)

then the structure has been strengthened by the subtle insertion of steel girders. The bridge can now cope with the demands of modern traffic but remains one of the most elegant bridges across the Colne.

Over the bridge the shared-use riverside path drops down beside Trotters Wine Bar and continues past a multi-story car park and more recent residential developments. Somewhere along here stood North Mill. This was one of the Colchester mills recorded in Domesday and was later used as a fulling mill, but by the 16th century had disappeared, probably due to its close proximity to Middle Mill, a mere half-mile downstream.

Beyond the last of the town's recent riverside developments the path stays by the river as it passes under a large road bridge. During the Victorian era, long before this was built, this section of the quiet, wide and slow flowing river was used as the town's first public bathing place. Then, during the early 1930s, Colchester's first bypass was built and this crossed the river near the

The town's first official public bathing place opened in 1883. It was a stretch of the river accessed from the north bank near Belle View Road.

The open-air swimming pool built in the early 1930s on the site of the riverside bathing place. (1933)

Colchester bypass bridge across the Colne. This was the first two-hinged arch reinforced concrete bridge in Britain. (1931)

No skimping on the reinforcing in this pioneering concrete structure. (1931)

The bypass bridge. For aesthetic reasons this, the first reinforced concrete arch bridge across the Colne, was clad in brick. (2004)

bathing place, which was refashioned alongside a new bridge as Colchester's open-air swimming pool. The bridge itself, although faced with bricks is a reinforced concrete structure. In fact, it was the first reinforced concrete hinged arch bridge to be built in Britain. The open-air swimming pool is now used by the Colchester Canoe Club and is sandwiched between the brick clad bridge and the newer bridge that carries the dual carriageway to North Station. This was built in 1981 to relieve congestion in North Station Road. The road is flat and I am sure that most drivers using it are unaware that they are bridging the river Colne. This is not surprising as the road is embanked as it crosses the floodplain and the bridge viewed from the river appears to be no more than two oversized concrete pipes.

THE COLNE

Slow moving traffic on Station Way Bridge, built in 1981
to relieve congestion in North Station Road. (2012)

As far as the river goes this is the end of urban Colchester. From here on the river meanders through meadows over its wide floodplain. This bridge also marks the limit of my exploration of the river by boat and of my riverside cycle rides. Upstream from here the river is not navigable even to the smallest of craft and for a variety of reasons the paths are not suitable for cycling. From here on, most of my journey was to be by boot. Fortunately, much of the river is accessible by footpath either along or close to its banks.

One summer lunchtime I was contemplating the river from a riverside style when I noticed what at first I thought to be a herd of cattle being moved by a stockman. As they moved closer I realised that it was not a stockman but a young lady and that she was being pursued by the herd. She was slowly walking backwards towards me, whilst holding her arms out, even so the cattle were almost on top her and almost nudged her over the style, which she finally reached after what must have seemed an eternity. I have never seen anyone so relieved to be on the right side of the fence. After a while, when she had regained her composure a very relieved Anna related how her lunchtime amble beside the river had turned into full blown drama. When she entered the field by the style, the cattle were far away and appeared to take no more notice of her than she did of them. A few minutes later, when she was a few hundred yards along the river but no closer to the animals she noticed that they were moving towards her. Being beside the river, the safest course of action was to turn around and retrace her steps, if a little more speedily. However the curiosity of cattle had been aroused and they were now stampeding across the meadow. Realising that she could not outrun them and not wanting to swim the river she decided to face them off. Most people who walk through fields where there are cattle are aware of the Ramblers Association's advice: 'Don't panic or run; most cattle will stop before they reach you.' The cattle that were facing Anna were not aware of this and did not stop before they reached her. Fortunately they did slow down when they saw her outstretched arms but stayed uncomfortably close to her until the style barred their way.

I have walked through numerous fields of cattle and never seen such aggressive behaviour. I have since learned that, although incidents of people being attacked by cattle are few and far between, they appear to be happening more frequently, even to people who are used to handling cattle. A few years ago a herd manager of over thirty years experience was attacked by one of his own cows. Despite waving his arms and shouting at the beast he ended up under the animal. Luckily he survived and now wonders if in the interests of profit, food additives or crossbreeding has resulted in some varieties becoming more aggressive. I decided to leave my walk across that particular field for another day and went by another route to Sheepen Bridge.

This footbridge is near the site of one of the earliest crossing places on the Colne used by the Iron Age inhabitants of Sheepen. These are thought to have been the Trinovantes who were at war with their western neighbours, the Catuvellauni who lived in what is now Hertfordshire. Eventually the Catuvellauni subdued the Trinovantes and their king, Cunobelin established his capital in the area around what is now Colchester. This tribal settlement would have occupied the whole of the area between the Roman River Valley and the river Colne and have been defended to the west by extensive

The ford and footbridge where Sheepen Lane crosses the Colne.
A snow scene from 1902

earthworks stretching between the two rivers. This area of about ten square miles was called Camulodunum, after the Celtic god of war, Camulus. Although described as a capital, it was not what we would recognise as a town, but more an area of scattered farmsteads and small groups of dwellings whose inhabitants were bound together by kinship or industrial activity. One of these groups was near the banks of the Colne here at Sheepen. It is known that the Iron Age peoples used shallow-draught boats and, at the time, the river was tidal up to here, so it is quite likely that there was a landing place and that the river was important to the community. Also, there is abundant evidence that extensive industrial processes were carried out on the site. One of the most notable activities was the production of gold coins. Excavations have revealed coin moulds and other paraphernalia associated with the mint where it is estimated that, during the reign of Cunobelin, about two million gold coins were struck. Following the Roman invasion of AD 43 a legionary fortress, which

The Sheepen crossing. The wooden footbridge has been replaced by a more substantial structure and the adjacent ford has all but disappeared. A snow scene from 2013

later became a colonia, was built on the hill, the site of the modern Colchester, about half-a-mile distant. The character of the Sheepen site changed under the Romans, but continued to be a thriving community of industrial artisans supplying some of the needs of Britain's first real town, up on the hill.

A gold coin struck at the Sheepen mint around 2,000 years ago. About the size of a modern 5p, it has an ear of wheat with the letters CAMU for Camulodunum and the reverse depicts a running horse with the letters CUNO for Cunobelin.

Today, as the river meanders through the pastoral meadows of Sheepen, there is no sign of any industrial activity. The area is known as Cymbeline Meadows after Cymbeline, the name given by Shakespeare to the Celtic King of Britain in his play based on an embellished, loose adaptation of the legends surrounding Cunobelin.

The 157 acre (63.5 ha) Cymbeline Meadows Farm is owned by Colchester Borough Council. The working farm is managed by a tenant farmer as an open access recreational facility. There are areas of arable fields, pasture, meadow and woodland all managed to encourage a diverse population of wildlife. The whole length of the Colne, which meanders through the meadows, is closed to fishing and boating, to ensure the protection and conservation of its wildlife. In addition there is a footpath along each bank; which one to choose? I have walked these meadows many times but, following Anna's experience with cattle, I set off from Sheepen Bridge along the bovine free side. This took me to another footbridge and on to the farm trail which led me to Spring Lane.

Cattle grazing on the banks of the Colne in Cymbeline Meadows. (2012)

This lane crosses the Colne by an iron bridge built in 1904; before then there was a wooden footbridge and a ford. The new bridge was built by Colchester Borough Council in less than six weeks with iron supplied by Rubery & Sons of Darleston. Some of the iron balustrades have been knocked down by careless drivers but what remain show that the design copied the diamond lattice pattern of the earlier wooden footbridge. In 2000, after nearly one hundred years of increasingly heavy use, cracks were found in the concrete foundations and plans were made to replace the structure, but so far this has not happened due to lack of funds in the County Council budget. I can't say that I am sorry, as the replacement will probably be a reinforced concrete structure with the functional, characterless balustrade seen on many of the replacement bridges that will be encounted further upstream.

A unique feature of the site of this bridge is that for several hundred years there were two entirely separate watermills less than a hundred yards apart. In 1455 the area was described as 'having two mills either side of the Colne.' One of these mills, to the south of the river, was driven by water from a man-made lake filled with the waters from Lexden Springs. This medieval millpond had banks of up to 15ft (4.5m) high that provided sufficient head to drive an overshot wheel. Originally a fulling mill, it was used for corn milling for a short while before returning to fulling in the hands of the last of the Colchester clothiers, Peter Devall, who also worked Bourne Mill. The mill underwent its last renovation in 1836 when one of the town's first auxiliary steam plants was installed, and it was changed back to flour milling. The mill flourished and was run by several different millers, the last, George Cross, died around 1910 after which the mill became derelict. It appears that the building was demolished well before the site was bulldozed during the construction of the new link road to the Northern bypass in 1970.

If you look over the bridge parapet you can see another WWII tank trap. This mass of concrete and iron is the only evidence remaining of the position of the former ford. The other mill, to the north of the river had an undershot wheel powered by the waters of the Colne. From before 1830 this was operating as an oil mill, continuing to do so, until 1878 when a disastrous fire burned it to the ground. Some of the mill's associated buildings survived and during the inter-war period a grist mill, driven by an oil engine, operated near the site.

Spring Lane follows the course of the Colne for about a quarter-mile, and then there is a footpath that crosses a golf course. Way above the footpath, the golf course and the river, soars the reinforced concrete bridge that carries the A12 duel-carriageway along Colchester's northern bypass.

Lexden Bridge was built by Colchester Borough Council in less than six weeks. (2012)

The first Lexden road bridge was built in 1904 with its distinctive diamond pattern balustrade, beyond is the derelict Lexden Mill. (1915)

Across the golf course is the highest bridge in the Borough, the brickbuilt seven-arch viaduct. This, the first railway bridge to be built across the river, was erected by the Eastern Counties Railway to carry the railway across the Colne Valley. The railway between London and Colchester was completed in 1843 and the opening ceremony is recorded by William Wire in his diary: 'The town is in a state of excitement and the bells ringing in consequence of a report that the Railway Directors and Shareholders are coming by the rail in four coaches drawn by an engine. Went to the station and after waiting there for two hours finding they did not make their appearance, came home, after which it was reported that a bridge at Mountnessing was not considered safe to cross. Daresay there were two thousand people collected to witness their arrival, and much disappointment prevailed at their non-appearance.' The fault at Mountnessing was remedied and the Directors' train eventually arrived two days late. Delays on the line are still commonplace but their duration has been somewhat reduced.

Opened in 1974, Colchester's Northern bypass crosses the Colne above Lexden Wood Golf Course. (2012)

The seven arch viaduct that takes the mainline over the Colne. (2012)

Close by the viaduct the river flows over a weir with associated gauging station. This is one of three such installations on the Colne that are used by the Environment Agency to monitor the flow of water in the river. The information is conveyed by telemetry to a central control facility where it is used to control automatic weirs that regulate the river level. At Seven Arches Farm the river is joined by the footpath that stays close to the riverside up to and beyond the confluence of Colne with St Botolph's Brook. This tributary is the ancient boundary of the parish of West Bergholt, the subject of my next chapter.

The Lexden gauging station that measures the flow of water into Colchester. (2012)

CHAPTER IX

West Bergholt

West Bergholt

The name Bergholt is derived from the Saxon 'Bergholta' which means 'the wood on the hill'.

The Domesday Book records that there were two mills in Saxon times but only one by the time of the survey.

When Robert Sackville became the lord of the manor in 1119 the name of the village was changed to Bergholt Sackville.

In 1848 White described the parish as being 3 to 4 miles west-northwest of Colchester, on the north side of the vale of the Colne. There were 822 inhabitants and 2,211 acres skirted on three sides by the Colne and two of its tributaries.

The recorded population in 2011 was 3,344.

The riverside path from Seven Arches Farm soon arrives at Newbridge, whose name belies its age. There has been a bridge on this site since at least 1204 and for many years was maintained by the lords of three manors, one in each of the parishes of Bergholt, Lexden and Stanway. Within living memory there has been a passable ford alongside the bridge but, as long ago as 1866, this was described as 'often being impassable except by the largest carts and wagons'.

The ford has now completely disappeared but within the last few years a sign has appeared that informs travellers that they are entering the village of West Bergholt formerly Bergholt Sackville. The name 'Bergholt' is derived from the Saxon and means 'the wood on the hill'. It appears that the Saxons were not the first to settle here as there have been finds of artefacts from the Prehistoric, Iron-Age, and Roman periods. The wood on

The ford and Newbridge with its iron railings as it appeared in the early years of the 20th century.

The latest Newbridge was built in 1983. It is of prestressed concrete with a brick parapet. (2012)

the hill is thought to have been near the manor house by the church. And it was when Robert Sackville became the lord of the manor in 1119 that the name of the village was changed to Bergholt Sackville. The Sackville family come to England during the time of the Norman Conquest and Robert was a member of the Royal Court and close friend of King Henry. He was a religious man who became the first official rector of St Mary's Church and donated a 240 acre (96 ha) estate in the village to St John's Abbey of Colchester. Later Sackvilles remained close to the crown and, although some found themselves out of favour, others achieved high office and were granted lands in other parts of the country. By the 16th century most of the family's estates were in Sussex; this led Thomas Sackville to sell Bergholt manor in 1578, so ending an association with the village of nearly five hundred years.

The official name of the village remained Bergholt Sackville until the early 20th century, although it was often referred to as West Bergholt or just plain Bergholt. Then in 1910, maybe to distinguish it from the other Bergholt in the area the official name was changed to West Bergholt. Today there are some villagers who prefer the former name, so maybe change is in the air.

THE FLOUR & GRIST MILL IS A SUBSTANTIAL SQUARE

Brick Boarded and Slated Structure of Three Floors,

CONTAINING (AND INCLUDED THEREWITH):

On Ground Floor—Catch Mill and Bins, Undershot water wheel for driving stones with spur wheels and all driving gear and connections complete.

On First Floor—Five pairs of 4ft. French burr stones, double flour mill, and sack room.

On Second Floor—Corn Bin storage for over 1,000 sacks of corn, and sack hoist.

The whole of the MACHINERY AND WATER WHEEL being in excellent running condition, and worked by a never failing supply of water to the mill dam from the river Colne.

Adjoining the Mill is a lean-to brick and tiled Chaff Cutting Place connected with the water power, and on the other side a brick boarded and slated Engine House, with Steam Engine and Boiler, pullies and shafts, and a brick chimney shaft.

Details of Argent's Mill as they appeared in the sale catalogue of 1906.

At the bridge the footpath crosses to the other bank and continues along the riverside to Newbridge Mill Farm. This may well have been one of the Saxon mill sites mentioned in Domesday, but the first specific reference to Newbridge Mill is in 1337 when it was sold to William de Mote. It remained in the family for over two hundred years and it is likely that during this time it was used as a fulling mill. The mill had a number of owners until the beginning of the 19th century when it passed into the Argent family with whom it remained long enough to be called Argent's Mill. During this time the power from the undershot wheel was supplemented by a steam engine which together could drive five pairs of stones.

When the family sold the mill in 1906 it was described as having an undershot wheel worked by 'a never failing supply of water to the milldam from the river Colne'.

The mill was still working in the 1950s, although powered by electricity. Then in 1960 it caught fire and, despite the efforts of firemen and the presence of six appliances, the whole of the substantial 200 year-old building was destroyed. Today the only evidence of its existence is the brick arch above the millrace outlet and a rather diminutive millpond. The mill house survived the fire and has since acquired a wall fashioned from four of the millstones.

Newbridge Mill with steam plant to one side and the mill house to the other. (1950s)

Newbridge Mill after the disastrous fire of 9ᵗʰ November 1960.

Beyond the site of the former mill the footpath continues due west while the river meanders to the south but remains in sight until it joins the path once more at Cook's Mill. This is less than a mile upstream from Newbridge Mill and is thought to have been the site of another Saxon mill. The earliest reference to Cook's Mill by name is in 1472 when it was described as a fulling mill belonging to the manor of Cook's Hall. It continued as a fulling mill until the 18th century, when its small wheel was replaced with a much larger one and a horse mill was built to provide additional power. At this time, before the availability of steam engines, the only method of providing a mill with auxiliary power was to harness the power of animals. The horse mill at Cook's Mill could be powered by up to six horses and was used to supplement the refurbished fulling mill. The new mills were designed by John Smeaton, the eminent engineer, scientist and builder of the Eddystone Lighthouse. He was a member of the Royal Society, which awarded him with one of their highest honours, for his research into the mechanics of waterwheels and windmills. So we can be sure that the new Cook's Mills were built to the best of designs. Unfortunately, the new mills did not have a very long life; as is so often the case, it was not the mechanics that failed but the markets. These new mills were built at the time when the wool trade was in decline and the reduced demand for fulling forced many mill owners to convert their mills to other purposes. After a mere fifteen years Cook's Mills were advertised as,

'Constructed by Mr. Smeaton, Engineer, to do a large quantity of business at the expense of a small quantity of water. The two mills are now fulling mills and quite distinct from one another, and may at small expense be converted into corn or oil mills, or otherwise. The mills are in extraordinary condition, being both entirely new set up a few years ago.'

It appears that from this date the carefully engineered fulling mills were converted for use as corn and oil mills. This they did for nearly a hundred years before suffering the all too familiar fate of burning down in 1873.

Today it is difficult to identify the sites where the mills once stood. The surviving Georgian redbrick mill house now occupies this beautiful location and its tranquil garden contains only traces of what was once a thriving hub of local activity.

Cook's Mill House. (2012)

Cook's Hall undergoing extensive renovation. The wandering roofline provides a clue to the evolution of the building. (2012)

The mill takes its name from the nearby Cook's Hall which itself is named after the 14th century owners of what was the former Netherhall. This medieval house was the seat of the lord of the manor and the building has been added to during practically every century since, evolving and blending into its surroundings. In the dying years of the 20th century the building suffered some dying itself but now change is afoot and the present century is seeing a transformation, more in the way of a total refurbishment, which hopefully will keep the building alive for many years to come.

Since Norman times Bergholt has been divided into two manors with two lords; one based at Cook's Hall and the other further up the hill at West Bergholt Hall. The hall that boasts the village name is a complete contrast and is described by Pevsner as 'a Georgian town house, not at all in harmony with its surroundings'. Never the less it is an imposing building on an ancient site close to the church of St Mary. This is where Bergholt started and from Saxon times to 19th century this was the hub of the village. Enclosure, along with other changes in the parish, caused the centre of the village to move and in 1904 a more conveniently located new church was built. Then in 1975 the old church was declared redundant and its care placed in the hands of the Churches Conservation Trust. Whatever your views about religion, church buildings are an inherent part of our history and an integral part of the English landscape. Most have evolved over centuries and deserve to be preserved. The Churches Conservation Trust was created in 1968 and now has over 340 churches in its care. Many are used by local communities for appropriate activities and events, and over one and a half million people visit them each year.

The oldest part of St Mary's is part of the north wall, which dates back to Saxon times and contains some reused Roman brick. Additions and alterations have been made ever since, with its unusual wooden bell turret being added during the medieval period. Aside from the fabric of the building, the church has had its share of troublesome vicars. During the 16th century, Reverend Edmund Tarrell managed to get away with a string of misdemeanors that included failing to turn up for services and spending too much time in the

The imposing West Bergholt Hall. (2012)

pub. Then there was Reverend Richard Kyrby who refused to conduct services in English after the introduction of the new Prayer Book, eventually he was removed as Rector. In 1650 Reverend Gregory Holland was called before the *Committee for Scandalous Ministers* for preaching Royalist sermons during the Civil War, along with drunkenness and swearing in Church; and so it goes on.

Today the church, in its rural solitude is peaceful and is enjoyed by many visitors, some of whom are travelling along the Essex Way. This long distance path passes the church before heading along the track to Cook's Hall and on through the parish's Colneside meadows.

The Essex Way, created in 1972, wends its way using footpaths and lanes right across the county from Epping to Harwich, a distance of 81 miles. Four of these are beside the Colne and the first is in the parish of West Bergholt. I walked along this beautiful path beside the meadows with the river to my left, and to my right the valley sloped up to a small hilltop wood. In the sunshine the leaves were glowing in their golden colours of autumn. This wood is thought to be the one that gave the parish its name and, appropriately, was bought by the villagers and is now managed by the Woodland Trust. The floor of this magnificent old woodland is crisscrossed by numerous paths that are enjoyed by many, particularly in the Spring when the heady scent of bluebells fills the air above a carpet of blue. Everyone hereabouts calls this ancient wonderland Bluebell Wood, but many do not know that it is marked on the map as Hillhouse Wood.

As the hilltop wood faded from view and the meadow ended with a style, I left West Bergholt and entered my next parish of Fordham.

Separated from the Hall by a trim yew hedge is
St Mary's Church, known locally as the Old Church. (2012)

Hillhouse Wood is thought to be on the site of the wood that gave Bergholt its name. (2012)

CHAPTER X

Fordham & Aldham

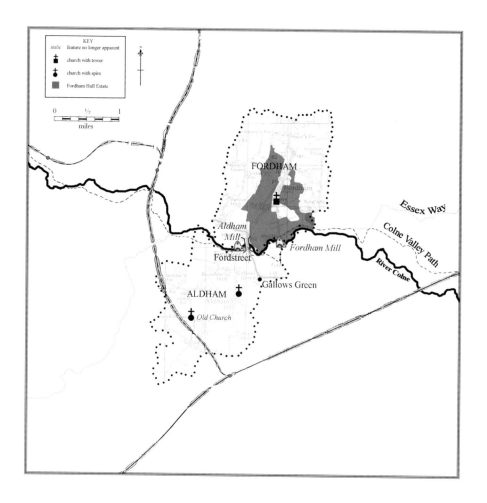

THE COLNE

Fordham & Aldham

The derivation of both these names is quite straightforward. 'Ham' is from the Old English and means an enclosure, homestead, manor or village. Giving us Fordham; the village by the ford, and Aldham; the old village.

Domesday records one mill in Fordham and none in Aldham.

In 1848 White described Fordham as a pleasant village of 739 souls and about 2,000 acres, sometimes called Great Fordham to distinguish it from Aldham or Little Fordham on the opposite side of the river. He went on to describe Aldham as a small pleasant village of 382 souls and about 1,790 acres including the village of Ford Street, sometimes known as Little Fordham, where there is a mill and a bridge on the river Colne

The population of Fordham in 2011 was 835, mostly up on the hill closer to the church than the ford. That of Aldham was 491 with two centres, one around the church and the other at Fordstreet.

Opposite: The Colne as it enters Fordham.. This is the site of a much earlier wooden bridge that had fallen down and was not replaced for many years, until, after lengthy appeals by local ramblers, this bridge was erected in 1996 to take the footpath from Fordham Heath into Fordham Hall Estate. (2012)

The riverside path reaches Fordham at a small copse of alder and willow. This parish was once practically all woodland, then over the centuries it was gradually cleared for cultivation until in 1837 when ninety percent of the parish was arable. By the early 21st century practically all of the woodland had gone. Then something unusual and mysterious happened that will change this parish for generations to come.

In 2002 Fordham Hall Estate was acquired by a mystery buyer who planned great changes for the 500 acre (200ha) farm. Very swiftly schemes were put in place to create the second largest new woodland in the country and work started on planting over a quarter of a million trees. Now, a mere ten years on, the landscape has been transformed and soon there will be a real woodland canopy over more than a quarter of the parish. The gently sloping land that surrounds the village has a network of over 12 miles of paths for walkers, cyclists and horse riders. This new native woodland and grassland linking the few remaining ancient hedgerows, marshland and ponds has created a haven for a rich variety of wildlife. As the river flows by this new, less agricultural environment it has gained a growing population of water voles and otters.

The pre-1976 iron Hammond's Bridge at Fordham. (1960s)

The Colne in full spate as it flows under Hammond's Bridge. (2011)

I continued along the riverside path beside the newly planted wood to Hammond's Bridge. This takes the road from Colchester up Mill Road to All Saints Church and the village centre. The church occupies a prominent hill top position that makes it visible from miles around. It would have been even more noticeable before 1796 when its spire fell down. At this time the river was crossed by no more than a ford and maybe a wooden footbridge. The last of these was replaced by an iron road bridge around 1910 and then this was replaced by the present concrete structure in 1976 and the ford has vanished.

As to the mill, this was first recorded in the Domesday Survey and there are records documenting its use as a grist mill, a fulling mill and a corn mill. It was rebuilt for the last time around 1780, from when it operated as a corn mill. In 1903 the mill was demolished by a builder who agreed to carry out repair work to make the adjoining mill house habitable in return for the mill materials and machinery.

Fordham Mill, the waterwheel was on the nearside of the building, protected from the elements by the black wooden structure. The double-bay mill house adjoined the far side and survives today. (c1900)

The gate to the riverside path as it approaches Hammond's Mill House down by the river. (2012)

The footpath skirts around the secluded mill house to rejoin the riverbank by the memorial seat erected in memory of Harvey and Carol Stephenson, who lived in the mill house for many years, enjoying the special quality of the river as it flowed through their garden. The path hugs the riverbank for a while before emerging from the *Shoulder of Mutton* garden in Fordstreet.

Iron-Age and Roman remains have been found near the ford, which indicates that Fordstreet could be one of the earliest settlement sites in Fordham. Place names that are based on the Old English 'straet', derived from the Latin 'via strata' which means paved way, are invariably associated with a Roman road. The Old English for river crossing is 'ford' so we end up with Stretfords and Stratfords all over the country, and in this case Fordstreet. When the Romans left our shores the country's roads fell into disrepair and by the time that the Saxons were building settlements some had all but disappeared. Today the majority of the surviving parts of the

Roman road that ran from Colchester to Godmanchester via Cambridge are outside Essex, but it is thought that the route from Colchester followed the Colne Valley to Yeldham and it is possible that there was a river crossing at Fordstreet. Then later Saxon settlers continued to use the Roman 'paved way' across the marshy ground and through the river. Written records of the ford go back to 1235 and it must have been quite well used as by 1485 it had acquired its first bridge. The route became increasingly important and in 1765 was turnpiked.

The long-distance road network in England is somewhat haphazard because it has evolved by the joining together of very many, very short local tracks between farmsteads and villages. Throughout our long history there have only been three periods of systematic road building; first the Romans, then the mainly 18th century turnpikes and finally the motorway network. Turnpike trusts were established to maintain the principle roads in Britain, with the power to collect tolls. These were collected at tollgates, or turnpikes, which were placed across the road by a tollhouse. This led to an improvement in the condition of the long distance routes in the country, which until then had been maintained by each parish to varying standards. The trusts were also obliged to mark their roads with milestones and maintain some of the bridges on their routes. The Colchester to Cambridge road exhibits examples of many features of a turnpiked route.

The Essex Turnpike Trust was responsible for many of the turnpike roads in the county including the section of the Colchester to Cambridge route that ran through the county from Lexden to Halstead and on to Sible Hedingham. Surviving from this period are four of the fourteen milestones and two tollhouses. One of these is up the hill from Fordstreet at Gallows Green and more relevant to our story is the fact that the Trust rebuilt Fordstreet Bridge in 1828, and it is still in use today. The responsibility for maintaining this bridge was taken over by the county in 1871. It was widened in 1963 and has since been restricted to traffic-light-controlled single lane operation.

If you had looked upstream from the bridge parapet a hundred years ago you would have seen a four storey brick and slate building astride a single arch bridge. This was the last mill to be built on this ancient site. A watermill

The Shoulder of Mutton *and Fordstreet Bridge with its pre-1963 parapet. (c1940s)*

Fordstreet Bridge, built by the Essex Turnpike Trust in 1828, with each keystone bearing this date. This redbrick, twin arch bridge was widened in 1963 with the addition of pre-stressed concrete beams carried on cantilevered supports for the footways. (2012)

was first recorded here in 1327 and its history follows the usual story of being used for corn milling and/or fulling depending on the economic return at the time. The 19th century owner, James Mercer Green, had ambitious plans for this small country mill. He built a completely new mill that housed the most up-to-date machinery. A water turbine was used to drive two pairs of stones, one for flour and the other grist. A large steam plant was installed to drive a proportionally sized roller mill. Mr. Green worked the mill until his death in 1900. New owners and changing times led to the closing and demolition of the mill roundabout 1917. The adjacent mill house survived and during the 1920s operated as a guest house with tennis and boating facilities. This enterprise was sold in 1930 and the operations were scaled down to non-residential tearooms, which continued until the 1940s. It is now called Bridge House and is a private residence.

From Fordstreet there is a footpath that passes Bridge House and then follows the raised mill leat to Millrace Nursery. Until the Middle Ages this side of the river was known as Little Fordham, but now it is in the parish of

Parts of Bridge House date back to the 15th century, this is the mid 19th century brick façade. (2012)

Fordstreet Mill and mill house. (c1900)

The single-arch bridge associated with the demolished Fordstreet Mill, now no more than a feature in the garden of Bridge House, the former mill house, which is now a private residence. (2012)

Aldham and just up the hill is Aldham church. To the casual observer this church with its slender spire, old porch and stone windows looks as if it has evolved over the centuries; it is in fact a Victorian creation. The original Aldham church was located way over to the west of the parish and although long established it was never smart and often in a state of disrepair. What with this and the fact that over the years the scattered population of the parish had migrated away from the old site, it was decided to build a new church closer to the new centres of population. The new church was opened in 1855 and was built to much the same plan as the old one with many of the original materials reused. These included 13th and 14th century windows and the beautifully carved 14th century porch, which was moved in its entirety. Also incorporated into the new church was a marble memorial to its most famous incumbent, the Reverend Philip Morant, author of *The History and Antiquities of the County of Essex*. This was published in the 1760s and was the first scholarly history of Essex. Written before the days of professional historians, this outstanding work by an enthusiastic amateur helped to establish later professional standards. Such is the standard of the work and presentation that it is still widely referred to today.

In 1966 the Essex Archaeological Society restored and moved the stone from Philip Morant's burial place, which was in the chancel of the old church, to a place inside the new church.

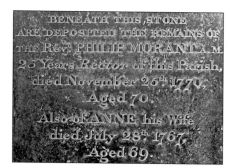

Philip Morant, author of The History and Antiquities of the County of Essex, *and Rector of Aldham 1745-1770.*

St Margaret's Church, Aldham was demolished in 1854.

This church of St Margaret and St Catherine, Aldham was built on a new site in 1854.

Many of the headstones from the old churchyard have been moved to the new one but the names of many of the occupiers of the unmarked graves have been lost to the village memory. I will resurrect one, the unfortunate Elizabeth Bailey, who suffered in life, had a cruel death and was reluctantly buried in Aldham after her body was found close to the parish boundary.

Extract from the Burial Register, 1795

Elizabeth Bailey Oct 17th – She was discovered in a clay pit in the south west corner of Ashfield on 14th inst: and found by the jurors of the Coroners Inquest murdered by William Clark late of the parish of Great Tey. Labourer, who was thereupon committed to the County Goal. He was acquitted at the ensuing assize for want of evidence.
N.B. The clay pit and three acres of land in the S.W. corner of Ashfield are in the parish of Great Tey. But the body having been ignorantly removed into the parish of Aldham, and the inquest there taken, it was buried in Aldham Church Yard and the parish put to a great deal of unnecessary expense.

Now back to Millrace Nursery, which opened in 1973 as a nursery, became a garden centre and has now diversified so much that it is difficult to say what it is. I have visited its café many times, by both bicycle and boot. Behind this is one of the few stretches of the freshwater Colne that is navigable and accessible. Here, at the head of the millrace, is a wooden jetty. Tied to this are a few rowing boats complete with rowlocks but lacking oars. I stood on the jetty and looked at the rippleless water. Downstream the river is wide and straight and I could see that within a short distance it entered the private grounds of Bridge House and the way was barred by the weir of the former mill; upstream looked a whole lot more interesting. I went back to the garden centre to look for a pair of oars.

The Millrace jetty and boats for hire. (2012)

No-one seemed to know how far along the river the boats could be rowed, but there were reports that some people had caught a glimpse of Chappel viaduct. I was set on going as far as I could and had come prepared with a day's food and a pair of waders. When the girl at the checkout asked if I wanted to hire the boat for one hour or two, I could only say that I hoped to be back before nightfall. She eyed up my rucksack and waders and for a modest deposit I was given, if somewhat reluctantly, a pair of oars.

I threw my kit into the boat, jumped in and cast off. It was a beautiful May day and the first time I had been afloat for quite a while. The first thing that struck me was the width of the river, in places it was 30ft (9m) or more. The banks were rich in vegetation beneath the willow and alder whose

The river Colne as it flows between Fordham and Aldham. (2012)

branches arched overhead creating patches of dappled sunlight, confusing the reflections on the surface of the water. Past the second bankside pillbox the course of the river began to meander but it was still comfortably wide making rowing a pure delight. The sunshine had brought out a mass of damselflies that hovered above the water, with much more elegance than my clumsy splashing. As the tree canopy receded, the riverbanks seemed to grow higher and before long I found myself being looked down upon by curious sheep. Somewhere along here, at a place not marked on the riverbank I left the parishes of Fordham and Aldham, and rowed my boat into Chappel. My story continues in the next chapter but I did return my hire boat, all be it five hours later, having had a wonderful day on the river.

CHAPTER XI

Chappel

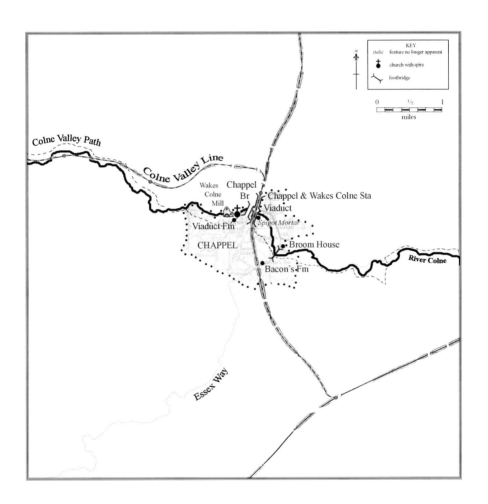

Chappel

Chappel is named after the chapel that was first recorded here in 1285 when this was part of the parish of Great Tey. The area was called Pontisbright, a Latinised derivation from Britric's Bridge. When the area became a separate parish in the 16th century it was called Chapel.

In 1848 William White described Chapel as a picturesque village on the south bank of the river Colne containing 429 inhabitants and 996 acres of land. It was anciently called Pontisbright.

The population in 2011 was 506.

I entered the parish of Chappel in a rowing boat. The river here was just wide enough for rowing, much to the surprise of walkers making the trek along the Essex Way which, for a short distance, hugs the riverbank before leaving the riverside at Broom House Bridge. In my progress towards this bridge I had encountered my first shallows and rowing had become difficult. I did manage to edge my way upstream by a combination of punting and holding on to clumps of reeds that had colonised much of the riverbed. I eventually reached the bridge where I took a rest on the riverbank. As I was sitting there in the sunshine I wondered why such an elaborate bridge had been built on this site. Although this is where five paths meet, the one that crosses the river could easily have done so by a ford or a simple wooden structure. And yet here, in the middle of nowhere, is this well engineered single span brick structure wide enough for a road. I later consulted my map collection and found that

The brick bridge that carried the lane that once ran between Broom House and Bacon's Farm. (2012)

The author approaching Chappel viaduct. (2012)

the bridge does not appear until the mid 19th century. From this time onwards there was a serviceable road between Bacon's Farm and Broom House, and, although probably never surfaced, it was marked as a road until 1953, after which it appears to have been downgraded to the existing footpath. The clue to the existence of this rather elaborate former road bridge maybe the nearby viaduct that was built around the same time and employed many men with the necessary skills to build brick arches.

Beyond the bridge progress in the boat was difficult, due largely to reeds and overhanging trees. Riverways, like highways need to be maintained to keep them passable. The Colne here is not really navigable, not because it is too narrow or too shallow, it is just overgrown. A little further upstream the river had been cleared and as it passed the gardens of the houses in Chappel I resumed rowing. By now the viaduct was in sight and I was soon propelling my small craft under this towering edifice.

Chappel viaduct is the second largest brick structure in England. It is 1,066ft (320m) long, has 32 arches each with a span of 30ft (9m) and its maximum height is 75ft (23m). It is the longest viaduct in East Anglia and was built in 1847 by Peter Bruff.

Peter Bruff has been called 'the Brunel of the Eastern Counties' because his many civil engineering projects have had such a profound influence on the region. He was a classic Victorian engineer who could turn his hand to practically anything. His first encounter with our area was as an assistant engineer with the Eastern Counties Railway (ECR) who were building the region's first railway, which we passed under earlier as we were leaving Colchester. This line was intended to go between London and Norwich, but as the line approached Colchester two things happened.

First the company ran into financial difficulties causing the line to terminate at Colchester. Secondly, the embankment at Stanway was not up to standard and this resulted in the dismissal of the engineer responsible for this section, who was the thirty year old Peter Bruff. This ambitious young engineer was more than up to the job, but was too trusting of his sub-contractors and maybe he was spending too much of his time on plans for other civil engineering proposals, which included a ship canal from Wivenhoe to Colchester that I mentioned in Chapter VII. In the event he did not proceed with any of these schemes but seized the opportunity to build the railway line past Colchester to Ipswich. To do this he secured funding from a consortium of Ipswich businessmen and the Eastern Union Railway (EUR) was born, of which Bruff was the resident engineer. He was also engineer to the Stour Valley Railway which was to lead to his most monumental construction, Chappel viaduct.

Before I detail this outstanding achievement I will just mention some of Bruff's other activities. He was clearly a man of his time who was passionate about the advantages that civil engineering projects could bring to communities and he also possessed the ability to persuade local dignitaries and businessmen to back his schemes. In practically every town in the region his name crops up in connection with one project or another. In Harwich he was responsible for the town's harbour works, the town's first pier and the water works. Shortly after completing these projects he bought a house and a considerable amount of land in the coastal town of Walton-on-the-Naze. Here he set about putting down an artesian well and installing steam engines to pump water to the whole of the town. He built sea defences with concrete walks. He built houses and an hotel, as well as a gasworks to provide street lighting.

Then he bought a large stretch of deserted coastline near to the inland village of Clacton. Here he planned to build a completely new town, Clacton-on-Sea. His grand plan was for the town to be an ideal seaside resort. Unrestrained by existing roads or buildings he designed the road layout and then started separate companies to build an hotel and a public hall. When he sold off individual building plots he laid down strict covenants and kept control of all services. He was, in effect, a one-man planning committee who kept control of all the town facilities, including drainage and paving, open spaces and the design of the buildings that overlooked them. The whole of the town centre, even today, is Bruff's town centre. The town began as a decorous Victorian resort, in accordance with his wishes, with villas occupied by genteel families, and hotels and boarding houses visited by similar folk. But the introduction of 'Bank Holidays', in 1871, brought a conflicting element, day-trippers, first by steamer and then by railways, many of Bruff's own creation.

Some years later his interest in Clacton-on-Sea waned and he restricted his activities to the design and construction of sewerage and water systems. These included a sewer system for Ipswich, the town in which he had lived since his early days with the EUR, and an improved water system for Colchester that included the landmark water tower 'Jumbo'. When Peter Bruff died in 1900, he had managed to leave his mark in just about every town in eastern England and had built Clacton-on-Sea from nothing, but his most monumental work is his viaduct at Chappel.

Peter Bruff (1812-1900)

The major obstacle on the proposed railway line between Marks Tey and Sudbury was the Colne Valley. Peter Bruff decided that this could be crossed by a viaduct and set about preparing a suitable design. This was to consist of a series of laminated wooden arches supported on brick piers. Then the discovery of a nearby plentiful supply of brickearth persuaded him to abandon these plans in favour of an all brick one. Work started in July 1847 and a mere twenty months later some seven million bricks had been laid to create what was, at the time, the largest brick structure in the country.

There are several remarkable features concerning the building of the viaduct. What was quite unusual for the time was that the whole structure was built without loss of life. And the story surrounding the laying of the foundation stone bears repeating. This was laid some two months into the project and can be seen about 10ft (3m) up in one of the piers between the road and the river. There were about 200 people at the ceremony and beneath the stone was placed a time capsule. This was a bottle containing a newly minted sovereign, half-sovereign, shilling, sixpence and a four-penny piece. Before anyone reading this thinks of attempting to recover this valuable hoard, think again, because you have been beaten to it. Within hours of the stone being laid it was discovered that it had been tampered with and the coins removed. Later that night a sharp-eyed barmaid spotted a newly minted coin and before long a bricklayer, William Coates, was arrested. We often hear of the harsh sentences imposed by Victorian courts for petty crimes but, in this case William Coates was clever enough to employ an even cleverer representative. Despite the certainty by everyone concerned of the guilt of the accused, his smooth-talking councel managed to persuade the court that 'The Company had no property in the money and that there was an entire absence of proof in the moral guilt of the prisoner', and the case was dismissed.

Chappel viaduct foundation stone, laid in 1847 shows Peter S Bruff as Engineer. (2012)

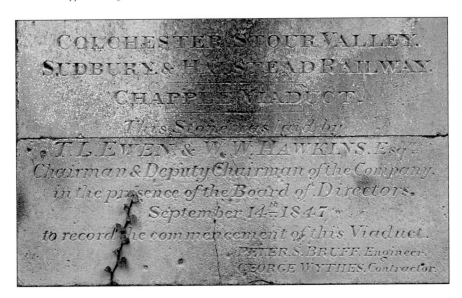

Now back to more recent times and the celebration of the millennium. This is when the Colneside land beneath the viaduct was transformed into the 'Chappel Millennium Green'. This highly successful open space provides a variety of facilities for both the local community and visitors. There are recreation areas, a nature reserve and a large grassed area that has been used for a variety of outdoor social events.

The area beneath the viaduct is also home to the remains of some WWII defences. Following the Dunkirk evacuation in June 1940 Britain was in imminent danger of an invasion by the German army. It was decided that a series of lines of protection would be constructed. The first line was the coast; if this failed then secondary lines further inland were designed to impede the progress of an invading army. One of these lines was the Eastern Command Line that ran from the mouth of the Colne, along the river as far as Chappel, before heading north through Suffolk and Norfolk to King's Lynn. In common with the other defence lines it utilised natural features such as rivers, railway cuttings and embankments. For the first twenty-one miles of the Eastern Command Line the natural feature was the River Colne. The estuary and its southwestern bank above Colchester was protected by a series of pillboxes. These were built of concrete or brick and reinforced with anything that came to hand. They derive their name from the original WWI pillboxes, which were circular with an overlapping concrete roof, and appeared similar to a Victorian pill box. The WWII structures look less like a pillbox and are usually hexagonal and many were camouflaged to look like farm buildings or haystacks. At the river's more vulnerable crossing places additional protection was provided in the form of tank traps and gun emplacements. Some of these I have mentioned along the way, but here at Chappel, where the defence line leaves the river to follow the railway, there are surviving examples of all three types of installation mentioned.

Beneath the viaduct stands a pillbox, and close by there are tank traps. Also on the riverbank there is a spigot mortar emplacement. This large, circular block of concrete with a short metal post at its centre was where the local Home Guard would mount their spigot mortar. This weapon was invented in 1941 and was intended to replace the anti-tank weapons lost after the evacuation of the army at Dunkirk. Many thousands were made but the Army refused to use them, so they were issued to the Home Guard. The weapon was a self-propelled, fin-stabilised bomb with a range of about 100 yards (90m). It is fortunate that these weapons never had to be used in anger, as not only would 'Dad's Army' have had to wait until the advancing tanks were perilously close but the weapon had the unfortunate characteristic that, when the warhead hit the target and exploded, the fins could fly back along the original line of flight and strike the crew operating the weapon. I have no idea if any of these were used by the Home Guard during exercises below Chappel viaduct, but will leave the reader to imagine which three of Captain Mainwaring's platoon he would have chosen to man such a weapon, and the likely farcical results!

From beneath the viaduct I continued my exploration of Chappel on foot. I walked by the river through the Swan yard to the road bridge. This is the bridge that gave Chappel its original name of Pontisbright.

The spigot mortar mount by the river under Chappel viaduct. Beyond is a new footbridge across the river, built in 1973 to connect the main road to the recreation ground. (2012)

A loaded spigot mortar on a mount ready for action. (c1942)

The opening of the new Chappel Bridge. (1907)

There has been a bridge here since at least 1140 when it was described as Britric's Bridge. It connected the two halves of the estate of Crepping Manor whose lord was responsible for its upkeep. In 1272 the bridge was referred to as 'Ponte Brichrich' which, over the centuries, was spelt in a variety of ways until, eventually, it became Pontisbright.

For many years the parish of Great Tey extended to the bridge. But being somewhat distant from the church, a small chapel was built for the community that grew around the river crossing. The building was first recorded in 1285 but it did not acquire the status of a parish church until the 16th century when this part of Great Tey became a separate parish, which took the name Chapel. When or why the double 'p' arrived I do not know.

The Swan *across a flooded river Colne at Chappel Bridge. (1990s)*

The 2011 reconstructed Chappel Bridge on the site of the bridge that gave Chappel its ancient name of Pontisbright. (2012)

Before I leave the village I will just mention a literary connection. The famous crime writer Margery Allingham lived at Viaduct Farm for four years before moving to Tolleshunt D'arcy in 1935. She is best remembered for her detective fiction featuring her aristocratic sleuth, Albert Campion whose adventures take him to the village of Pontisbright. Her only non-fiction title, *The Oaken Heart*, was written in 1941 at the request of her American publisher to inform his countrymen about what life was like in England during WWII. In this the names of towns and villages were changed for security reasons and Chappel became Pontisbright once more.

The lane that leads from the bridge to the church soon comes to an end and diverges into two footpaths. One keeps to the south of the river and

Chappel's church of St Barnabas with its squat wooden belfry and elegant spire. (2012)

26 of the 32 arches of the viaduct that towers 75ft (23m) above the village of Chappel. (2013)

passes through water meadows to the parish boundary with Earls Colne. The other crosses the river and immediately passes an impressive mill building. This is Wakes Colne Mill and we are into another chapter of our journey.

The plaque built into the 2011 bridge across the Colne at Chappel.

CHAPTER XII

The Four Colnes; Wakes Colne, Earls Colne, White Colne & Colne Engaine

THE COLNE

Wakes Colne, Earls Colne, White Colne and Colne Engaine

All of these parishes derive part of their name from the river. The other distinguishing part is that of a family that was, at one time, associated with one of the manors in each of the relevant parishes.

Wakes Colne from Baldwin Wake who acquired land, in the former Great Colne through marriage in the 13th century.

Earls Colne, formerly Great Colne, after the De Veres, Earls of Oxford.

White Colne, anciently Colne le Blanc, was held by Dimidius Blancus in 1086.

Colne Engaine, formerly Little Colne, was held by Vital Engaine in 1219.

Domesday records two mills in Earls Colne, one from before the conquest, as is the one in Wakes Colne. Another two mills are recorded in Colne Engaine, again one from before the conquest.

In 1848 White described Colne (Earls) or Great Colne as a large well built village pleasantly situated on the south side of the river Colne and on the opposite side of the river are the three parishes of Colne Engaine, Wakes Colne and White Colne.
The parish of Earls Colne contains 1,385 inhabitants and 2,959 acres of land; Colne Engaine, 685 souls and 2,444 acres; Wakes Colne, 444 inhabitants and 1,837 acres, rising boldly from the river; White Colne, 419 souls and 1,780 acres.

The populations of the four parishes in 2011 were recorded as; Earls Colne: 3,693, Colne Engaine: 1,008, Wakes Colne: 538, and White Colne: 540.

Today Wakes Colne Mill and mill house are private residences set in a scene of rural tranquillity. This is a far cry from when the hammering noise of the oil mill stampers reverberated along the valley, loud enough to be heard in the next village. But that would have been nothing compared to the explosion that blew the top off the old mill early in the 19th century. Flour milling is a dangerous business and the highly combustible mix of flour dust and air has caused innumerable fires in mills and bakeries, and probably the great fire of London. When there is enough flour dust suspended in a cloud in a confined space all that is needed for an explosion is a source of ignition. Millers were well aware of this and took sensible precautions but every now and again explosions occurred that were attributed to spontaneous combustion. The real cause was often heat generated from machinery or some source of static electricity.

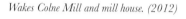

Wakes Colne Mill and mill house. (2012)

The working Wakes Colne Mill shortly before it closed in 1974.

Following the explosion at Wakes Colne a new mill was built, which is the one that stands today. The first mill to be recorded on this site was in 1086, and the grinding of corn appears to have continued until the 16th century when the first mention of a fulling mill occurs. This activity continued into the early 18th century when an oil mill, with its noisy stampers, was added to the site.

The present mid 19th century building is described by Benham as 'a handsome corn mill, brick-built with an elaborate mansard-style slate roof, flanked at one end by its mill house and at the other by a wooden oil mill.' He goes on to describe the mill's unusual machinery, which he was fortunate enough to visit during the last years of its operation. The mill was driven by an enormous iron wheel, 20ft (6m) in diameter and 10ft (3m) wide, so large that the water available could only run it for an hour or two at a time.

All Saints' Church, Wakes Colne with its wooden bell turret and stumpy tower. (2013)

Instead of the conventional drive from the wheel shaft used in all the other mills on the Colne, this giant wheel had, around its rim, a set of inverted iron teeth which drove a 3ft (0.9) iron pinion. This was mounted on a shaft which carried five pit wheels, each driving a pair of stones; too many for the power available, making it impossible to operate them all at the same time. This well engineered and beautifully constructed mill was just too large for its situation. Despite this, it did manage to operate at a reduced capacity until about 1945 when two pairs of stones were removed and electric grinders installed. The modified arrangement continued to function until all milling finally ceased in 1974.

The oil mill, first recorded in 1777, appears to have always been a separate entity, with its own waterwheel used to drive an old-style stamper press. This

251

was later replaced by hydraulic ram presses powered by an eight horsepower portable engine; this continued to operate until the early 20th century.

From the mill there is a path that leads up the hill to the road and All Saints' Church. Parts of this building are Norman, but its distinctive wooden bell turret and stumpy spire date from the 15th century.

The church overlooks the valley but there is a better view from along the road and further up the hill, at the railway station. When this was opened in 1849 it was simply Chappel but later this was changed to Chappel & Wakes Colne and it is now the home of the East Anglian Railway Museum. Perhaps now is the appropriate time for a brief overview of the Colne Valley railways.

At various times there have been proposals to build railways along the whole length of the Colne. I have already mentioned the lines that have followed the lower reaches from Brightlingsea up to Colchester and the first railway to cross the valley by the seven arch viaduct to the west of Colchester. We are now at the start of the only railway in the valley that bears the name of the river, the Colne Valley & Halstead Railway (CV&HR). This company would not have come into existence if the earlier 'Colchester, Stour Valley, Sudbury & Halstead Railway' had fulfilled its obligation to build a line to Halstead. This earlier company built a line from Marks Tey to Sudbury with intermediate stations at Bures and Chappel, but then ran out of steam. By the time that the CV&HR was incorporated in 1856, the Sudbury line was being operated by the Eastern Counties Railway (ECR) with whom negotiations were made for the Halstead line to join the network at Chappel. The route of the new line was designed by Peter Bruff, but his expensive expertise was not utilised in its construction.

When the line opened to Halstead in 1860 there was only one intermediate station, this was called Colne. Then, after two years, another station, Ford Gate, was opened. Some years later the railway company proposed the closure of the earlier Colne station. These plans were met with considerable local opposition and, following a local meeting, a deputation of local businessmen, including Reuben Hunt, pleaded with the board to keep the station open. This was ignored and in 1889 the station was closed. One wonders about

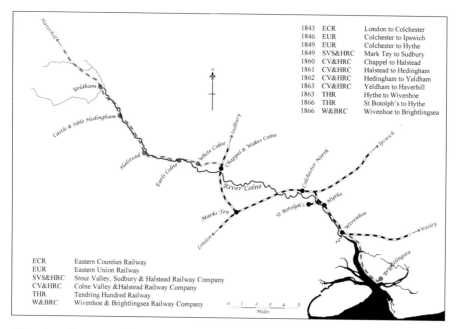

1843	ECR	London to Colchester
1846	EUR	Colchester to Ipswich
1849	EUR	Colchester to Hythe
1849	SVS&HRC	Mark Tey to Sudbury
1860	CV&HRC	Chappel to Halstead
1861	CV&HRC	Halstead to Hedingham
1862	CV&HRC	Hedingham to Yeldham
1863	CV&HRC	Yeldham to Haverhill
1863	THR	Hythe to Wivenhoe
1866	THR	St Botolph's to Hythe
1866	W&BRC	Wivenhoe to Brightlingsea

ECR	Eastern Counties Railway
EUR	Eastern Union Railway
SVS&HRC	Stour Valley, Sudbury & Halstead Railway Company
CV&HRC	Colne Valley &Halstead Railway Company
THR	Tendring Hundred Railway
W&BRC	Wivenhoe & Brightlingsea Railway Company

The various railway companies and the railways they built along virtually the whole length of the river Colne.

the sincerity of Mr. Hunt's plea, as a short while later he provided land and finance for the development of a new Ford Gate station that just happened to be down the hill from his factory, rather than at the other end of the village. Meanwhile the protestations continued and within a few years, following changes on the board of the railway company, the original station was re-opened. But not as Colne, as this name had been transferred to the new station. So the reopened station took the name of the parish in which it stood, White Colne. The final station name change on this short stretch of line occurred in 1905 when the station that opened as Ford Gate had its name changed from Colne to Earls Colne, ostensibly to avoid confusion with Calne in Wiltshire and Colne in Lancashire. But we must not forget that by now R Hunt & Co had a thriving export business and were known throughout the world as being at Earls Colne.

Chappel & Wakes Colne Station. The present station was built at the end of 19ᵗʰ century; it is a somewhat grander building than the original station built in 1847. This is now a private residence still standing diminutively beyond and beside the newer station. (2013)

During the years following the opening of the CV&HR to Halstead, the line was gradually extended along the valley, first to Hedingham, then on to Yeldham and eventually to Haverhill, where it joined the line into Cambridge. The line had an enormous impact on the economies of the towns and villages through which it passed, as we will see as we continue along the river.

Returning to Chappel & Wakes Colne station, from here I walked down the hill to the river and the village sign. This, like the station, bears the names of both parishes, Chappel on one side and Wakes Colne on the other, for the river here both divides and unites these two parishes. This unusual sign was dedicated to the memory of a local landowner and the dedication service was attended by a member of the Wake family who claims to be a descendent of Hereward the Wake. A name that has been associated with the village since the 13ᵗʰ century when Baldwin Wake acquired land in the former Great Colne through marriage.

The legends surrounding that champion of English liberty, Hereward the Wake, have been told and retold so many times and for so long that it is difficult to separate fact from fiction, but of some things we can be certain. Hereward was a rebellious 11th century historical figure of Anglo-Saxon' or Anglo-Danish, origin but certainly of noble birth. He is described as, 'being short and stoutly but agile, with long golden hair, an oval face with eyes light in colour and not matched'. And he certainly had a considerable following of anti-Norman Englishmen centered around his fenland stronghold on the Isle of Ely, which became a notorious refuge for like-minded dissidents. From here they managed to subvert Norman rule for a full five years until in the autumn of 1071 William gathered together an army supported by a fleet and prepared to blockade the Isle of Ely. Eventually, after a long siege the Isle was taken and here history gives way to myth. Hereward may well have been killed but legend has it that he escaped and the stories that surround him are many and varied. In general, Hereward is made to follow the traditional route of a fictional hero, rescuing a princess, being pardoned and suffering a noble death. None of this is substantiated but we all like a good story, as did the 12th century chroniclers who first recorded the supposed exploits of Hereward. It was not until several years later that the Wake family adopted Hereward as their ancestor and the two names became associated, coincidently at about the same time as one of the Wake family acquired a Colneside manor now known as Wakes Colne.

It is unusual that the village signs of these two villages are mounted on the same post at the boundary between the two, by Chappel Bridge. (2012)

THE COLNE

I left Wakes Colne by crossing over the bridge and for a short time was back in Chappel, making my way along the Colne Valley Path. This follows the edge of the floodplain past a relatively new fishing lake and through water meadows to the parish boundary with Earls Colne. Here the character of the path changes abruptly as it follows the bricked lane leading to Swanscombe Farm, now a smart private residence, a little at odds with its surroundings. The footpath continues alongside this property's high, close-boarded fence as far as the riverbank where rural charm is resumed as the path enters Chalkney Wood.

This really ancient woodland has probably been in existence since the last Ice Age and during the 10,000 years since has acquired a rich diversity of wildlife and more than a few signs of human activity. The wood is crossed by a massive holloway that still has traces of its boundary banks. It is thought that these are the remnants of a Roman road, which is claimed by some to be part of the Via Devana, the lost route between Colchester and Cambridge. There are other boundary banks in Chalkney Wood that date from the medieval period when it was owned by the De Veres, Earls of Oxford, who used it as a wild boar enclosure. For the last 400 years or so much of the wood has been managed by coppicing. That was until a substantial part of it passed into the ownership of the Forestry Commission who introduced alien conifers that threatened to destroy the native fauna and flora. When Oliver Rackham wrote his authoritative book about ancient woodlands in 1980 he said that despite the introduction of conifers 'Chalkney still gives one of the best impressions of a medieval wood'. A few years later the Forestry Commission saw the error of their ways and began the staged felling of the conifers. To their credit they employed local contractors to do this work and the final alien tree was removed in 2011. The native species have re-established and some of this area has been returned to traditional coppicing; a practice that has been carried out for many years by Essex County Council who own another significant part of the wood. Coppicing involves the periodic felling of trees from different areas of the wood and then allowing the cut stumps to regrow to be harvested in the future. The plan in this wood is based on a 25 year cycle and the first cycle, completed under County Council ownership, was completed in 1999.

*The working Chalkney Mill with its 19th century addition, unusual lucam
and chimney rising from the steam plant. (1897)*

*Chalkney Mill and mill house. The door enclosing the millwheel has been removed to expose
all that remains of the mill machinery, the Whitmore & Binyon wheelshaft. (2012)*

Chalkney Mill's cast iron wheel shaft made by Whitmore & Binyon of Wickham Market. (2012)

I last walked the riverside path through Chalkney Wood on a glorious June day, with the sun creating patches of dappled light as leaves quivered in the hint of a breeze that kept the temperature down to just the right level for the adventurous stroll I was making towards Halstead. The path leaves the wood as it enters the yard and buildings associated with Chalkney Mill. This is now a private residence but the river still rushes through the millrace in the middle of the building where all that remains of the original waterwheel is its octagonal axle.

This is an ancient mill site, first recorded in 1086, and then from 1140 until the Dissolution it belonged to Colne Priory. During its long history there have been times when it was recorded as a corn mill or fulling mill. It is known that in 1802 its breastshot wheel was driving two pairs of stones. Later in the century an addition was made to the side of the mill building and a steam plant installed which kept the mill operating as a corn mill until the early 1930s. The building then remained derelict for many years before the 19th century addition was demolished and the earlier mill converted for residential use in 1986.

From the mill there is a choice of paths, one on either side of the river. I chose to cross by the bridge in front of the mill and continue my journey in the parish of White Colne. A short distance along the lane I turned on to a rather overgrown riverside path. The inclement weather experienced earlier in the summer had obviously suited the nettles that had grown to shoulder height along much of this path. I soon emerged, relatively unscathed, between houses at the foot of Colneford Hill. Close by is the bridge and the former *Anchor* pub, now the *Riverside Spice*, Indian restaurant.

White Colne Green looking towards Colneford Bridge. (c1900)

Up the hill is White Colne Green, and around the corner, is the former White Colne railway station, now the village hall. And quite a bit further away, somewhat isolated from the village is the parish church of St Andrew.

In 1860 Colne station was the only intermediate station on the line. It was later renamed White Colne.

Since 1976 the former White Colne station has been used as the village hall. (2013)

259

St Andrew's Church, White Colne, where there may be parts dating from the 12th Century, but the whole building was extensively restored by the Victorians who added the shingle spire. This has recently been reclad, as woodpeckers had attacked the original. (2013)

The name, Colneford Hill, must be ancient indeed as there has been a bridge at its bottom on and off since 1155. The early wooden bridges often fell into disrepair leaving travellers no option but to wade through the adjacent ford. Even the stone and brick bridge built by the Earl of Oxford 1560 was allowed to fall into disrepair while disputes over maintenance lingered on. By 1825 the river was crossed by yet another wooden bridge. This was adopted by the Essex Turnpike Trust who widened it in 1833 before it was taken over by the county in 1860. This, the last wooden Colneford Bridge, was replaced by a stronger and wider concrete structure in 1909. The strength of the new bridge was demonstrated at its opening by allowing two steam rollers, with a combined weight of 24 tons, to drive, abreast of each other, across the bridge. This structure coped with the ever-increasing A604 (now A1124) traffic until 1995 when it was replaced with the existing pre-stressed concrete bridge and for the first time, provision for fording the river was removed.

The last wooden Colneford Bridge was not strong enough to take heavy carts or early motor vehicles, these had to use the adjacent ford. (c1900)

The new Colneford Bridge being tested by the simultaneous crossing of two steam rollers. (1909)

The Colne Valley Path continues along the river by way of a concrete access road. From here, looking across the river there is nothing but greenery, but this is the site of the former Colneford Mill. This was probably the site of one of the two Earls Colne mills recorded in Domesday and became the property of Colne Priory at its foundation and descended with the priory manor thereafter. The mill

The 1995 Colneford Bridge. (2012)

was rebuilt in the early 17th century as a double mill for both corn and fulling, then in the 18th century this building was replaced by a new, three storied structure with three pairs of stones worked by a large diameter undershot wheel. During the 19th century, when many mills were kept viable by the installation of steam engines, the priory mill languished because the owners of the neighbouring Colne Priory House would not allow a steam engine to be installed so close to their house. This probably contributed to the mill's early demise around the beginning of the 20th century.

The priory was founded in 12th century by Aubrey De Vere, the friend and brother-in-law of William the Conqueror. The DeVeres were a powerful family for hundreds of years and became the Earls of Oxford. At the Dissolution the priory passed into private hands, the hands of the De Veres, who converted parts of the priory building into a grand mansion. The present house, which contains many features and materials from the earlier building, was built in 1825 to the west of the earlier building. At one time this new house contained the elaborate monuments to the De Veres that survived from the destruction of the family mausoleum at the Dissolution. They have since been removed to St Edmund's chapel at Bures. But there is still much about the village, apart from its name, to associate it with the family. The family emblem of the five-pointed star, or mullet, is seen on many buildings including around the top of the church tower.

The church of St Andrew stands on higher ground and is thought to be built on a Saxon site. There are no Saxon remains in the present church whose most outstanding feature is its 16th century embattled tower. A notable vicar of Earls Colne was Ralph Josselin, not so much for his achievements but for the fact that he kept a detailed diary that provides us with a window into the world of the mid 17th century.

The Reverend Ralph Josselin became the Vicar of Earls Colne in 1640 and, from then until his death in 1683, he kept a daily record of events in the village and beyond. The ordinary and mundane is enlivened every now and again with such events as the arrival in the village of a troop of Royalist soldiers during the civil war.

> June 1648
> On Monday morning the enemy came to Colne, were resisted by our townsmen. No part of Essex gave them so much opposition as we did. They plundered us and me in particular of all that was portable, except brass, pewter and bedding.

On many days the diary records the weather and when it is read, you realise that our so-called extreme weather events are nothing new. 1648 seems to have been a particularly wet year and in 1661 gales swept the country.

> June – August 1648
> The summer was wonderfully wet; floods every week, hay rotted and much was carried away with the floods, much ruined and very dirty, and dangerous for cattle; we never had the like in my memory. It continued to August, and commonly we had floods weekly, or indeed in the meadows there was a continuous flood. A very great flood with the great rains last day & night. Continual rain spoiling much grass, and threatening of the harvest.

> February 1661
> In the night it rained, the wind rose and was violent beyond measure, overturning a windmill at Colchester, wherein a youth killed. Diverse barns, stables, outhouses, trees, and divers dwellings were rent apart. Few escaped loss; chimney stacks were thrown down and Lady Saltonstall was killed in her bed, by her house falling. Some orchards were almost ruined with 27 trees blown down within priory wall.

Inclement weather did not always quell the vicar's zeal for preaching, which must have been doubly disheartening for his parishioners who would have had to endure such marathons as he describes for one day in November 1646;

> It was wet in the morning, so we did not go to church until eleven and I continued preaching until the sun was set.

Perhaps it is not surprising that the new Quaker meetings in the village became more and more popular. The original Quaker Meeting House, dating from Ralph Josselin's time still stands and is now the oldest in the county.

Ralph Josselin 1616-1683

Earls Colne Quaker Meeting House, the oldest in Essex was built in 1674, originally a redbrick square box with a pyramidal tiled roof befitting the unpretentious Quaker philosophy. The building was considerably altered in 1986 when a new annexe was added. (2013)

St Andrew's Church, Earls Colne with a frieze of DeVere mullets in knapped flint around the top of the fine 16th century tower. (2013)

My walk was now taking me along the trackbed of the former CV&HR. I soon arrived at a small bridge over the diminutive tributary, the Peb. This small stream rises above Pebmarsh and in earlier times its waters powered two mills before tumbling into the Colne. The first of these is visible from the old railway and has been known as Overshot Mill since the beginning of the 20th century. The original mill on this site was a fulling mill built around 1640 when the Peb was diverted into the newly dug millpond providing a 17ft (5.1m) head of water. Around 1790 the mill

Two children watching a CV&HR train cross the Peb. (1949)   *The present bridge across the Peb is made from old sleepers resting on the original abutments. (2012)*

was rebuilt as a four-story corn mill powered by a 12ft (3.6m) diameter overshot wooden wheel. Sometime later, a larger 16ft (4.8m) iron wheel was installed. This may have increased the efficiency of the mill while it was working, but it was too large for the millpond, which could only drive it for a limited time, and too powerful for the mill structure which suffered a daily shaking. At the time of the demise of many country mills during the early 20th century, it was fortunate that Overshot Mill and the adjoining farm were acquired by the Marsh family who were the mill's custodians for three generations. From very early on, the mill was used for the production of domestic electricity as well as for grinding animal feed for the family's livestock. It was also used for grinding a mixture of homegrown grains to produce a range of products, including cereals and biscuits, that were marketed to the local population as a preventative of rickets. A health food before the term had been invented! This wholefood business prospered until 1944, and then during the 1960s the family converted the mill into a home. All the mill machinery was kept in situ but the waterwheel was removed and replaced by a turbine, which was used to drive a 4 kW alternator to provide domestic electricity.

Overshot Mill in its working days. (c1900)

*Since the 1960s Colne Engaine's Overshot Mill has been
an attractive private residence. (2013)*

Overshot Mill was not the only mill on the Peb to bring innovation to the Colne Valley; further upstream in the village of Pebmarsh stood the brook's other mill. In 1798, this village corn mill was where George Courtauld set up the county's first silk throwing mill, and so began the long association of the Courtauld family with the Colne Valley. Within a few years the family's activities had expanded into other locations, including the nearby town of Halstead a little further up the Colne. I will detail the growth of the fortunes of the company when I get there in the next chapter. But for now, back in Pebmarsh, the village mill continued as a throwing mill employing up to 95 people. The water power of the Peb was supplemented by a steam engine in the later years before finally closing in 1883. A few years later the mill and mill house was bought by George's grandson who demolished the mill and extended the house, which still stands today.

Back at the old railway bridge, where the Peb is nearing its confluence with the Colne, I wandered off across the meadow to the riverbank. The meadow is one of several that go to make up an 'open access area' that has been established along the banks of the river. These meadows are managed under the Countryside Stewardship Scheme in an environmentally friendly way, with no fertilisers, limited grazing and in these particular meadows the grass is allowed to grow to be cut for hay. On the June day when I arrived here I had made good progress on my walk along the Colne Valley Path and although it was really too early for lunch, it was in my mind that I should linger here for a while. I soon found myself a spot in this riverside meadow that epitomised the idyllic view we have of summertime in England. I sat in the grass, unpacked my sandwiches and poured a coffee from my flask. The tall grass lazily moved in the imperceptible breeze accompanied by the hum of myriads of invisible insects, all under a cloudless blue sky. It was difficult to leave but I still had a fair way to go and today was not for rushing.

At the end of the meadow the CV&HR crossed the Colne by an iron girder bridge. The iron was removed soon after the closure of the line but the crumbling brick abutments remain. Across the river are the neatly manicured greens and fairways of the Colne Valley Golf Club, whose re-profiling of the terrain has removed all trace of the course of the former line. As my path left the trackbed on this side of the river it plunged into an overgrown thicket, before following the riverbank through another open access meadow.

The flow of the river here is impeded by another weir and associated gauging station, similar to the one we encountered by the seven arch viaduct in Colchester. A little further upstream the path leaves the riverside and after passing a small wood emerges on to the minor road connecting Earls Colne to Colne Engaine. Before I continued along the river I explored what lies along this road. To the left, the river is bridged by a modern steel reinforced concrete bridge with steel railings. It is not known when the first bridge was built at this Colne crossing. A ford was referred to in 1612 and again in 1876, and land was acquired for a bridge in 1873. It seems likely that the demand for a bridge may have coincided with the opening of the nearby railway station in 1862. As mentioned earlier a new station on this site was financed by R Hunt & Co. whose premises were just up the hill in Foundry Lane.

Station Road Bridge. (2013)

Robert Hunt, a travelling millwright, from Cambridgeshire came to Earls Colne in 1824. Here he met and married Mary Ann Rogers and set up a millwright's business. In 1855, Reuben, one of his five sons took over the business and developed it into a major exporting company with customers all over the world.

The firm's Atlas Works expanded as Reuben developed products for the expanding farm machinery market. The company's products included rollers, harrows and hay rakes, as well as the hand operated grinding and cutting mills, which had been the firm's original stock-in-trade.

Ford Gate station opened in 1862 on the site of the later Earls Colne station. (1903)

The new Earls Colne station. (1906)

Earls Colne station before it closed in (1965).

After the railway closed the station yard and buildings were developed as industrial units. (2013)

'Atlas' has come to mean any collection of maps, a long way from the mythological Greek deity who held up the celestial sphere. He is commonly used in western culture as a symbol of strength and stoic endurance, an image that Reuben Hunt thought fitting for his engineering enterprise at Earls Colne. (2012)

Reuben Hunt 1836-1927, a short stocky man with hazel eyes that missed very little.

The company prospered and by 1915 was employing nearly 300 people in its, now extensive, Atlas works. This success was due to the high standard of workmanship of its products and this could only be achieved by a dedicated workforce. Reuben realised this and kept many of his employees for life by providing them with high quality housing and social facilities. The company's first houses were built in 1872 and by 1915 the firm had provided 120 new houses for its employees. Despite all his philanthropic works, Reuben could not have been the easiest person to work for, if the following description by Patricia Burton-Hopkins, in her book about the Hunt family enterprise, is anything to go by:

'Reuben Hunt was not anything remarkable to look at, a short stocky man with enormous hands. However he had hazel eyes that seemed to miss very little, and he was a man who liked having his own way very well indeed, and with a devil of a temper if thwarted in his endeavours. A captain of industry and a useful public figure, he believed in the rights of men such as himself to pay their employees as little as possible although unlike some he was always concerned about their welfare. Reuben worked hard and through his own enterprise inspired others to achieve their potential.'

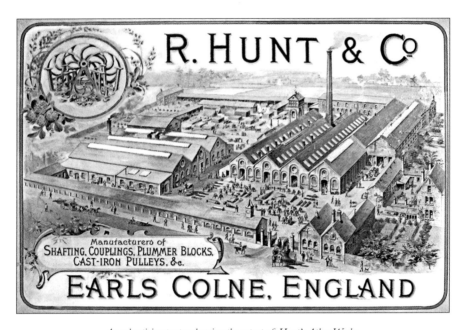

An advertising poster showing the extent of Hunt's Atlas Works.

Following the death of Reuben in 1927 the firm was run by other members of the family until 1983 when it was sold to Christy's of Chelmsford who closed the Earls Colne site a few years later. The loss of the Atlas works was a bitter blow to its employees, but the name of R Hunt & Co will be forever associated with the village.

It is now time to return to the river, but before proceeding further along the Colne Valley Path I made a slight diversion up the hill into the village of Colne Engaine, whose hilltop position is dominated by the church of St Andrew. This site has been inhabited since Roman times indicated by the substantial amount of reused Roman brick used in the 12th century nave walls. The church also has a fine Tudor brick tower and an impressive crow-stepped porch with a niche from which a small statue of St Andrew looks over the valley and the neighbouring *Five Bells*.

273

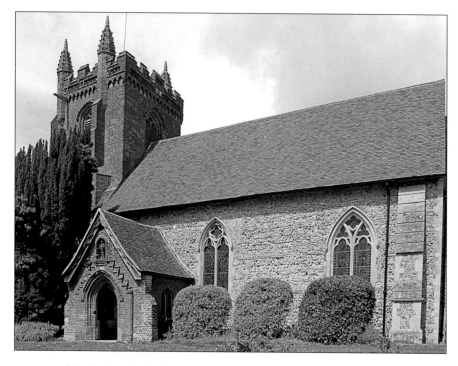

Colne Engaine church of St Andrew with his statue looking across the valley. (2012)

It is in the village pubs that I often pick up interesting local stories and then spend weeks trying to unearth their origins, often to find that they are based on a relatively ordinary event that has been made into a good story by numerous embellishments in the telling. When I dropped into the *Five Bells* to refresh myself for the rest of my journey, I did not overhear any such stories but I did find on the bar, a couple of books published by the local history society that contained a wealth of information about the village. I will briefly mention a couple of items that took my eye.

The first concerns the towering monument in Colne Park in the east of the parish. This stands in what was Shrives manor, which was bought by Michael Hills in 1762, inherited by his son, also Michael, who died a bachelor, bequeathing the manor to his young friend Philip Astle providing that he took the name of Hills. This he did, and to honour the memory of his benefactor he commissioned the eminent Neo-Classical architect, John Soane, to design a monument. The great classical column still stands, visible between the trees from nearby lanes and paths.

More recently, on an August day in 1940 there was commotion in the air over the village as a Heinkel 111 bomber was shot down by an RAF Huricane. The stricken plane crash-landed in the north of the parish at Peverel's farm with one crew member dead, three wounded and one unharmed. After token resistance by the single uninjured German, the survivors were soon taken prisoner.

I left the pub, walked down the hill and resumed my travels along the Colne Valley Path that continues by following the river along Elms Hall Road. A short distance along here is a track that leads to the site of a Colne Engaine mill. Very little is known about this mill but it was recorded in 1599 and was later known as Ford Mill. More recently it was called White's Mill after the

Colne Park Monument stands 70ft 5in (21m) high and is surmounted by an 8ft (2.4m) copper vase, erected in 1791 to a design by the eminent Neo-Classical architect, John Soane. (1937)

A Heinkel 111 crash-landed in Colne Engaine on 30 August 1940. Many people went to view the plane during the week or so before it was removed and over £100 was raised from them for the local 'Fighter Fund'.

last miller who ceased working it shortly before it was demolished in 1917. Now, only the 16th century mill house remains as a reminder of the former mill's existence.

Past the driveway to the mill house, a path continues on to the embankment of the former CV&HR and the site of the bridge that brought the railway back to the north side of the river. This was the only bridge to survive for any length of time after the closure of the line; all of the others went for scrap when the line was dismantled. Then in 1980 this sole surviving CV&HR steel bridge was relocated to the Colne Valley Railway (CVR) heritage railway based further along the valley in Hedingham. A light steel girder footbridge used for occasional access to a Water Authority facility now occupies its place in Colne Engaine.

276

White's Mill, Colne Engaine, formerly known as Ford Mill. (c1903)

Ford Mill stood immediately to the left of the remaining 16ᵗʰ century mill house. (2012)

In 1980 the last surviving CV&HR bridge across the Colne was replaced by this footbridge. (2012)

Just above the site of this bridge the Colne is joined by its second longest tributary; this is also the second of its tributaries to bear the name Bourne Brook. This rises in Wethersfield and by the time it reaches the Colne has flowed nearly ten miles, on its way passing through the expanse of Gosfield Lake. This was made by damming the stream after Louis XVIII had said, whilst staying at Gosfield Hall, that some water would improve the landscape. Below Gosfield the Bourne meanders its way to Greenstead Green where a mill stood until 1874. This former fulling mill spent the last fifty years of its life as the only water powered paper mill in the Colne Valley.

You may recall that fulling mills were used to bond the fibres of newly woven cloth by pounding the wet material with large wooden hammers.

These were attached to arms that were raised and lowered by cams driven by the mill. Excessive hammering would cause the cloth to fall to pieces; and it was this process that was used during the 18th century to break up rags into fibres to be used for making paper.

Papermaking was practiced by the Chinese as early as the 2nd century BC but it took over a thousand years to reach Europe and the industry was not established in England until the late 16th century. The early mills used woollen rags to make brown paper and it was not until the late 17th century that French and Dutch papermakers came to England with the art of white papermaking using cotton rags.

When Greenstead Mill was converted into a paper mill in 1823 it was probably installed with machines called Hollanders. These machines were more efficient than the earlier water-powered hammers at macerating the rags. Each machine consisted of an oval trough in which a mixture of rags and water was churned and pulped by an iron roller with projecting blades. The resulting pulp, called 'stuff', was transferred to a vat where it was kept agitated.

The vatman used a shallow wooden frame, with a bottom made from a fine wire mesh, to dip into the vat to remove a layer of fibres. Sometimes a fine wire pattern was attached to the mesh; this caused a permanent impression in the fibres resulting in what is known as a watermark. When the water had drained away, the wet sheet of paper was turned over onto a sheet of felt by another workman, called a coucher, who built up a stack of sheets of paper interleaved with felt. This was then placed in a press and the remaining water squeezed out. The sheets of paper were then hung on long ropes in the drying room before being pressed and polished in the finishing room.

The mill at Greenstead Green prospered for a number of years and then, shortly before it was demolished, the paper making equipment and an eight horsepower steam engine were moved to Halstead where Alfred Potter continued to produce about 20 tons of paper per week for another fifteen years. By which time papermaking machines had been developed that could use wood pulp to produce continuous rolls of paper, which rendered small paper mills uneconomic, forcing them to close down.

An 18th century engraving showing a vatman on the right dipping a wooden frame into the stuff, on the left is a coucher laying a sheet of felt on to a pile of paper.

Below Greenstead Green, Bourne Brook flows in a steep-sided valley to its confluence with the Colne at Ford Mill. From here I continued my journey along Elms Hall Road and, within half a mile, arrived at Langley Mill. This small country mill was converted into a rural residence in 1975. Its history of being a fulling mill, then a corn mill, is unremarkable, but its last miller George Hart was something exceptional. He took over the running of the mill after the death of his father in 1948. He fitted new paddles to the waterwheel and was skilled at dressing the stones, but found that driving them from a tractor more reliable than using the intermittent flow of the Colne. In 1969 he abandoned the watermill and established his business in an industrial unit on the Earls Colne Station industrial site where he continued to grind grain for local farmers with his diesel-powered mill. A traditional miller at heart, who was prepared to change the rumble of the waterwheel for the thump of an engine, to keep doing what he loved most.

By Langley Mill the road crosses the Colne near where the CV&HR crossed the road by a level crossing whose precise location can be identified by the kink and rise in the road. The old trackbed is now a private drive but the Colne Valley Path continues between it and the mill into our next parish, Halstead.

Langley Mill Bridge, dating from the early 20th century, has brick abutments, a concrete deck supported on steel beams, and later balustrade of timber posts and steel rails. (2013)

Langley Mill in its working days. (c1900)

In 1975 Langley Mill was converted for residential use. (2013)

CHAPTER XIII

Halstead

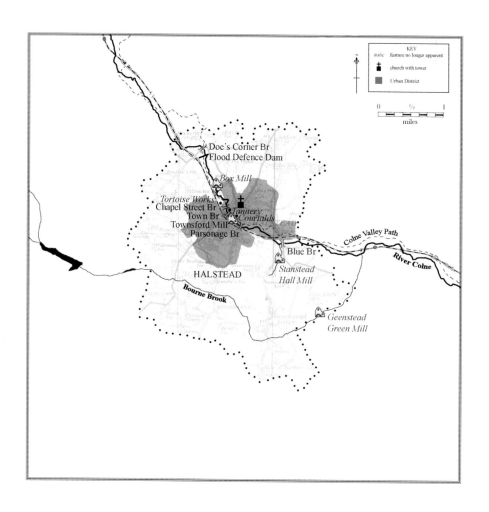

Halstead

Halstead is Old English for 'the settlement on the valley-slope' from 'heald', the side of a valley, and 'stede', a settlement. This was probably centred close by the site of St Andrew's Church and the clear water stream that ran down the hill, later to become the High Street.

The Domesday Book records 3 mills in the Halstead area, it is likely that one was on the site of the Townford Mill, another where the later Box Mill stood, and the third could have been Langley Mill, now outside the town.

In 1848 White described Halstead as a neat but irregularly built market town pleasantly situated on both sides of the valley of the river Colne. The town rises picturesquely on the opposite acclivities of the valley, and has three large silk and crepe factories, belonging to Messrs Courtauld & Co who employ about a thousand hands. The population had risen to 5,710, and the parish extended over 5,425 acres.

By 2011 the population had risen to 11,000 but boundary changes had reduced the area to 1,232 acres.

I approached Halstead along the Colne Valley Path that follows the line of the CV&HR as far as the Blue Bridge Industrial Estate. This complex was built in the 1960s, since when the many and varied industries using this site have provided the townspeople with employment opportunities that were lost with the closure of the older town centre factories. The official route of the Colne Valley Path passes through this industrial estate but, as I approached, I noticed a well-trodden path along the edge of the meadow that separates the industrial units from the river. I chose the meadow route and was soon by the river where it is crossed by the major road that runs between Colchester and Halstead, now the A1124, but still referred to by those of an older generation as 'the 604'. I clambered over a gate onto the road and stood on Blue Bridge where I gazed into the shallow water below.

This crossing was originally a ford beside which there have been many bridges. These have been known by several names; Ashforde Bridge after a family who owned a nearby farm, Coggeshall Bridge after the owners of the

Children playing in the shallow waters below Blue Bridge. (c1900)

ancient house part way up the hill, and most recently Blue Bridge. It has been claimed that this name is a corruption of 'Below Bridge' as it is situated below the town, both downhill by road and downstream by the Colne. Strange as it may seem, a more likely derivation is to do with a local butcher, John Morley, who bought the old timber framed house part way up the hill in 1712. Within two years he had built a fine brick mansion with the Arms of the Worshipful Company of Butchers and his name, cut in stone over the entrance porch. He was not one to forget the trade that had enabled him to rise from humble beginnings to owning a butchers shop in the High Street and on to making a fortune buying and selling land to provide the capital for his prestigious new house. With the acquisition of this property came the responsibility of maintaining the bridge; this he did and for the first time it was painted blue. So, of course it soon became known as the Blue Bridge. In 1845 Morley's first bridge was replaced by a new wooden bridge paid for by the Turnpike trust that was then responsible for maintaining the road between Colchester and Halstead. And this was painted blue as was its successor. The bridge was still being painted a colour befitting its name into the 1920s when, following a series of accidents white posts were installed to improve its visibility to the increasing number of night time motorists. It has since been replaced several times and now, sadly, the only trace of blue is in its name.

Blue Bridge is now crossed by the busy A1124. It is no longer a suitable place for children to play. (2013)

Blue Bridge with John Morley's early 18th century Blue Bridge House beyond. (2013)

John Morley's imposing early 18th century house with his name and the arms of the Worshipful Company of Butchers above the entrance. (2013)

Close by Blue Bridge the Colne is joined by a small, almost unnoticed, tributary. This rises no more than half-a-mile away in the grounds of Stanstead Hall and enters the Colne via a culvert that takes it under the road from Greenstead Green. In the mid 17th century this diminutive stream filled a large lake, the water from which powered an overshot mill. Both mill and lake have long since disappeared. They are not even shown on Chapman & André's map of 1717.

From Blue Bridge there is a choice of footpaths that lead on into the town. I chose to cross the road and continue along the one that heads across the water meadows to the south of the river. This soon rejoins the course of the CV&HR to emerge near the foot of Tidings Hill close by the town's next river bridge, Parsonage Street Bridge. The alternative route to this bridge is along the north bank of the river. This path has been improved recently as part of the new Nether Court Public Open Space. This extends along most of the length of the river between the two bridges and was created along with a housing development on adjoining land. The riverside open space is managed so as to create many diverse habitats for wildlife that both residents and visitors can enjoy all year round.

The riverside walk through Halstead's Nether Court Public Open Space.
The path was resurfaced in 2012 to a standard suitable for wheelchair users. (2013)

Parsonage Street Bridge is situated at an ancient crossing place and in the early 18th century the historian, William Holman, refers to there being a bridge here. The earliest picture of a bridge dates from the early years of the 20th century. This shows a fine double arch brick structure, but is clearly suffering structural problems, probably caused by the excessive loads transported across it by a local timber merchant. By 1909, despite having been reinforced with four iron tie rods, the ancient bridge was virtually rebuilt, but the double arches were retained. Then about half a century later the whole bridge was replaced by the present single span, pre-stressed concrete structure.

The reinforced two-arch, brick-built Parsonage Street Bridge. (pre1909)

Parsonage Bridge after rebuilding. (1950s)

Parsonage Street Bridge of pre-stressed concrete rebuilt in the 1960s. (2013)

The 1986 Mill Bridge with Townford Mill just visible through the trees. (2013)

From here on, into the town, factory sites surround the riverside. I continued to follow the river by proceeding along Factory Lane West and was soon at the next bridge, Mill Bridge. This was built to provide access to the new development of houses, shops and car parks that were built following the demolition of the vast Courtauld mill complex in 1986.

A little further along the river is the white weatherboarded Townford Mill where Samuel Courtauld set up his first enterprise in the town. This ancient mill site has a long history stretching back to Saxon times. For hundreds of years this and the town's other mill, less than half a mile upstream, worked in relative harmony; then in the 1780s both were rebuilt and both tried to take more from the river than it could provide. After some initial disagreements the mill owners came to a compromise and both agreed to work their new mills below full potential for their mutual benefit. This gentlemens' agreement worked well until Samuel Courtauld came on the scene and installed a new waterwheel in his newly acquired Townford Mill. For this to work efficiently the town's other mill was choked and could only run for half of its previous number of hours. Courtauld needed all the power he could get from his mill and would not compromise. This led to a protracted legal dispute that ended with a judgement against Courtauld who then installed a steam engine. A situation that did not please him at all; not only had he to suffer the ignominy of losing the case but also had the ongoing expense of running his new machine, which he described as 'a terrible coal eater'.

Samuel Courtauld was the son of the George Courtauld who had set up the silk throwing mill at Pebmarsh. Since those early days the Courtaulds had acquired mills in Braintree and Bocking but it was at the Halstead mill where the business really took off.

Samuel Courtauld 1793-1881

The Townford Mill's steam plant was installed in 1827 and by 1850 the firm were employing over a thousand workers, transforming raw silk into finished fabric. The first stage of production, called throwing, involved a number of processes. First, the raw silk was released from the silk moth cocoon; this very fine and delicate fibre was then reeled, cleaned, twisted and doubled into a usable thread. The whole process involved about a dozen steps, many of which required the use of machines, which were housed on the first and second floors of the mill. The prepared yarn was then taken to the ground floor where some 500 women, each working at a power loom, transformed it into finished fabric. Very soon the firm was making a fortune and became the foremost British producer of black mourning crepe, a material that had become fashionable for middle and upper class Englishwomen to wear after the death of a relative.

Like many successful 19th century industrialists, Samuel Courtauld was a man of strong personality and drive. He was a religious man who believed in the virtues of hard work and high moral standards, not only for himself but also for his employees. He had a strong social conscious and favoured social reform, but on his own terms. He opposed the 1833 Factory Act, arguing that: *'Legislative interference in the arrangement and conduct of business is always injurious, tending to check improvement and to increase the cost of production.'* With a workforce of less than 10% men, his reforming zeal stopped short of anything that would prevent him from paying his workers more than was necessary to keep them. In 1838 he was paying adult males 7s. 2d. (36p) a week, women less than 5s. (25p) and girls under eleven only 1s. 5d. (7p). The firm may not have paid their employees very well, but it did provide them with opportunities for self-improvement, all be it under the control of the company. During the 1850s Samuel Courtauld organised a school, adult education classes, a library and institute, nursery, mothers club, sick fund, amusement society, and a lodging house for workers from outlying districts. He also provided many of his workers with good quality houses, many of which still stand today.

After Samuel's death in 1881 the company went into a short decline, but his successors diversified and in 1904 made a move that was to secure the firm's future for many years to come. They purchased the British patent rights for the new viscose process for making artificial silk or rayon, a fibre produced by chemically treating wood pulp. Within a few years Courtaulds were producing 40% of the world's rayon and the company soon become an industrial giant that flourished into the 1970s with the Halstead factory expanding to cover a vast area and becoming the town's major employer. There then followed another decline, this time the combination of a world recession and increased foreign competition led to closure of the Halstead site in 1982.

Throughout its long association with the town, the company continued to uphold its founder's principles and built many more houses, as well as funding a wide range of civic amenities including a school, the Public Baths, the Public Gardens and the Cottage Hospital.

From the mill it is easy to see the Town Bridge, anciently called Town Ford Bridge because it is built near the site of the town ford from which the mill takes its name. Until sometime in the late medieval period the river here was quite shallow making it easy to ford. Then the mill was rebuilt and the

Townford Mill, the former Courtaulds steam plant is now the Blacksmiths Tearoom and the attached mill house, formerly the Mill Manager's residence, is now the Town Council Offices. (2012)

The Courtaulds factory was closed in 1982 and demolished in 1986, now the site consists of shops, houses, supermarket and car park.

miller stopped more water and a new bridge was erected. This was on the mill side of the ford and this repositioning of the crossing place meant that the bottom of the High Street acquired a curve, which it still has today. Every time that the mill was rebuilt the water became deeper; what with this and the increasing amount of traffic, the bridge was rebuilt or widened several times. In 1846 the wooden structure had become so dilapidated that it was replaced by the town's first brick bridge. This new single arch bridge was later widened twice and then lengthened with the addition of a second arch. But then, in 1912, another completely new bridge was erected. Despite the many and various modifications and even a complete rebuild in 1980, some features of the 1912 bridge survive in the present structure.

One of the most attractive views of Halstead is from the bridge looking along the Causeway to Townford Mill. The names Causeway and Townford provide a clue to how this scene would have looked before the mill was rebuilt in 1780s. In medieval times the Causeway would have been a narrow, raised walkway across a marshy area by the river. As rubbish from the dwellings up

The first brick Town Bridge, built in 1846, originally a single arch with a brick parapet, later a second arch was added, then iron balustrades were erected as shown here. (1897)

This new Town Bridge was built in 1912,
the misalignment of the High Street with the bridge is clearly seen in this photograph. (c1914)

The present Town Bridge was built in 1980
with many of the features of the earlier balustrade incorporated into its design. (2013)

The Causeway with the houses built in 1886 by Samuel Courtauld for his mill overseers and mechanics. (c1900)

The Causeway looks much the same today, but behind the façade the mill is now a restaurant and antiques centre. (2012)

296

the hill accumulated in the marsh, it slowly became dry enough for humble dwellings to be erected. Eventually the whole area became covered with tightly packed cottages and the Causeway remained a low riverside path. Towards the end of the 19th century the whole area was transformed by Samuel Courtauld who demolished the tumbledown dwellings and replaced them with a smart new row of houses along the length of a newly raised Causeway.

Courtauld was also responsible for major changes on the other bank of the river. Until he built his factory here, this had been the site of the tannery, one of Halstead's oldest industries. Established by the river in 1573 the successful business moved a little further upstream to Chapel Street where it continued to thrive into the 1950s. In its later years the tannery's hides arrived by train, some from as far away as Argentina, but its oak bark was obtained locally. The combination of Colne water and Essex oak used in the Halstead tannery ensured that their products were much sought after and sold world-wide to make high-class boots, shoes and other leather goods.

Traditional tanning is a smelly industry. Animal skins, often with traces of meat and sometimes maggots, are first soaked in lime pits for several weeks. The hides are then transferred to tanning pits containing a mixture of oak bark and water. Here they remain for months before being removed for scraping and drying. The prepared leather is then ready for the finishing processes of hardening and polishing.

From the Town Bridge I wandered along Bridge Street and was soon at the site of the former railway station. This was the headquarters of the CV&HR and as well as passenger facilities, had extensive sidings where a wide range of goods could be handled. The station operated for very nearly a hundred years, during which time it allowed many of the town's industries to grow and prosper. It opened in 1862 and was closed 1961 to be demolished six years later.

On the other side of the Town Bridge is the High Street. Any High Street is important to its town but Halstead owes its very existence to its High Street. For many centuries this was the course of a clear, fast flowing stream, then in the mid 19th century it suffered the ignominy of being piped underground.

On the banks of the Colne, the Tan Yard, Chapel Street. (1950s)

Inside the Halstead Tannery. The lime and tanning pits, seen in the floor, were 4-5ft (1.2-1.5m) deep, convenient for any worker to climb out of if he happened to slip in. The drying and finishing processes were performed on the floor above. (1950s)

*The earliest photograph of Halstead station, a steam engine
with mixed passenger and goods rolling stock waiting to leave. (1870s)*

*Halstead station and sidings that were vital
for the town economy for nearly a hundred years. (c1950)*

The broad High Street and the extent of medieval Halstead before the railway and the influx of people that the 19ᵗʰ century industries brought to the town. (1750)

Today it remains hidden beneath the High Street to flow, via a conduit into the Colne underneath the Town Bridge.

I have mentioned one of the High Street's former eminent residents before, namely John Morley, the local butcher who made good. Another who achieved considerable notoriety was the ironmonger, Charles Portway, who occupied a shop with an adjoining warehouse. This was bitterly cold in winter so Charles set about designing a stove to heat his premises. Within a short time he had designed and built a compact iron stove, which soon became the envy of his friends and neighbours. Seeing the potential of his invention, Charles went into production and as demand continued to grow he bought the former Halstead Iron Works premises close by the railway and opened the Tortoise Works. 'Slow but Sure' was the motto of the efficient little stove that was produced in its thousands for nigh on a hundred years to heat innumerable workshops, halls, churches, barracks and WWII Nissen huts. The site of the factory is now a car park, but it does contain a monument to Charles Portway & Son Ltd who were major employers in the town and whose products have warmed many a soul the world over.

At the top of the High Street is St Andrew's Church built on the site where the ancient route along the valley crossed the clear water of the brook that flowed down the hill to the Colne. It could well have been a place of religious significance to the pre-Christian inhabitants of the area. The church's dedication to St Andrew may indicate that the early Christians arrived here by following the routes of earlier invaders, into the heart of the county, by following the Colne. You may not have noticed just how many churches along the Colne Valley have been dedicated to St Andrew; I certainly had not until it came to listing them. This set me wondering as to why this should be. Although St Andrew is a popular saint he only ranks 5th in popularity in English churches as a whole, but along the Colne he is the out and out leader, with almost twice the number of dedications of his nearest rivals. Jim Kimmis, in his book of Essex church dedications, suggests that this may be because St. Andrew was regarded with special favour by the early missionaries from the Celtic sanctuaries of Iona and Lindisfarne. It was a monk of the latter place, St Cedd, who spread the gospel into Essex during the 7th century, and it may be that the St Andrew's churches along the Colne Valley received their dedications at this time. If this is so then this would indicate that, in those times, movement along the valley was important in bringing new peoples and ideas to the region.

Charles Portway (1828 -1909)

Portway's trademark and the Tortoise Stove that remained virtually unchanged throughout its 120 years of production.

THE COLNE

Although it is almost certain that a Saxon church stood here, the oldest parts of the present building date back to the 14th and 15th centuries. And there has been much rebuilding since; during the 18th century the spire was struck by lightning twice, being replaced each time. This was before Benjamin Franklin developed an understanding of atmospheric electricity and invented the lightning conductor. This proved to be a far more effective way of protecting tall buildings than by prayer alone. But the problems of St Andrew's were not over; in the 19th century the west tower collapsed. Whatever the cause, an act of God, subsidence or structural weakness, the tower was not rebuilt but a new tower was erected to the west of the old one, and this one is still standing.

I had enjoyed my walk from Colchester to Halstead but now as the evening was drawing in I decided to seek out a place to stay. Conveniently

St Andrew's Church, Halstead, parts of which date from the 14th century, but its commanding tower is a Victorian addition. (2013)

situated near the Town Bridge is the *Bull*. The deceptively regular façade of this historic building conceals a maze of rambling bars with many nooks and crannies. I enjoyed a pint of IPA and indulged in idle chatter at the bar with a few others, some of whom had walked to the hostelry but none further than a few hundred yards and no one was aware of the Colne Valley Path let alone where it went. I then went up to my room, past more nooks and crannies; these with the uneven floors and sloping walls made the real age of this building apparent. People had been sleeping in my room since 1398 and I'm sure the walls have a tale or two to tell. I had unpacked my rucksack in a jiff, but took longer in the shower where the detritus of the day was washed away. Newly invigorated I returned to the bar where I partook of an excellent meal of mushroom pappardelle pasta, followed by Bramley apple pie served with warm custard. I did not find anyone with whom to share my interest in the minutiae of local history, so I joined the happy crowd and watched the football on the plasma telly. It was quite late when I retired to my room and even later when I went to bed. All buildings talk in the small hours, but timber framed ones positively chatter as the central heating cools and ancient beams relax in their tired joints. None of this kept me awake, and it was eight o'clock before I was down for breakfast and gone nine before I was back on the Colne Valley Path.

I crossed the Town Bridge and followed the path through Oak Yard to the Sainsbury's car park where there is a footbridge across the river. This is not far from the position of what was probably the earliest bridge across the Colne in Halstead. Looking over the footbridge today there is no trace of the ancient bridge, but surprisingly, it could still be there. In 1969, during the demolition of a riverside building, the river was drained to allow the bank to be reinforced. Under the silt in the riverbed, workmen discovered the preserved remains of a packhorse bridge.

Until wheeled transport became commonplace, goods were carried overland by packhorse. When the routes followed by these animals crossed rivers, bridges were built. A typical packhorse bridge was stronger, but no wider, than a pedestrian bridge and if there was a parapet at all, it was low, so as not to obstruct the panniers, in which the animals carried their load. Most of these bridges have been replaced by later bridges, but where the packhorse route became abandoned or, as in the case of Halstead, the river crossing place was relocated rare examples remain.

In Halstead, when the riverside work was completed, the bridge was reburied in the silt where it remains to this day. The fact that this find was well below the present riverbed shows that the water level has risen considerably since medieval times when this packhorse bridge crossed the river by the town ford.

The footbridge between Bridge Street and Sainsbury's car park. A little downstream from here is the submerged packhorse bridge that once crossed the river by the medieval town ford. (2013)

The Paper Mill and bridge. (1880s)

I followed the riverside path along the riverbank beside this deepened stretch of river to Chapel Street Bridge. This is close to the site of the relocated tannery and also the steam driven paper mill that was moved here from Greenstead Green in the early 1870s. After fifteen years the paper making activity was moved to another location further along the river and the Chapel Street mill was sold. After years of various uses, in the 1980s, the building was converted into a row of dwellings.

I crossed Chapel Street and continued along the river as it left the town and entered an area of unkempt wilderness where many townsfolk enjoy their varied outdoor pursuits. This has long been a popular spot for recreation and even saw winter sports activities during the cold weather of 1947 and 1963.

The old Paper Mill building and bridge. (1964)

The converted Paper Mill building and Paper Mill Bridge, also known as Chapel Street Bridge. Only the balustrade has been changed since the 1960s, the stumps from the earlier one remain in the deck which is no longer suitable for motorised traffic. (2013)

The frozen Colne near Chapel Street Bridge. (1947)

Today there are not many who practice another river related activity enjoyed by their forebears. Here at a particular bend in the river known as Moor's Hole was the town's first bathing place. This was opened in Victorian times when both men and women were allowed to bathe, but at strictly controlled different times. All regulated by the caretaker who also taught youngsters to swim with the aid of a harness attached to a pole. This popular facility attracted thousands of visitors who played in the water or took part in some of the many and varied organised swimming and diving events. This outdoor bathing facility was closed in 1915, just one year after the new indoor baths had been opened near Parsonage Street Bridge.

A short way beyond Moor's Hole the Colne Valley Path leaves the riverside as it crosses the meadow to Box Mill footbridge. From here the view upstream is of the meandering river across wooded meadows, with not an interesting building in sight. Go back just over a hundred years and the view was something completely different. When Morton Mathews, Halstead's local

Halstead Victorians enjoying the old bathing place at Moor's Hole. (c1900)

artist captured the scene in 1882 there was a charming group of buildings straddling the river. The centrepiece was the watermill, with the handsome mill house attached to one side and the other flanked by a post mill.

It is thought that one of the Halstead mills recorded in Domesday was on this site and by 1555 it was recorded as Boxe Mill. The name 'Box' occurs in several place names and is derived from the old English box or boc, which relate to either the box or beech tree. Presumably Box Mill was named because of its association with one or other of these trees. The watermill was rebuilt during the 18th century, 'on the newest principles', enabling its waterwheel to power three pairs of stones for grinding corn into flour. The conveniently adjacent windmill, built in 1775 was also used for grinding corn and must have caught the wind well as it whistled down the valley. That was until 1882 when, during a gale, it caught a little too much, and the whole structure tumbled into the river. Sadly, this was not the only tragedy to befall this site. Six years later, on a more peaceful morning, the

*Box Mills as depicted by Morton Mathews in 1882
with the wooden footbridge across the Colne in the foreground.*

The wooden Box Mill Bridge with a CV&HR train passing by. (pre1908)

All the mill buildings have gone and the wooden footbridge has long since been replaced. (2013)

mill worker, Walter Wicker, arrived at the mill to find his bearded master, George Ruffle, in a sorry state, entangled around the rotating machinery, caught by his facial hair the poor man must have suffered an horrific death. Despite this calamity the mill continued to work until the early 1920s before being demolished in 1926.

Before these horrific disasters, this must have been an enchanting place with its footbridge, watermill, windmill and nearby railway. The wooden bridge was repaired and replaced many times until 1908 when the first iron bridge was built. Traces of this structure can still be seen, integrated within the present steel bridge.

From Box Mill Bridge I continued along the river through the water meadows and soon arrived at the Halstead flood defence installation. This civil engineering project was completed in 2005. It is comprised of an earth embankment, some 20ft (6m) high built across the valley, with an automatic sluice to control the flow of the river into the town. In extreme conditions the farmland above the barrier can be temporarily flooded to protect the town. Until this was built parts of Halstead were flooded every few years; most recently in 1979,1987, 2000 and in 2001 when over 300 properties

The 2005 Halstead flood defence installation. (2013)

were inundated. The new embankment has successfully protected the town to date. It is designed to cope with all but the most extreme situations which are likely to occur only once in every seventy-five years.

When I walked over the meadow above the barrier the river was quietly flowing within its banks. This whole area is used as a rather pleasant picnic site where families can relax while the children play in the summer shallows of the Colne.

The footpath continues to the main road where it emerges near the road bridge, which was rebuilt when the road was realigned in 2005. I crossed the road and, for the first time on my journey, I was forced to make a significant diversion from the riverside. There is a footpath that crosses a field to where

The tranquil waters of the Colne above the Halstead flood defence installation. (2012)

the river was once crossed by the CV&HR, which soon enters the next parish of Great Maplestead. But this was not to be. My progress across the field had been difficult and when the path reached the river there were several signs warning of shooting in the area. Then, in the thicket by the old railway, where I expected a style, I was confronted by an impenetrable tangle of barbed wire. It was then that I decided to return to the road and follow the Colne Valley Path. This follows the driveway to Hepworth Hall, then across several fields to emerge on the Dynes Hall Road. By the time that I had reached this point I had the distinct impression that the landowner was trying to make the use of footpaths across his land as inconvenient as possible. By now I had strayed into the next parish and another chapter of my saga.

Sometimes known as Hepworth Hall Bridge, this pre-stressed concrete bridge, built in 2005 carries the A1124 across the Colne near Doe's Corner. Otters do not like swimming under bridges and are often killed when crossing the road. The board on the right abutment provides a safe route for them to cross under the road. (2012)

Hepworth Hall Bridge looking towards Doe's Corner. (early 1900s)

CHAPTER XIV

Great Maplestead, Sible Hedingham & Castle Hedingham

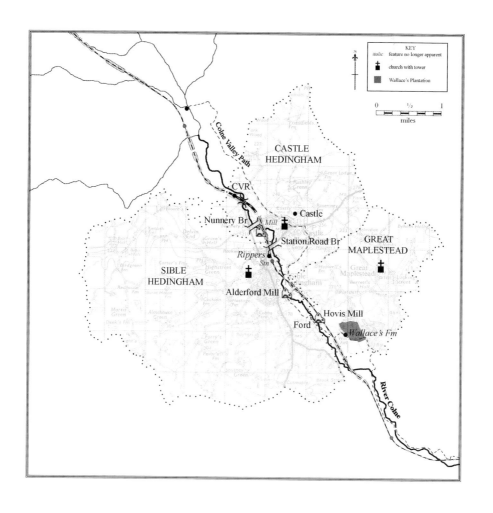

THE COLNE

Great Maplestead, Sible Hedingham and Castle Hedingham

There is no great mystery as to the origin of Maplestead. 'Stead' is from the Old English meaning 'place' or 'settlement'. Simply the 'settlement by the maple trees'.

Hedingham consists of three elements; 'ham' meaning 'settlement' and is the origin of our word 'home', 'ing' which means 'named after', and a persons name 'Hedin' or 'Hethin'. That is, Hedingham is 'the settlement or home named after Hethin's or Hedin's people'. The prefixes were added later to differentiate between landowners. The 13th century Sybil, wife of Geoffrey de Laventon, was one of the very few women to own land, so unusual an occurrence to merit a parish to carry her name.

Domesday records one existing mill in Hedingham, and that there had been two in Saxon times.

In 1848 White described the three parishes as follows: Great Maplestead is a scattered parish of 452 souls and 1,892 acres of land finely undulated, and bounded on the west by the river Colne

Sible Hedingham is an extensive and pleasant village on the western side of the vale of the Colne, opposite Castle Hedingham. The parish contains 2,322 inhabitants and 5,248 acres of fertile land rising in gentle undulations from the river Colne and several of its tributary streams.

Castle Hedingham is a well-built village situated on a pleasant acclivity on the east side of the river Colne. The parish contains 1,343 inhabitants and 2,431 acres of land

The populations of the three parishes in 2011 were;
Great Maplestead: 343, Sible Hedingham: 3,994, Castle Hedingham: 1,201.

Just along Dyne's Hall Road is Wallace's Plantation. When I walked the Colne Valley Path in the summer of 2012, the path through here had been well rutted by the enormous tyres of forestry vehicles that were being used for harvesting some of the mature trees in this wood. Through the plantation, on its southern edge, is the derelict Wallace's Farm. This is a beautiful location overlooking the Colne Valley and was just one of the many farms in the scattered rural parish of Great Maplestead. The demise of these, once working farm buildings is but a symptom of the increased mechanisation of agriculture and the shift of employment opportunities from the parish to further afield. During the past hundred years or so, the proportion of parish residents engaged in agricultural activities has fallen from about three-quarters to well below a quarter. Their houses have either fallen into ruin or become the homes of those who commute to employment away from the village.

The church of St Giles, Great Maplestead with its Norman tower partially rebuilt in brick, following the 1612 lightning strike. (2013)

Most of the dwellings in the parish are clustered around the parish church of St Giles, perched on the top of a hill far from the Colne. This is an ancient site and the church is probably built where the pre-Christian inhabitants of this area worshipped. The present Norman building, dating from around 1100, still subtly dominates the village with its massive western tower, which was for many years covered with plaster. When this was removed in 1861, it was found that part of the tower was brick and the date 1612 was revealed. It is believed that this was when half the tower, together with the west end of the aisle, were destroyed by a lightning strike.

The derelict Wallace's Farm buildings. (2012)

The derelict Wallace's Farm house. (2012)

Past the abandoned Wallace's Farm, the path drops down into the valley, crosses the dismantled CV&HR to follow close by the river to Hull's Mill. Here the path crosses the river by a footbridge beside a ford; this is now the last remaining such crossing over the Colne. As we have seen on our journey along the river, the increased use of crossing places by mechanised vehicles had led to the building of stronger bridges, that in turn has led to the abandonment of the earlier fords, but here at Hull's Mill the traveller can still enjoy the delight of a water splash. This is a somewhat ironical situation if Benham is to be believed. He claims that during the 17th century the mill was known as Hull Mill, which he thinks could be a corruption of Hall Mill, or more likely the obsolete word 'hull' used to describe a waterway running under a road, as is the derivation of the Yorkshire town of Hull, and possibly the Hull Mill that we encountered by Distillery Pond in Colchester. He could well be right as Hull's Mill in Great Maplestead has never been owned by anyone with the name of Hull, but it did take the name of the owners who acquired the mill shortly after WWI.

In 1836 Richard Smith was born in the Mill House, Stone, Staffordshire. When he grew up he became a successful miller like his father before him. Then, as he approached middle age, he conceived the novel idea of extracting the highly nutritious wheatgerm from the wheat, lightly cooking it to preserve the nutrients, then putting back into the flour many times more wheatgerm than it originally contained. The resulting flour was known as 'Smith's Patent Germ Flour' and the bread produced from it 'Smith's Patent Germ Bread'. The process was patented and the products became very popular but the name was a bit of a mouthful, so a competition was held to devise a better name. The winner was an Oxford schoolteacher, Herbert Grime, who suggested 'Hovis' as a contraction of the Latin couplet 'Hominis Vis', which means 'the strength of man'. By 1895 Hovis had become established as a household name and was selling over a million loaves a week. Richard died in 1900 but his product lived on and, in 1918, 'Hovis Limited' was launched as a public company. To keep pace with the ever-increasing demand for its products this organisation went about acquiring country mills, one such was Hull's Mill. The Hovis Company eventually became part of the Rank-Hovis-MacDougal (RHM) conglomerate, which in turn became part of the giant food manufacturing company Premier Foods who still market the Hovis brand. But for those of you who wish to capture the distinctive taste of Hovis from yesteryear, just add a generous spoonful of wheatgerm the next time you use your breadmaker.

When Hovis took over Hull's Mill it still had a working waterwheel and stones, but was also equipped with a roller mill. This was powered by an internal combustion engine driven by gas, which was generated on site by heating anthracite in a fan-assisted furnace. Hovis replaced the waterwheel with a turbine that was used to power a single pair of stones and to drive a dynamo to supply light to the mill house and mill cottages. The new owners

Hovis Mill in its working days.

The ford by Hull's, Hovis or Great Maplestead Mill is the only remaining ford across the Colne. (2012)

not only kept the mill equipment up to date but also maintained the fabric of the building to a high standard. Throughout most of this time the mill was known as Hovis Mill and was operated by Harry Noble, followed by his son John who was born in the mill house and ran it until its eventual closure in 1953.

Hull's Mill is on the north bank of the river and is therefore in the parish of Great Maplestead and is now sometimes referred to as Great Maplestead Mill, but because of its proximity to the village of Sible Hedingham it is regarded by many as being in this parish. The path from the mill soon leaves the riverside and heads across arable fields before returning to the river and Alderford Mill, which is definitely in Sible Hedingham.

The setting of this weatherboarded mill is not quite as attractive as Hull's Mill but behind its white façade is a treasure waiting to be explored. Its recent history is fascinating and unique, but before I go into that I will briefly describe its more distant past.

This mill was first recorded in 1547 but there may well have been earlier mills on the site, possibly even as far back as Domesday. The present timber framed structure dates back to 1720 when its new waterwheel was capable of driving two pairs of stones. About a hundred years later a brick extension was added, to house a steam engine, which was used to drive an additional three pairs of stones. This steam engine was later replaced by a more economical oil engine that kept the mill producing wholemeal flour into the 1940s. After this date the mill produced animal feed until its eventual closure in 1956, although during the later stages of its working life the machinery was driven by electricity.

Hull's Mill, Hovis Mill or Great Maplestead Mill is now a private residence. (2012)

This was not the first time that the mill was associated with electricity. When Frederick George Bishop owned the mill during the early years of the 20th century he generated electricity, which he sold to the villagers to light their homes. There is a story that a local garage proprietor was using the supply to charge batteries and not paying for what was used. When the mill owner became aware of this he decided to reverse the polarity of his supply. This would have had no effect on those lighting their cottages but a rather disastrous effect on batteries.

In 1926 the mill was taken over by the Rawlinson family who ran it until it ceased grinding in 1956. The building was then used as a feed store for a few more years. By 1994 the structure was beginning to deteriorate but it still contained a unique selection of mill machinery.

Since 1945, Essex County Council had adopted a policy of purchasing a representative selection of the rapidly declining number of mills in the county. By the 1990s they had acquired several windmills and the tide mill at Thorrington, but they had not yet gained possession of a representative country watermill. By this date, all the county's once numerous watermills had ceased working and many had been demolished or converted for domestic use, never likely to work again. Then in 1994, the County Council had the opportunity to buy Alderford Mill and this historic building entered the last chapter of its long history.

The first task was to make the building weatherproof by carrying out repairs to the roof and the weatherboarding. Then came the job of securing the mill's water supply by carrying out works to the upstream riverbanks and the bypass sluice. By 2003 all the external repairs and renovations had been completed. Work on the internal machinery continued under the direction of the County Millwright; the equipment and millstones were slowly brought back to working order. A major task was the replacement of the 100 year-old wheel shaft, which had partially rotted. First, a suitable piece of timber had to be found. After a long search a straight trunk of field oak approximately 18ft (5.4m) long, some 2ft 6in (75cm) in diameter and weighing in excess of a ton was obtained. Then a way of shaping the shaft had to be devised. This involved cutting square shoulders to mount the pit wheel, octagonal sections to mount the wheel frames and turned ends for the main bearing pinions. The turned ends were produced by rotating the shaped trunk using a specially devised bicycle powered lathe. With all the refurbished parts assembled in 2008, for the first time in 52 years, the waterwheel was turning once more. At the time of writing it is hoped that by 2013 this unique Essex watermill will be once again producing wholemeal flour from the power of the water flowing in the Colne. Even if the enthusiastic band of volunteers fail to achieve this, the mill will be open to the public on every second Sunday of the month from April to September.

The restored breastshot Alderford Mill is now the only working country watermill in Essex. (2012)

As I left the mill I caught a glimpse of the Hedingham Riverside Walk. This is only a few yards away, but across a stream and unfortunately is at present inaccessible from the mill. This riverside amenity will eventually provide a path from Alderford Mill to Station Road Bridge but at present only part of it is open, and that can only be accessed from a central point.

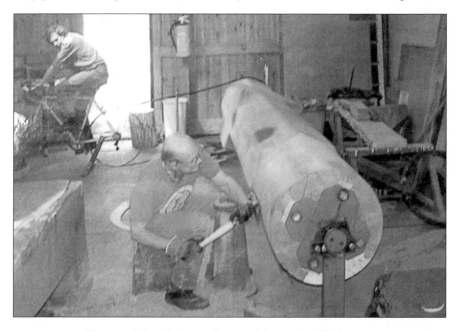

The new wheel shaft weighing about a ton being turned by bicycle power.

The future progress of this project has no timetable because it is dependent upon several developers and other agencies. I am sure that it will be completed one day, but until then travellers who wish to venture further along the river have to leave its banks and follow me up the hill towards Castle Hedingham. A short way along the lane I crossed the CV&HR and turned on to a footpath that took me across a couple of fields, past several farm buildings and rows of poly-tunnels to find myself ambling through a riverside wood. Emerging

Station Road Bridge stands on the parish boundary between the Hedinghams,
seen here with its adjacent ford still usable. (1926)

The three arch, redbrick Station Road Bridge, built in 1736 is the
oldest surviving bridge across the Colne. (2013)

from the wood the path continued along the north bank of the Colne soon to arrive at the Colne's next bridge. This is the oldest surviving bridge across the Colne. It is now called Station Road Bridge, but when it was built in 1736, long before the railway had arrived, it replaced an earlier wooden structure on what was then River Lane or Water Lane. The stone carriageway of the adjacent ford can still be seen beneath the water but the access either side is now impenetrably overgrown.

This impressive bridge was built at the instigation of Sir Henry Houghton, the then owner of Hedingham Castle who donated £60 towards the cost of its construction; the balance of £420 was made up of equal contributions from the parish and the Turnpike Trust. The original bridge was enlarged in 1819 and then restored in the 1980s to cope with the increasing demands of modern traffic. The inscription on the badly eroded keystone is now barely visible, but just about decipherable is the date of 1736. Earlier observers have recorded the name of the builder as Robert Poole. He was a local man who became the County Surveyor. The Station Road Bridge was not a county bridge but a private venture, which has become his enduring legacy.

The bridge joins the two parishes of Sible Hedingham and Castle Hedingham. Because of the historical association with the castle the latter is the better known and has been, at times, the more important. But its neighbour, Sible, is the larger and has its own interesting past. Station Road leads to an industrial area that grew up around the railway. One of the most significant enterprises to flourish on this site was the joinery works of Ripper's Ltd. This all started in the 1890s when three brothers turned their general building activities into a highly successful specialised woodworking enterprise. The factory worked throughout WWI making wooden components, such as propellers, and then during WWII supplied a large variety of wooden components for the war effort. During the post war period the company returned to its beginnings by supplying all manner of joinery products to the booming building industry. Then, during the 1970s, there followed the familiar story of being taken over by a multinational only to be closed down a few years later. The site is now awaiting a housing development.

St Peter's Church,
Sible Hedingham. (2013)

Sir John Hawkwood (1320-1394), the
Hedingham born medieval mercenary.

Beyond the industrial area is the main road. Many people form their impression of the village from this often congested and not very attractive thoroughfare. For those who venture beyond, there are many attractive features in this extensive rural parish. The church of St Peter stands in a commanding position with a surprisingly steep access from the village street below. This largely 14th century building contains a memorial to the parish's most famous celebrity, Sir John Hawkwood.

John Hawkwood was born in the village in 1320, the son of a tanner. He became a soldier who fought under King Edward III, and after the battle of Poitiers received a knighthood. He then formed a group of mercenaries known as the White Company who fought for various Italian states. Sir John was an outstanding soldier, a charismatic leader with an intellectual mastery of military tactics; this, with a skilful use of spies, made him a formidable adversary. For a man who had chosen this way of life, he lived to a surprisingly old age and was still fighting into his 70s. It is said that he had hoped to return to England but this was not to be. He died in Italy in 1394 and was given a state funeral and his memorial can still be seen in Florence Cathedral. In his home village this

Medieval graffiti, a representation of the Devil in St Peter's Church, Sible Hedingham.

soldier of fortune has a less auspicious memorial of which only the canopy remains, and this has been defaced with medieval graffiti.

The wall scribes of this era seem to have been especially active in this particular church leaving their scratched Christian symbols all over the place. And there is one notable rendering that I'm not sure is Christian at all, a rather unusual depiction of the Devil.

The belief in the power of the Devil through the aegis of his disciples, his witches, seems to have lingered in Sible Hedingham longer than in most places. As recently as 1863 one unfortunate resident of the parish died as a result of an 'ordeal by water'. A local girl, Emma Smith, accused Dummy, a somewhat eccentric, elderly deaf and dumb tramp, of putting a spell on her. Apparently she caused such a scene in the local inn that the unfortunate man was beaten, and dragged into the brook, only to be re-immersed several times as he tried to climb out. A post mortem concluded that he had died of pneumonia brought about by immersion in water. Emma Smith and an accomplice, Samuel Stammers, were subsequently charged with his death and tried at Chelmsford Assizes, where each was sentenced to six months hard labour.

With this chilling tale I will return to Station Road Bridge and continue my walk along the Colne. The path, now on the Sible Hedingham side of the river, sneaks along beside a crudely fashioned fence surrounding a builder's yard, before entering a meadow where it continues alongside the river as it meanders towards Nunnery Bridge. There has long been a bridge on this site, which takes its name from the Benedictine Nunnery established here in 1191 by Aubrey de Vere, a man who, along with other members of his family, has had an enormous influence on the Colne Valley, and Castle Hedingham in particular.

The castle is built in a position of natural dominance in a location that has been fought over from the earliest times. Before the castle was built, successive incursions of settlers from Europe defended the stronghold with a massive ditch and rampart earthwork.

After the Conquest, King William rewarded his brother-in-law, Aubrey de Vere, by giving him estates in six counties, including the manor of Hedingham in Essex. This became the place chosen by Aubrey to build his power base. In 1140 a descendent, another Aubrey, built the Norman keep, which remains among the most magnificent and best preserved in Europe. The other significant Norman building in the village is the church of St Nicholas. This is the most complete Norman parish church in the county. For centuries these two buildings dominated the life and fortunes of the villagers whose fates were inextricably linked to those of the de Veres. Then in the 17th century the wool industry brought a new prosperity to the area and the village prospered and became a thriving market town. Within the medieval network of village streets there are many buildings from this period. Then, with the demise of the wool industry, many of the villagers were thrown back to the agricultural activities of their forbears, but for some there was a new source of employment, the cottage industry of straw platting. This had been introduced to the area in 1790 by the Marquis of Buckingham who lived at Gosfield Hall, and many cottagers spent their days weaving straw into plaits for the booming straw-hat industry.

By this time one of the most successful local agricultural activities was hop growing. This crop, traditionally associated with the southern counties, most notably Kent, was once grown commercially in Hedingham. Hops had been grown in the area since Tudor times, but on nothing like the scale that was reached in the 19th century when over 250 acres (100ha) were devoted to

Hedingham Castle as depicted in Thomas Wright's History of the County of Essex *published in 1835.*

St Nicholas' Church, Castle Hedingham, a rare Norman parish church with a beautiful wheel window in the nave. The War memorial in the foreground, erected in 1921, incorporates the village's ancient Saxon cross, rescued from the cellar of the Falcon Inn. (2013)

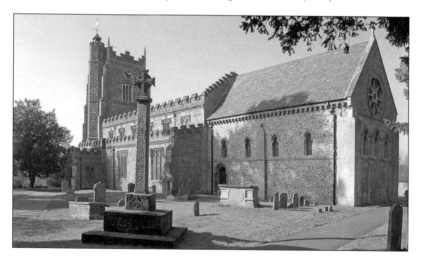

this crop. Hedingham hops were prized for their size and flavour but the best does not always succeed in the market place and by 1887 all commercial hop growing in North Essex had ceased. Even so, hops can still be found, growing wild in the hedgerows of the parish, especially those down by the river.

With the coming of the railway in 1861 another local activity that had been going on, in a small way, for some time expanded rapidly. By 1900 the local brickmaking industry was employing around 500 men who were making over seven million bricks a year. There was abundant brickearth in the Hedingham area and the rate of brick production was only limited by the ability of the CV&HR to transport away the finished products.

Deposits of brickearth occur in various places in Essex; they are the result of windblown deposits of dust during the extremely cold conditions of the ice age some two hundred thousand years ago. This easily dug material was first used in pre-historic times for pottery making and the first bricks to be made in Britain were made by the Romans. When they left, the art of brickmaking was lost until the arrival of the Flemings towards the end of the 15th century. Some Hedingham clay has been used in each of these periods.

St Nicholas' Church 800 year-old Norman south door, known as the skin door because it is said that the skin of a thief who once tried to rob the church was nailed to it. (2013)

Brickmaking is a long and interesting process. Clay is dug in the autumn and allowed to over-winter in heaps, being turned over several times to allow it to weather. Sand and water are then mixed with the clay in a pug mill. The brickmaker then takes an amount of this clay, kneads it, and throws it into a sanded mould with sufficient force to fill the mould. The surplus clay is cut off and the mould removed from the newly formed brick. The bricks are then dried for several weeks in long, open-sided sheds before being fired in a kiln. This is the final stage in transforming the soft malleable clay into a hard and extremely durable material, which will last for thousands of years.

'Hedingham Reds' became well known and were exported as far afield as Ireland and Egypt, and, closer to home, over a million were used in the building of Colchester Town Hall. As the brickmaking industry became more mechanised, the Hedingham products fell out of favour and the decline set in. Fortunately, for the many employed in this industry, this happened at the time when the woodworking activities of Rippers were expanding, who rapidly became the most significant employer in the area.

Some of the hop growing and some of the brickfields were on the banks of the Colne, and it is to the river that I must now return. A 1592 map of Castle Hedingham shows a mill with a millstream near the site of the present

The Nunnery Mill as shown on Israel Amyce's survey of Castle Hedingham. (1592)

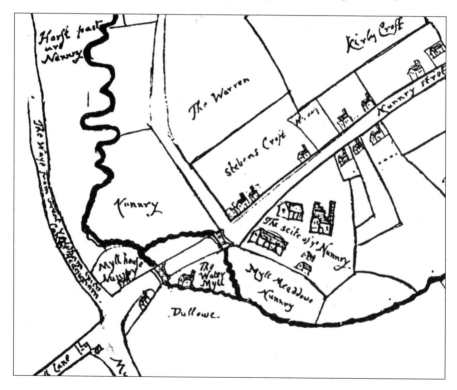

Nunnery Bridge over the Colne. The mill itself belonged to the Benedictine nunnery that stood on the site of the present Nunnery Farm. On the south side of the bridge there was, until quite recently a ford, a very significant ford that gave its name to the Hinckford Hundred.

Back in the tenth century, or maybe before, counties were divided into Hundreds. These originally contained a hundred hides, or family holdings, each of somewhere between 60 and 120 acres (25-50 ha). In medieval England the Hundred was an important administrative unit responsible for, amongst other things, law and order. Each Hundred had its own court which was called a 'moot'. The Hundreds often took their name from the location of their open-air moot or meeting place. This was often an easily found landmark such as a mound, mere or ford.

There is no town, village or any other feature on a modern map that gives a clue to the location of 'Hinckford'. So we must resort to historians, some of whom claim that it is a corruption of the Domesday description of the ford at Hedingham as 'Hidingford' or 'Hedingford'. A little to the west of the ford is a small triangular area of about one-third of an acre which is raised about 6ft (1.8m) above the roadway and flood level. It is thought that this may have been where the moot held their meetings. This idea is supported by the fact that this area was anciently known as Mustoe Green, itself a corruption of 'mote-stow', which means 'meeting place'. This is also the original location of the Saxon cross that was removed at the Reformation to be used as a prop in the cellar of the Falcon Inn until it was rescued in 1921 to be used as part of the village War Memorial. So there seems to be quite a lot of evidence to suggest that this ford is indeed Hinckford.

If you look over the bridge parapet the remains of this historical ford can still be seen, but any remains of the mill and nunnery have long gone, leaving only a name. Until 1870, Nunnery Bridge was a three-arched brick structure similar to Station Road Bridge. When it was replaced, the road was leveled and the two side arches were filled in, leaving the central piers to be spanned by cast iron girders. These were supplied by Symington & Atterton, Engineers who were, at the time, operating the Halstead Iron Works. The bridge, as seen today, was restored by Essex County Council in 1922.

The 1870 Nunnery Bridge, and beyond on the extreme right is Mustoe Green, the moot meeting place. (2013)

The original ironwork supplied by Symington & Atterton, Engineers who were working from the Halstead Iron Works.

The bridge bears a plaque recording the restoration by ECC in 1922

The route of the Colne Valley Path crosses the bridge to continue along the Castle Hedingham side of the river. I walked along this path, separated from the river by a plantation of young trees, up to the gated foot crossing that crosses the Colne Valley Railway (CVR).

The story of the CVR starts in 1973 when two enthusiasts walked a one-mile stretch of the former CV&HR between mileposts 60 and 61 near Castle Hedingham. Although there was never a station on the site and the track had been lifted, they had a vision to recreate a part of the railway including platforms, signal boxes and bridges. By 1974 a company had been formed and volunteer helpers gathered to form the Colne Valley Preservation Society to assist the company in building and running the railway. Since then a tremendous amount has been achieved, two platforms have been built and the original Sible and Castle Hedingham station was moved brick by brick from a mile down the track. The Signal boxes from Cressing and Wrabness

The Colne Valley Railway (CVR), the only true steam operated railway in Essex, the other examples being museums rather than railways. (2011)

Hedingham Station on the occasion of the Coronation of King Edward VII. (1902)

During the 1970s the Hedingham Station building was moved, brick by brick from its original location to its new site at the CVR. (2011)

In 1980 this unique CV&HR steel girder bridge was brought from its original location in Earls Colne to the CVR site where it now crosses the Colne considerably further upstream. (2013)

and the station footbridge from Stowmarket have augmented the collection. And most significantly for my story, the last remaining CV&HR steel girder bridge from Earls Colne now crosses the Colne on this site.

The CVR is a unique preservation project and the enthusiasts have plans for still further expansion. It has become a popular tourist attraction and the organisers claim that it is the only true steam operated railway in Essex, the other examples being museums rather than railways. The working CVR is open to visitors on most weekends and bank holidays from April to October.

I continued my walk along the Colne Valley Path, which followed the contour above the river, first by footpath then country lane before becoming a footpath once again to a footbridge across a minor tributary. I was now beyond the well-trodden paths of the local dog-walkers and was venturing on to a less well-used length of the Valley Walk. Along here I came upon an old railway wagon decaying in its dying days, used as an animal shelter and wondered if the enthusiastic restorers at the CVR, just across the river, knew of its existence. I was soon back on the riverside where I could hear the sound of water cascading over a weir; this was associated with the third gauging station on the Colne. The river here is only a few feet wide and on most days the flow is modest and one could be forgiven for wondering why there is a monitoring station here at all. The many small streams feeding the river above this point drain a large agricultural area and, following periods of heavy rain, the changing flow patterns recorded at this station provide advance data for the control of flood management installations further downstream. As I looked upstream from here I was looking into the next parish and the last chapter in my chronicle of the Colne.

A reused railway wagon on farmland overlooking the CVR site. (2013)

Pool Street Gauging Station with the CVR beyond. (2013)

CHAPTER XV

Great Yeldham and Beyond

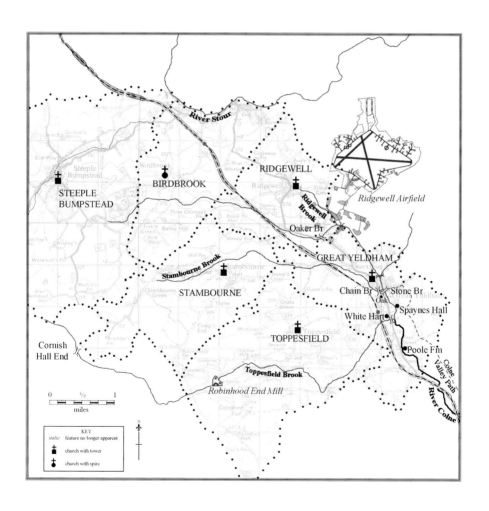

THE COLNE

Great Yeldham and Beyond

Yeldham is derived from the Old English word 'geld' that means a 'payment' or 'tax', and Ham is from the Old English and means an 'enclosure', 'homestead', 'manor' or 'village'. Presumably, at some stage during the Saxon period this 'ham' had to pay some sort of tax.

The Domesday Book records that there was a mill in Yeldham during Saxon times but by the time of the survey it was no longer.

In 1848 William White said of Great Yeldham or Lower Yeldham, (he also refers to Little Yeldham as Upper Yeldham); it is a neat and scattered village, on the high road, and on the banks of the small river Colne and two of its tributary streams. It contains 726 souls and 1,793 acres.

White's entries for the adjoining parishes that mention the Colne or its tributaries are:

Ridgewell is described as a pleasant village, built round a large green, on a commanding eminence near the sources of the river Colne.
Birdbrook is described as a pleasant village, on a bold eminence, near the chief source of the Colne.
Stambourne is described as a long scattered village, pleasantly situated near the source of a rivulet.
Toppesfield is a pleasant retired village on a commanding eminence on land rising boldly from a tributary stream of the river Colne.

By 2011 the population of Great Yeldham had risen to 1,844.

The footpath by the Colne enters the parish of Great Yeldham by a double row of pylons that stride across the valley. These are part of the complex electricity distribution system that ensures our generating stations can deliver power whenever and wherever it is required. For that convenience I am more than happy to accept these towering giants marching across the landscape, and sometimes wonder if those who campaign so passionately for their removal are the same folk who complain about electricity prices and the occasional power cut.

The path runs along the upper edge of the riverside meadow to Poole Farm, whose buildings are now used for a variety of purposes. One of the oldest is being used by a pet and animal feed supplier. During the 19th century Walter Whitlock, one of the largest farmers in North Essex, lived and worked here and one of his many interests was in the business of supplying forage or animal feed. This was at the time when the first machines

Pylons carrying the high voltage grid across the Colne on the Hedingham/Yeldham boundary. (2013)

were being introduced into farms and Walter bought several machines for cutting forage. These early machines were not always reliable and spare parts were frequently unavailable. To remedy this situation and to maintain some independence from suppliers Walter decided that two of his four sons would train as engineers. Meanwhile, Walter's youngest son continued the forage business and Whitlocks Chaff Works was built in 1909. Eventually the engineering brothers set up their own works near the railway station, which was to become a major employer in the area.

On one occasion when I visited Poole Farm I left by the bridleway that leads up the hill behind the farm. At the top of this farm track I turned to the left across an extremely muddy field that was supposed to be a footpath. I trudged on through the glutinous soil that tenaciously stuck to my boots, making them heavier with every step, until I reached the corner of a copse. Here I was reassured that I was following the right, but invisible, path by

The ornate brickwork at Whitlocks Chaff Works, Poole Farm. (2013)

The vehicular access to Poole Farm is via a steel and concrete bridge across the Colne. (2013)

This wide, substantial, brick-built bridge is now used only by those walking the Colne Valley Path. (2013)

the presence of a well-camouflaged waymark. I managed to dislodge most of the accumulated clods of friendly mud that had become attached to my boots and continued along the woodside path. This had not been ploughed and was easy going right to the end of the trees and another waymark. This directed me straight across another ploughed field and I was soon back to lifting pounds of mud with every step, but it was downhill which made the going less exhausting. At the bottom of the field, the gap in the hedge turned out to be a bridge that crossed one of the numerous minor streams that flow down the valley sides into the Clone. Although the stream was little more than a ditch, the brick-built bridge would have been wide enough and sufficiently strong to take any farm vehicle of its day.

The path across the field on the other side of the bridge was not as heavy going because there had been more time for the path to become consolidated since its autumn ploughing. At the end of this field of winter wheat that was struggling in the cold and wet spring, the path emerged on to a well-compacted farm track that took me down to Spaynes Hall.

This 16th century house is built on the site of a much earlier one and is currently undergoing a major restoration following a fire in 2012. It is named after its ancient owners, the de Hispania family, who came from Spain in the 13th century. For many years the house was known as Spains Hall, as were two other properties in Essex that were originally owned by the same family.

It is said that the unusual spelling of the Yeldham hall was changed during the 19th century to distinguish it from the others. The hall has had many owners since the de Hispanias; I will mention only one, Peter Muilman. He was born into a wealthy family in Amsterdam and moved to London as a young man where he became a successful merchant. Peter fancied himself as an antiquary and shortly after his marriage, in 1749, established himself in his adopted county. He managed to buy the manor of Little Yeldham along with four estates in Great Yeldham including Spains Hall, which also made him lord of this manor. From his newly acquired country seat at Spains Hall, he pursued his antiquarian interests with fervour and it is known that he corresponded with Philip Morant to whom he supplied information about the Yeldhams. Some years later in 1770 the six volume *Gentleman's Guide to Essex* was published anonymously, but it is widely thought that the author was Peter Muilman.

It is said that Peter was perspicuous and had a high opinion of himself and this is amply illustrated by the many references to himself in the tome attributed to him. One example is the reporting of a parish meeting at which:

'Peter Muilman Esq. acquainted the parishioners that all lanes shall be thirty feet wide, the ditches two feet deep and the hedges be laid so that the wind and sun may have admittance.'

When I read this I thought it was refreshing to hear of a lord of a manor who had the money and pride to provide his manor with such facilities that would be useful and convenient for all parishioners and visitors, as well as being a showpiece to all around. But I had forgotten that many men of wealth and influence manage to coerce or force others to do their bidding and Peter Muilman falls into this category, as later in the report of the meeting:

'the said Gentleman then observed that persons frequently received alms who were not so infirm but that they might do some little service to the public. He proposed therefore that a sufficient quantity of light sticks six feet long with iron scoops about eight inches long three wide fixed at the ends thereof, be provided by the parish for such poor as receive alms, to be employed in the said lanes and byways to let out what water may be standing in the roads and open what drains they may find stopped.'

Today the maintenance of roads is no longer the responsibility of the parish but there are still those who would advocate Peter Muilman's approach to alleviating the problem of our increasingly potholed roads.

The road to Spaynes Hall crosses the Colne by a single arch brick bridge that is badly in need of some maintenance. The bridge's problems are not being helped by all the vehicles now using it in connection with the extensive renovation of the hall following the disastrous fire. The bridge is currently supported by four acrows. These adjustable building props were invented by the Swiss born inventor, William de Vigier, who arrived in London in 1935, with an idea and £50 pounds in his pocket. The solicitor who helped him set up his company was Mr. A Crowe and although it took a while for the idea to catch on, the solicitor's name quickly became the building industry byword for the ubiquitous adjustable prop.

The elegant but structurally unsound Spaynes Hall Bridge is temporarily supported by four acrows. (2013)

The earliest known photograph of Yeldham Station. (1860s)

Yeldham Station, the clearance of trees and creation of a footpath in 2010 has revealed the platform. (2013)

The lane from Spaynes Hall joins the main road near Toppesfield Road, formerly Station Road. A short way along here was a level crossing and the former Yeldham Station. This opened in 1862 and as well as providing a regular passenger service provided a freight service that enabled local companies to develop and thrive, one of these was Whitlock Bros.

Alongside the station is where the Whitlock brothers set up their works in 1899. The site was well chosen with access to a siding and near the main road. The firm became agents for many agricultural machinery manufacturers and could also offer a repair and manufacturing service in their well-equipped workshops. This combination enabled them to provide the entire local agricultural community with a comprehensive supply and repair service. They were also manufacturing their own products and, by 1907, had established an enviable reputation. The chaff cutter that they produced in their Yeldham works won a gold medal in an international competition and was subsequently marketed as the Whitlock Gold Medal Chaff Cutter. The company evolved with the times and became a significant manufacturer of mechanised products. Around 1950, they were the first British company to manufacturer a backhoe loader, which they called the 'Dinkum Digger'. Not long after this, Joseph Cyril Bamford produced a similar product. Mr. Bamford was a great self-publicist who vigorously marketed his product, which he called the JCB. These are still manufactured in the UK and the company is one of our few thriving engineering companies exporting all over the world. The fortunes of Whitlocks followed a different path; this business evolved and expanded to a peak in 1967. With over 400 employees, Whitlock Bros. was one of the biggest manufacturers of earth-moving and industrial equipment in the country. Since then, by way of amalgamation and takeover, all trace of this once flourishing concern has completely disappeared.

Whitlock Bros. vigorously campaigned against the proposed closure of the station, sadly to no avail and the station closed to passengers in 1961 and goods in 1964. Today all that remains is the platform. The station site was cleared of encroaching vegetation and the trackbed opened up as a footpath in 2010 by the County Council, who now own the site.

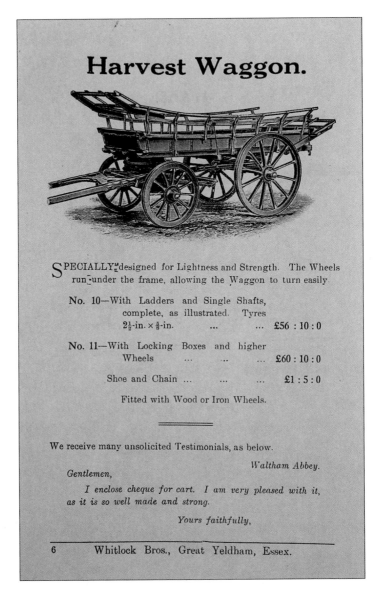

A 'Harvest Waggon' from an early Whitlock Bros catalogue. (c1910)

During the 1950s and 60s Whitlock Bros manufactured large numbers of their
'Dinkum Diggers', the first British backhoe (JCB). (2012)

From the station site, it is but a short way along the main road to the centre of the village and its famous oak tree. It seems that any ancient oak of extraordinary proportions attracts stories and legends and Great Yeldham Oak is no exception. Sometime, someone estimated its age and suggested that it was growing at the time when the Domesday survey was taken, and this soon became miss-reported as the tree was actually mentioned in the survey, this is simply incorrect. There are also completely unsubstantiated stories connecting the tree with the historical figures associated with oak trees, Robin Hood and Dick Turpin.

So, what can be said reliably about this undoubtedly ancient tree? One of the earliest accounts written in 1769 by the local antiquarian, Peter Muilman states,

'The remarkable large oak tree supposed to be upwards of three hundred years old, the stem of which measures in circumference twenty-seven feet three-quarters, but the height is not in proportion to the bulk, the stem from the ground to the first branches being not above

twelve feet high: and the height of the whole not exceeding eighty feet. A person of this parish, near one hundred years of age declares, that when she was a child, heard a person, who was older than her by eighty years say, that from his infancy this tree was distinguished by the appellation of the Old Oak.'

The Victorian villagers were obviously proud of their venerable tree but realised that it would not live for ever and, thoughtfully, funded by public subscription, planted a young tree for the benefit and enjoyment of future generations. This was carried out in 1863 to commemorate the marriage of the Prince of Wales to Princess Alexandra of Denmark, later King Edward VII and Queen Alexandra. This young tree now towers above its predecessor whose trunk was corseted in concrete and iron bars in 1949.

The age of some ancient trees has been determined accurately by counting their annual growth rings, and those of many more by measuring their girth. My interpolation of this data indicates that at the time Peter Muilman made

The plaque which was attached to Yeldham Oak in 1959.

THE GREAT OAK
GREAT YELDHAM, ESSEX

THE HISTORY OF THIS OLD OAK IS OBSCURE
ALTHOUGH IT WAS SHOWN ON MAPS IN 1777 AS
THE GREAT OAK AND MARKED THE FORD IN THE RIVER
AT THIS ROAD JUNCTION.
THE YELDHAM OAKS MAY WELL HAVE BEEN THOSE USED
FOR SHIPBUILDING IN THE TENTH CENTURY.
THE ROAD CONNECTING COLCHESTER TO CAMBRIDGE
IS BELIEVED TO BE AN OLD ROMAN ROAD.
RECORDS SHOW THAT THIS TREE WAS ALIVE AFTER 1860
AND ATTAINED A GIRTH OF NEARLY 30FT., A
HEIGHT OF 80FT. AND IS REPUTED TO BE OVER
300 YEARS OLD.
THE TRUNK WAS ENCASED AND PRESERVED BY PUBLIC
SUBSCRIPTION IN 1949.
THE YOUNG OAK ADJACENT WAS PLANTED TO
COMMEMORATE THE MARRIAGE BETWEEN KING EDWARD VII
AND QUEEN ALEXANDRA IN 1863.
THIS PLAQUE WAS ERECTED BY PUBLIC SUBSCRIPTION
IN 1959 AND THE FUND WAS OPENED WITH A SUBSCRIPTION
FROM LEILA STONE OF CALIFORNIA U.S.A. WHO SHOWED
GREAT INTEREST IN THIS RELIC OF A PAST AGE.

A. CARLETON WHITLOCK.
CHAIRMAN YELDHAM PARISH COUNCIL

Early photograph of Yeldham Oak, c1860, before the new tree was planted in 1863.

The ancient Yeldham Oak, corseted in concrete and iron, is struggling to stay alive in the shadow of the 150 year old youngster at its side. (2013)

his measurements on the Yeldham Oak it was about 750 years old, which means that it is now nearly 1,000 years since that particular acorn sprouted. This implies that our tree is not quite old enough to feature in the Domesday Survey, but it was certainly growing within the Norman period.

The Yeldham Oak is significant as much for its position as for its age, and could well be the sole survivor from a grove of ancient trees that marked the ford at the junction of four roads near the confluence of two streams. The importance of this location may well be the reason why Yeldham is here at all.

Such ancient sites are often the places chosen by Christians to build their churches so as to supplant earlier beliefs. This is not the case in Yeldham where the church of St Andrew is situated in a dominating position overlooking the spreading village. Its most imposing feature is its late 15th century tower built with a pleasing mixture of flint, brick and puddingstone topped with stepped battlements, pinnacles and figures of angels.

From the church lychgate can be seen a most unusual wall. This crinkle-crankle wall is one of only a small number that exist in East Anglia. Despite

St Andrew's Church, Great Yeldham, as depicted in Gentleman's Guide to Essex. *(1770)*

St Andrew's, Great Yeldham, parts of which date from the 14ᵗʰ century, but its most impressive feature is its 15ᵗʰ century west tower, built after an earlier south tower was abandoned, the base of which forms the massive south porch. (2013)

its sinuous configuration, this form of construction economizes on bricks, because it can be made just one brick thin. The alternate convex and concave curves in the wall provide stability, obviating the need for buttresses in such a tall, thin wall. This wall design is attributed to Dutch engineers, who introduced it to the boggy parts of East Anglia, when working on draining the fen country during the 17ᵗʰ century. Today the majority of surviving examples are in Suffolk but there are a handful in Essex. Most of these date from the Victorian era when they became a desirable feature of country garden design. The one at Yeldham is a mere youngster, being built in 1968

Yeldham's crinkle-crankle wall bordering Change House. (2013)

from reused handmade bricks. Never the less, its sinuous nature is an unusual and attractive feature noticed by many as they pass through the village. Not so many notice the inconspicuous, some would say invisible, village bridges.

At least five tributaries of the river Colne converge within the parish and three of these are bridged in the village. It is from these bridges that I will start the second part of this chapter in which I will explore the Colne Valley beyond Great Yeldham.

Up from Hedingham the valley becomes less well defined and the landscape begins to roll as the underlying chalk has its softening effect on the contours. It is in these chalk uplands of northwest Essex that the Colne rises. To determine precisely where is somewhat contentious as it depends upon which definition is used, which tributary is followed and which of the authorities you choose to believe.

I will start with the stream that is crossed by the main road to the south of the village by the *White Hart Inn*. During the time when this road was turnpiked, the bridge that was rebuilt by the Turnpike Trust was described as being across the

Colne. This stretch of water that flows beside the Inn is now called Toppesfield Brook, after the parish through which it flows for much of its length. Beyond the *White Hart*, the brook passes under the CV&HR, past the site of a former mill at Robinhood End and under several small roads before its last bridge, on the minor road at Cornish Hall End. From here the brook continues across fields for about half-a-mile to the Finchingfield/Steeple Bumpstead parish boundary, which it follows for another half-a-mile or so to what could be the source of the Colne at 350ft (105m) above sea level.

There are those who would say that this is the source of Toppesfield Brook and not the Colne. But it all depends how the source of a river is defined, and this is something that geographers have preferred to keep mysteriously muddied. Sometimes it is an area of marsh, sometimes the position of melting glaciers and sometimes, as in the case of the Nile, it is the distance from the mouth to the most distant headwater, irrespective of the name. This river ends at Lake Victoria, but this is not its source as the lake is fed by a number of rivers, the longest of which is the Kagera. Using this definition, the Nile becomes the longest river in the world, rather than the fourth or fifth. And if this definition is applied to the Colne, then as Toppesfield Brook is significantly longer than any of the other headwater streams, it can claim to lead to its source. Interestingly

The bridge crossing Toppesfield Brook by the White Hart. (2013)

The White Hart *with its 16th century towering chimneys. The timbers were exposed in the 1930s when the fashion was to mediaevalise many old buildings.* (2013)

the OS Explorer Map labels the river Colne just below the *White Hart* but near Cornish Hall End it has become Colne Valley.

Now back to the *White Hart* and a rival headwater that takes us to the centre of Great Yeldham where this stream is crossed by Stone Bridge, close by the Oak. Within a very short distance this rivulet is joined by Stambourne Brook. This is a significant headwater but has never been in the running as a contender for the honour of being the source stream. It is, however, crossed by the third of the village bridges, Chain Bridge. This is on the road between the Oak and St Andrew's Church and is not at all obvious as the main road sweeps across it, but it is the oldest and one of the most interesting of all the village bridges. Although not crossing the Colne it is probably the oldest bridge in the valley but its history has been woefully under recorded. In 1869 the Hedingham Highway Board reported that the 200-year-old bridge was in need of repair as it had been damaged by a 'steam cultivator passing over it, a portion of the arch being forced in'. The bridge has been repaired and

The widened and rebuilt Stone Bridge with 1935 style parapets. (2013)

The narrow Stone Bridge before it was widened in 1935. This attractive view from the ancient Oak is now obscured by an ugly, wholly inappropriate 1980s development of eleven cramped dwellings. (c1920s)

Looking past Yeldham Oak towards Stone Bridge with the 1980s development marring the view. (2013)

widened several times since, but it still retains its original double brick arch and a stone bearing the date 1682. This bridge is hardly noticeable to the road user and is small, even by Colne standards, but it can lay claim to being the oldest in the valley.

Beyond Chain Bridge, in the grounds of Yeldham Hall, Stambourne Brook now flows beside, what Vernon Clarke calls, a series of monastic fishing ponds. If these are indeed ancient ponds then this may also be the site of the long vanished Saxon Yeldham Mill. By the time of the Domesday Survey, in 1086, the mill was no longer in existence and has not been recorded since, so any attempt to establish its location is no more than a guess. When I have visited Yeldham in the winter and peered over its bridges, any one of them

Still supporting the modern carriageway is the oldest bridge in the Colne Valley. The date, 1682, is engraved on a stone, almost obscured by ivy, built into the double-arch Chain Bridge. (2013)

*St Andrew's hill top position beyond Chain Bridge where the A1017,
formerly A604, crosses Stambourne Brook.*

*A similar view looking towards the church, now completely obscured by trees,
with the now inconspicuous Chain Bridge in the foreground. (2013)*

could have been the site of the Saxon mill but the flow under Stone Bridge together with its strategic location, to my mind, gives it the edge.

From the Oak I crossed Stone Bridge and walked along North Road. This follows the riverside that is now protected from erosion by a concrete bank. Several simple concrete bridges span the river every few yards to give access to the dwellings to the left of this road. The road soon veers away from the river but a short way up the hill a footpath took me back to riverside, now hiding behind back gardens and St Andrew's School playground.

North Road and the river are protected from each other by a concrete bank. (2013)

The concrete footbridge to the riverside footpath as it leaves the back gardens of Yeldham. (2013)

I last walked this path on a crisp spring day. The early morning sun, behind its high altitude veil, was just strong enough to cast soft shadows as I clambered over the stile that separated the enclosed urban path from the open fields that lay before me. The well trodden, grassy path followed the field margin alongside Spencer Grange. This extensive area of woodland covers the valley floor and extends way up the other side. The brook meanders through the wood as far as the footpath to Tilbury Juxta Clare, which crosses it by a simple plank footbridge before continuing across the rather boggy valley floor by means of a boardwalk. I did not take this path but continued to follow the brook by its southern bank. My path hugged the ancient field boundary that kept to the edge of the high ground, just a few feet above the floodplain, until I arrived at a functional WWII brick and concrete bridge and the confluence of two streams. Here there is also a joining of footpaths. One path follows an inviting stream which I will come back to later, the other crosses the WWII bridge before continuing along the other brook to Oaker Bridge. This bridge, at the foot of Oaker Hill, is where the main road passes by the land formerly occupied by the Land Settlement Association (LSA).

The LSA was a scheme set up by the Government, with the help of a couple of charities in 1934, to re-settle unemployed workers from depressed industrial areas. Over a thousand smallholdings were established in 26 separate rural locations. As a child I often visited my uncle Eddie who lived and worked on his LSA market garden. He never visited me because he was always at work, and when I visited him he seldom stopped. He was in love with his plot, his glasshouses and his crops and, as his admiring nephew followed him along his furrows, he would find time to convey the wonder of how plants grow. He taught me much without either of us realising it. On one occasion, when I was cleaning a toy that I had dropped he asked me what I was doing, 'Wiping the dirt off' I replied. His response has stayed with me for a lifetime. 'That's not dirt, that's soil, and that's where all your food comes from.'

The site at Yeldham consisted of nearly 100 smallholdings. Each was provided with a house for a family and outbuildings suitable for rearing poultry or pigs and a few acres of land. After WWII the running of the scheme was transferred to the County Councils and some of the units were sold to sitting tenants. At Yeldham much of the land was returned to agriculture and the dwellings were used as retirement homes for LSA tenants from other sites. There are still a few original LSA houses that have not been altered and extended to be almost unrecognisable. But only one, standing within a sizable plot, that provides its occupants with a livelihood from horticulture. This, 'Plants that Grow' business, is run by the descendents of the Fisher family who moved here in the 1940s when the holding was being sold for £220.

The relatively unchanged LSA house at 'Plants That Grow',
the only ex-LSA holding still being run as a horticultural business. (2013)

The waterside footpath ends at Oaker Bridge but the rivulet passes under the road and continues across the fields. Mr. Fisher informed me that he was told by the River Authority that the Colne ended at Oaker Bridge, and beyond there it was classified as a ditch. This was important to him as it affected his rights to discharge water from his land. He also said that he thought the source of this ditch was in Steeple Bumpstead.

It is difficult to follow this brook beyond Oaker Bridge but it can be seen from several places where it is crossed by a lane or minor road. The first of these is near where the brook was crossed by the CV&HR. It is near here that the railway climbs to its highest point as it leaves the Colne Valley and crosses the watershed into the neighbouring Stour Valley.

The stream that we are following then passes close by the village of Birdbrook where it is crossed by a couple of lanes before entering Moynes

The deep cutting through which the CV&HR passed as it left the Colne Valley to cross the watershed into the Stour Valley, where it joined the Stour Valley Railway at Haverhill. (2013)

Park and petering out at 300ft (90m) above sea level in the parish of Steeple Bumpstead. This parish straddles the watershed between the Colne and the Stour and as we have seen, two of the principle headwaters of the Colne rise within its boundaries, but the village itself is located on a tributary of the Stour and is certainly within the Stour Valley catchment area. It is for this reason that Steeple Bumpstead is often denied as being the source of the Colne. It is the attractively named, neighbouring parish of Birdbrook, with its village centre much closer to the infant rivulet, which is sometimes claimed to be the source of the Colne.

I have spent many hours cycling the gently undulating lanes of these relatively high Essex parishes where the expansive landscape often affords views of developing valleys. Hidden in one of these is the third Colne headwater that has been claimed by some to lead to its source. This is the brook that rises in the village of Ridgewell and, unlike the other headwaters, has a footpath close to its bank for its entire length. In terms of height, length or any other statistic, this tributary can make no claim to lead to the source of the Colne, yet many believe that it is; and a case can be made to suggest that Ridgewell is the spiritual source of the river.

In 1848 William White was diplomatically vague on the subject, stating that 'Ridgewell is a pleasant village, built round a large green, on a commanding eminence near the sources of the river Colne'. A century later, E. Auston tried to identify the true source of the river by asking the people of Yeldham. He says he heard a rumour that the source could be found at Steeple Bumpstead, but the local experts assured him that it was at Ridgewell, wither he went.

When I left Mr. Fisher at Oaker Bridge I retraced my steps back to the confluence of the two streams that I mentioned earlier and followed in Auston's footsteps. From the WWII bridge the brook is followed by a wartime concrete road which was a former access road to some of the many peripheral sites associated with Ridgewell airfield. This started life in 1942 as an RAF bomber base, then in 1943 was expanded and used by the USAAF as its only bomber base in Essex. After the war the base was used by the Air Ministry as

One of the few remaining WWII buildings associated with Ridgewell airfield. (2013)

a bomb store until it was sold in 1957. Since then the land has been returned to agriculture and most of the runways, hardstandings and buildings have been removed. But alongside the remains of the road I was following were a few derelict and overgrown survivors.

I emerged onto the minor road to Tilbury Juxta Clare. Across the lane the brook continued, slowly rising to the top of the field. Alongside the stream there is a farm track following the course of the remains of another WWII road, but there are two official footpaths that run parallel to this, each about a hundred yards to either side of the brook. I chose the farm track, which was joined by the two paths at the top of the field, where I entered a small wood. Emerging from this I caught my first glimpse of Ridgewell church.

The path continued along the field margin, which ran beside the long, thin wood that followed the fast flowing brook for nearly a quarter of a mile. Every now and again I ventured down into the wood following the paths made by wild animals as they sought refreshment from the clear flowing brook. From the overgrown stream the wood appeared no more than a sunken,

My first glimpse of Ridgewell church, from here the path follows the brook for another half-mile to emerge by the spring behind the church. (2013)

The last bridge crossing Ridgewell brook, in its small and narrow, wooded valley incised in the landscape. (2013)

wide hedge. Here I was put in mind of the holloways described by Robert Macfarlane. These ancient ways are found in areas where the sub-terrain is a soft stone, usually a chalk or sandstone. They are formed by the wear of countless feet, wheels and water; some date back to the Iron Age and many follow a route incised into the landscape by the flow of water. If a holloway was subject to frequent flooding the path would move to one side or the other. This is what appears to have happened to much of the path that follows the brook from Yeldham to Ridgewell. Beyond the wood the official path crosses the brook for the last time and from here there is a choice of paths. All of these follow the stream but at varying distances from it, the highest being the official route.

I started on the official path but was soon hopping from one to another of the lower ones as they crept up the water meadow. All of these paths converge in the humperty-bumpy field that contains several springs that are the source of Ridgewell Brook and, what I like to think of as, the source of the Colne. It is the only headwater that has a defined, year round location and is publicly accessible. And more significantly has an ancient right of way leading to it that follows the brook all the way from Yeldham.

I am of the opinion that people have been following this route for centuries, even millennia. The earliest peoples realised that water was vital for their existence so it is quite understandable that they would seek out and revere the places from whence it came. And very soon these sites would acquire mystical significance and all sorts of irrational properties. The fame of at least one of Britain's springs was known throughout the ancient world, and when the Romans arrived, they lost little time in building a temple dedicated to the Celtic goddess Sul and the Roman goddess Minerva on the site and a town soon grew up around the thermal spring which was named Aquae Sulis, now known as Bath. Few settlements that have grown up around springs have such a reliably documented history, but some can be guessed at. In Essex, many place names have Anglo-Saxon origins and the Saxon word for a spring is 'wella', which gives rise to all those place names that end in 'well'. Ridgewell is one of only a dozen or so such names in the county. The first part of this name has changed over the years and its derivation is uncertain. It could be a

*The decaying Victorian pump that was placed over one of the springs in the field
next to the church of St Lawrence at Ridgewell. (2013)*

corruption of the word for 'reeds' or refer to a personal name. The name was certainly in use before the Norman church was built close by the spring that is thought to be the 'wella' that gave the village its name. It is not known if there was an earlier church or if this is built on an earlier pagan site. Anyway, the spring never gained any Christian significance, nor did it continue to be venerated as a pagan well, spa or wishing well. But there does seem to be a lingering folk memory that it is the source of the river Colne.

When Auston arrived here in 1950, villagers were still drawing water from the ever-flowing spring. Many praised its quality and purity, and some even claimed that 'the crystal stream gives the river a mystical charm throughout its course'. It is with this thought that I end my journey along the Colne.

The source of the Colne? One of several springs in the field next to the church of St Lawrence at Ridgewell. (2013)

APPENDIX 1

Principal Components of a Watermill

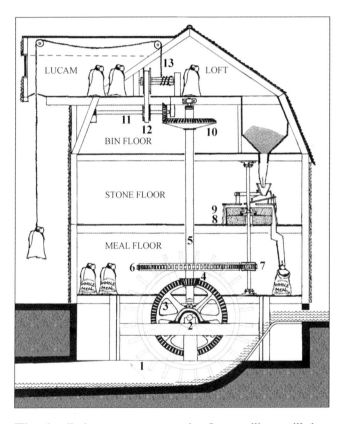

1 water wheel
2 axle tree
3 pit wheel
4 wallower
5 main shaft
6 great spur wheel
7 stone nut
8 bed stone
9 runner stone
10 crown wheel
11 lay-shaft
12 belt drive
13 sack hoist

The detailed arrangement varies from mill to mill, but
all have the basic components listed above.

APPENDIX 2

Colne Valley Mills

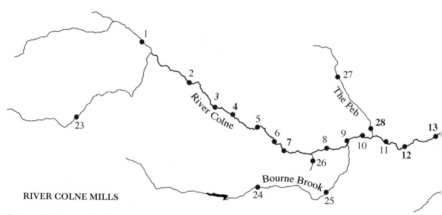

RIVER COLNE MILLS

Bold indicates mill still exists   *Italic* open to the public

No	map ref	page	name
1	?	356	Yeldham
2	TL779354	330	Nunnery
3	*TL784339*	*319*	*Alderford*
4	**TL793332**	**316**	**Hull's**
5	?	--	Hepworth Hall
6	TL809313	307	Box
7	**TL813303**	**290**	**Townford**
8	**TL834298**	**280**	**Langley**
9	TL846298	275	Ford
10	TL855289	--	--
11	TL866289	262	Colneford
12	**TL875284**	**258**	**Chalkney**
13	**TL892284**	**249**	**Wakes Colne**

TRIBUTARY MILLS

23	TL714358	353	Toppesfield
24	TL793291	--	Gosfield
25	TL825277	278	Greenstead Green
26	TL825295	287	Stanstead Hall
27	TL853331	268	Pebmarsh
28	**TL860299**	**265**	**Overshot**

Bold indicates mill still exists   *Italic* open to the public

No	map ref	page	name
14	TL919271	223	Aldham
15	TL928272	221	Fordham
16	TL948271	211	Cook's
17	TL958267	209	Newbridge
18	TL973255	201	Lexden
19	TM074247	192	North
20	TL998257	185	Middle
21	**TM007253**	**175**	**East**
22	TM016247	167	Hythe

29	TL973255	201	Lexden Springs
30	TM038278	165	**Spring Valley**
31	TM035270	165	Wallswood
32	**TM031262**	**164**	**Crockleford**
33	*TM005239*	*158*	*Bourne*
34	**TM011239**	**157**	**Cannock**
35	TM016239	156	Hull
36	TM023219	--	--
37	TM041219	125	Wivenhoe
38	TL936239	--	Stanway
39	TL955215	--	--
40	TL956212	--	Birch
41	**TL980206**	**--**	**Layer**
42	**TM030205**	**97**	**Fingringhoe**
43	*TM082194*	*59*	*Thorrington*
44	?	34	Brightlingsea
45	TM014152	26	Strood
46	TM115155	9	St Osyth

APPENDIX 3

Principal Colne Crossings

No	map ref	page	name	date, etc.
1	TL759385	354	Yeldham Chain Bridge	1682, the oldest surviving bridge in the Colne Valley.
2	TL761384	354	Yeldham Stone Bridge	1935
3	TL774361	334	CVR Railway Bridge	The only surviving CV&HR steel girder bridge.
4	TL776355	331	Nunnery Bridge	1870
5	TL781350	323	Station Road Bridge	1736, the oldest surviving bridge across Colne.
6	TL784339		Alderford Sreet Bridge	
7	TL795331	316	Hull's Mill footbridge	The only remaining ford across the Colne.
8	TL801324	312	Hepworth Hall Bridge	2005
9	TL808320	309	Halstead Flood Defences	2005
10	TL810310	306	Box Mill Footbridge	
11	TL812307	304	Chapel Street Bridge	
12	TL812306	303	footbridge	Near the site of an ancient packhorse bridge.
13	TL810305	292	Town Bridge	
14	TL815301	288	Parsonage Street Bridge	
15	TL826299	285	Blue Bridge	
16	TL836298	281	Langley Mill Bridge	
17	TL849299	269	Colne Engaine Bridge	
18	TL868289	260	Colneford Bridge	
19	TL875284	257	Chalkney Mill Bridge	
20	TL896283	243	Chappel Bridge	

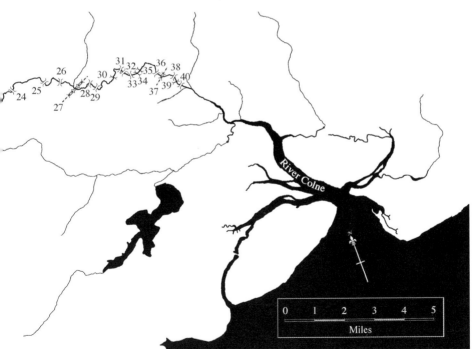

APPENDIX 4

River Colne Catchment area

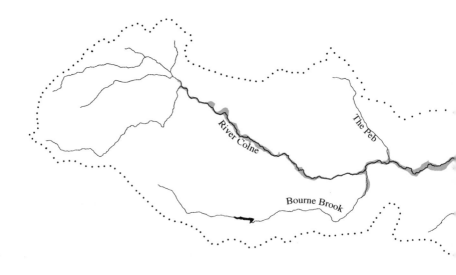

The Colne catchment area covers approximately 250 square miles.

Several headwaters converge in Great Yeldham to form the infant Colne.

It is joined by its second longest tributary, Bourne Brook, just below Halstead; the longest being Roman River which joins the Colne opposite Wivenhoe.

The mean, average annual rainfall is about 22 inches, of which around 3.5 flows into the river. This provides a mean annual flow through Colchester in excess of 20 billion litres.

Areas liable to flood are show in grey.

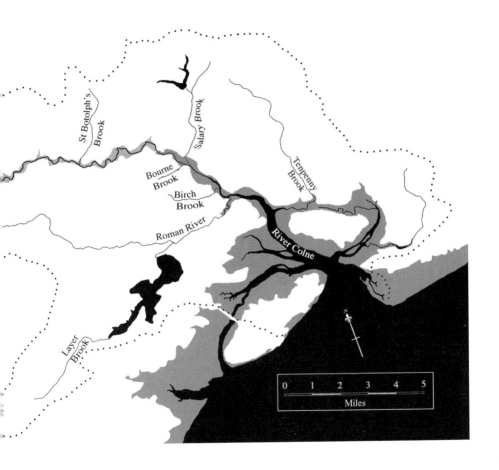

GLOSSARY

abutment	the foundation structure at each end of a bridge.
axle tree	the wooden shaft on which is mounted a waterwheel.
bed stone	the fixed or bottom millstone.
belt drive	a flexible belt used to transmit power from one shaft to another.
bin floor	the floor near the top of the mill where the grain is stored in bins.
bowstring	a form of bridge truss with an arch tied at each end by a horizontal element.
balustrade	a railing along the side of a bridge.
catchment area	the area of land bounded by watersheds draining into a river.
collier	a ship used to transport coal.
crown wheel	the large cog wheel at the top of the mill main shaft to engage bevel gears to drive other machinery.
deck	the main surface of a bridge over which traffic passes.
elliptical arch	an arch with two smaller radii at each end of a larger one.
flume	the channel bringing water to a mill wheel.
girder	a metal or concrete beam.
great spur wheel	the large wheel mounted on the mill main shaft to transmit power to the millstones.
grist	animal feed.
hard	a firm landing place on an otherwise soft or muddy shore.
headrace	the stream of water above a mill.
keystone	a central stone at the apex of an arch.
lade	the channel bringing water to a mill wheel.
lay-shaft	a shaft for transmitting power to additional equipment such as a sack hoist.

leat	the channel bringing water to a mill wheel.
lighter	a flat-bottomed barge used to unload larger vessels or lighten their load.
lucam	a dormer-like projection from the roof of a mill, it contains the hoist used to raise sacks of grain to the top of the mill.
main shaft	the large upright shaft in a watermill that transmits power from the pit wheel to everything else.
meal floor	the floor of a mill below the stone floor where the ground products are collected.
mill site	a typical layout.

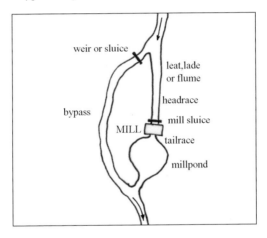

parapet	a low wall that forms a barrier along the outer edge of a bridge.
pier	the vertical element of a bridge that supports horizontal elements, such as beams or trusses.
pit wheel	the gear wheel parallel to a waterwheel, inside a mill.
roller mill	a mill with grooved metal rollers instead of millstones.
runner stone	the upper or revolving millstone.
sack hoist	the hoist used for lifting grain up to the top of a mill.
smack	a sailing vessel used for fishing, sometimes equipped with a well for keeping the catch alive.

span	the distance between two supports or piers of a bridge.
stackie	a sailing barge used to transport large quantities of hay or straw.
stone floor	the floor of a mill that houses the millstones.
stone nut	the pinion which engages with the spur wheel and drives the millstone spindle.
tailrace	the stream of water below a mill.
tranship	to transfer cargo from one vessel to another.
wallower	the small toothed wheel on the mill main shaft in gear with the pit wheel.
waterwheel	a water driven turbine fitted with vanes or buckets.
waterwheels	

overshot: water falls over the top of the wheel, suitable for locations with a high fall.

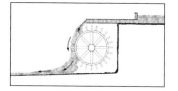

undershot: wheel driven by the impulse of water passing underneath, suitable for locations with a very low fall.

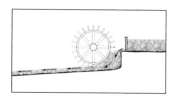

breastshot: wheel struck by water at or just above axle height.

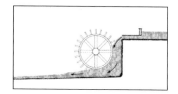

Select Bibliography

Auston E *The Colne Valley* Standard P & P 1951

Bamberger Percy *Discover Halstead* Halstead & District Local History Society 2000

Bamberger Percy *Halstead in old Picture Postcards* European Library 1987

Barton Dick *Wivenhoe* Dick Barton 1975

Benham Hervey *Some Essex Water Mills* Essex County Newspapers 1976

Bird Charles James *Castle Hedingham in Old Photographs* Halstead & District Local History Society 1990

Brown, Paul *The Wivenhoe and Brightlingsea Railway* Henry 1995

Burton-Hopkins P J *Hunt for Machinery* Halstead & District Local History Society 1995

Butler Nicholas *The Story of Wivenhoe* Quentin Press 1989

Clarke Vernon *Essex River Colne* Vernon Clarke 1991

Clarke Vernon *The Four Colnes and their Rivers* Earls Colne Society 1993

Collins John & Dodds James *River Colne Shipbuilders* Jardine Press 2009

Corder-Birch Adrian *A History of Great Yeldham* Halstead & District Local History Society 1994

Corder-Birch Adrian *A Pictorial History of Sible Hedingham* Halstead & District Local History Society 1988

Corder-Birch Adrian *Our Ancestors were Brickmakers and Potters* Adrian Corder-Birch 2010

Craze David *Wivenhoe: A Portrait in Old Picture Postcards* SB 1998

Denney Patrick *Colchester* Tempus 2004

Denny Patrick *Old Heath Past & Present* FRT Publications 2006

Dickin Edward P *A history of Brightlingsea* D H James 1939

Downey Mary *Morton Mathews* Halstead & District Local History Society 2004

Evans William James *Old and New Halstead* East Essex and Halstead Times 1886

Farries Kenneth *Essex Windmills, Millers & Millwrights V* Charles Skilton 1988

Fleming Jill *Reflections on our village* Colne Engaine History Society 2004

Forsyth Laurie *Island of Wildlife* Essex Wildlife Trust 2005

Foxon Lawrence A *The Village of St Osyth over Past Centuries* Aylott 1992

Gibbons TG *Holman's Halstead* East Essex and Halstead Times 1909

Greatorex Jane *Overshot Mill Colne Engaine* Manors, Mills & Manuscripts 1991

Greatorex Jane *The Benedictine Priory of Castle Hedingham* Jane Greatorex 2008

Hedges John *Alresford* H & C Publications 2000

Hendy Phyllis *A Toosey Twelvemonth* Phyllis Hendy 2006

Hendy Phyllis *St Osyth Parish Council Centenery 1894-1994* Phyllis Hendy 1994

Jay Brian *Mersea Memories* Brian Jay 1990

Josselin Ralph *Diary 1616-1683* OUP 1976

Karbacz Elsie M *A Short History of Mersea* Mersea Island Museum Publications 1987

Kent Peter *Fortifications of East Anglia* Terence Dalton 1988

Kimmis Jim *Essex Church Dedications* Essex Landscape Mysteries 1981

Leather Margaret *Saltwater Village* Terence Dalton 1977

Lucy Gerald *Essex Rock* Essex Rock & Mineral Soc 1999

Macfarlane Robert *Holloway* Faber & Faber 2012

Marriage John *Mersea Island* Sutton 1999

Morant Philip *A History and Antiquities of the County of Essex* 1768

O,Dell Sean *Skillingers of Brightlingsea* History Press 2011

Osborne David *Halstead and Colne Valley* Tempus 1999

Pevsner Nicholas *The Buildings of England: Essex* Penguin Books 1976

Polley Bernard *Pillboxes and Other WWII Defences around Colchester* 2003

Potts Doreen *People at Work in Halstead and District* Halstead & District Local History Society 1993

Potts Doreen *A look back at Halstead* Doreen Potts 2003

Potts Doreen *Halstead's Heritage* Halstead & District Local History Society 1989

Rackham Oliver *The History of the Countryside* J M Dent & Sons Ltd 1987

Rex Peter *Hereward The Last Englishman* Tempus 2005

Scarfe Norman *Shell Guide to Essex* Faber & Faber 1968

Southern L W *An Odd Cinque Port* Southern L W 1953

Southern L W *Stories of the Colne* Southern L W 1949

Stratford Ian *Lost Chappel & Wakes Colne* Ian Stratford 1999

Thompson Chris *The Man Who Would Have Flown* Chris Thompson 2009

Thompson Paul *Sea-change Wivenhoe Remembered* Tempus 2006

Thompson Paul *Upstreet, Downstreet, Rowhedge Recorded* Rowhedge Heritage Trust 2012

Wakeling A L *Brightlingsea in old picture postcards* European Library 1983

Wakeling A L *Images of Old Brightlingsea* Ella 2004

Wakeling A L *Looking Back* Ella 2001

Wakeling A L *Echos of the Past* Scribe 1984

Wallis Andy T *Colne Valley & Halstead Railway* Amberley Publishing 2011

Watson Peter (Ed) *Colne Engaine The Story of an Essex Village* Colne Engaine History Society 1992

Willingham Edward *From Construction to Destruction* Halstead & District Local History Society 1989

    Fingringhoe Past & Present   Fingringhoe Historical Recorders 1998

    Fordham: A Photograph Album Fordham Local History Society 2000

    Rowhedge Recollections Rowhedge Village Association 1977

    Victoria History of the County of Essex IX, X OUP 2001

Picture Credits

INDEX